ROYAL DISCORD
THE FAMILY OF GEORGE II

ROYAL DISCORD
THE FAMILY OF GEORGE II

Veronica Baker-Smith

ATHENA PRESS
LONDON

ROYAL DISCORD – THE FAMILY OF GEORGE II
Copyright © Veronica Baker-Smith 2008

ISBN 10-digit: 1 84748 067 5
ISBN 13-digit: 978 1 84748 067 5

First Published 2008 by
ATHENA PRESS
Queen's House, 2 Holly Road
Twickenham TW1 4EG
United Kingdom

Printed for Athena Press

March 1734

It was the first marriage of a Princess Royal for over a hundred years, and it had captured the public imagination as such events always do. Anne, daughter of George II, was the bride 'in whom each Grace and all the Virtues join', leaving her adoring brothers and sisters to wed a handsome prince whose very name stirred memories of greatness, William of Orange. The newspapers were happily exploring every detail: brocaded silk for the wedding dress in the fashionable colours of blue and silver had been sent from France, the pillars of St James's Chapel were being swathed in velvet and gold lace under the direction of William Kent, and Mr Handel had composed a wedding anthem for his 'flower of princesses'. As the Hanoverians revived the two Stuart alliances, romance and nostalgia were in the air, inspiring even Cambridge dons to song:

> His amorous suit he sighs in Anna's ear
> And views his Goddess while he makes his pray'r,
> His prayer is heard, the my stick knot is wove,
> Anna and William are but one in love.

Such is the mystique of a royal marriage that only a very few witnesses of the splendid ceremony saw a woman of twenty-five, badly marked by smallpox and 'with a great tendency to fat' being escorted to the altar by her two brothers with whom she was barely on speaking terms, to join a political nonentity whose physical deformity made her mother weep.

The majority were right to ignore such details; on the personal level the union was a happy one, and it was to bring the ambitious bride to a position of power in a foreign country never matched by an English princess.

Group portrait of Frederick, Prince of Wales (1707–1750), son of King George II, with his brother the Duke of Cumberland (1721–1765) and their five sisters, by William Aikman (1682–1731). Copyright © The Devonshire Collection, Chatsworth.

Preface

It is a strange fact that the only English princess ever to wield power in her own right in a foreign country has languished in total obscurity. When Anne, Princess Royal, left England on her marriage to William of Orange in 1734 she 'was as much forgotten in three weeks as if she had been buried three years.' I discovered her when looking for a research topic while living for some years in Amsterdam, and the result was a volume in the Sir Thomas Browne series published by Brill of Leiden.

This relied heavily on Anne's private correspondence, which had seldom been studied even in the Netherlands. I am grateful to Her Majesty Queen Beatrix for permission to work in the Koninklijk Huisarchief in The Hague, where the staff, under the then director Dr B Woelderink, were unfailingly helpful and tolerant of a *buitenlander*'s effort to come to grips with the troubled history of their eighteenth century.

When I returned to England I became interested in Anne's family as a whole – a lost generation which appears to have slipped through the historical net. Ragnhild Hatton's monumental work on George I and much attention on George III has left the thirty-three year reign of George II almost untapped. The last worthwhile biographies of this Hanoverian and of his wife, Caroline of Ansbach (a Queen Consort of great intelligence and influence), date respectively from 1975 and 1901. Frederick, Prince of Wales and the Duke of Cumberland have received some attention, but few historians could name their five sisters. This book brings them all into focus – their public quarrels and private thoughts – against the background of social life in England and tumultuous political and military events in Europe.

I am grateful to my friend Clarissa Campbell Orr for her constant interest in my work, and for including my piece on the daughters of George II in her volume *Queenship in Britain*.

I should also thank the Athena Press for their acceptance of my manuscript, and my editor for his meticulous correction of it. His firm request for five hundred and twenty-two footnotes proved a Herculean task, but of course he was right.

Finally I acknowledge my husband's encouragement of my intrusion into his academic world and his exemplary patience as I monopolised his e-mail and tangled myself up in his computer. This is a small offering to him.

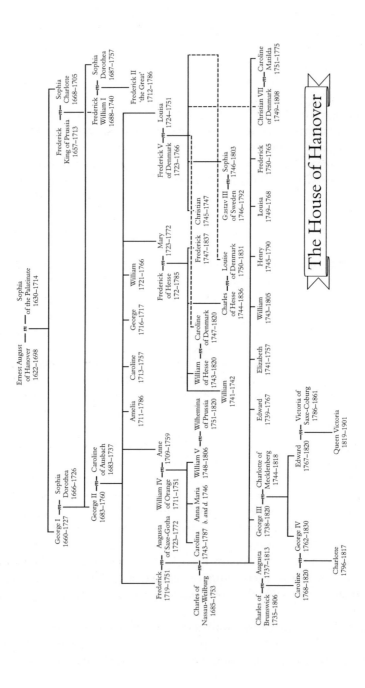

The House of Hanover

Ernest August
of Hanover
1622–1698 — m — Sophia
of the Palatinate
1630–1714

George I
1660–1727

Sophia
Dorothea
1666–1726 — m — George II
1683–1760 — m — Caroline
of Ausbach
1683–1737

Frederick
King of Prussia
1657–1713 — m — Sophia
Charlotte
1668–1705

Frederick
William I
1688–1740 — m — Sophia
Dorothea
1687–1757

Frederick II
'the Great'
1712–1786

Frederick
1719–1751 — m — Augusta
of Saxe-Gotha
1723–1772

Amelia
1711–1786

Caroline
1713–1757

George
1716–1717

William
1721–1766 — m — Mary
1723–1772

Louisa
1724–1751 — m — Frederick V
of Denmark
1723–1766

Charles of
Nassau-Weilburg
1685–1753 — m — Carolina
1743–1787
b. and d. 1746
Anna Maria — William V
of Prussia
1748–1806 — m — Wilhemina
1751–1820

William
1741–1742

William
of Hesse
1743–1820 — m — Caroline
of Denmark
1747–1820

Frederick
of Hesse
172 –1785

Charles
of Hesse
1744–1836 — m — Louise
of Denmark
1750–1831

Frederick
1747–1837 — m — Christian
1745–1747

Gustav III
of Sweden
1746–1792 — m — Sophia
1746–1803

William IV
of Orange
1711–1751 — m — Anne
1709–1759

Augusta
1737–1813 — m — Charles of
Brunswick
1735–1806

George III
1738–1820 — m — Charlotte of
Mecklenburg
1744–1818

Edward
1739–1767

Elizabeth
1741–1757

William
1743–1805

Henry
1745–1790

Louisa
1749–1768

Frederick
1750–1765

Christian VII
of Denmark
1749–1808 — m — Caroline
Matilda
1751–1775

Caroline
1768–1820 — m — George IV
1762–1830

Edward
1767–1820 — m — Victoria of
Saxe-Coburg
1786–1861

Charlotte
1796–1817

Queen Victoria
1819–1901

Chapter One

I have just received the good news of the birth of a daughter at which I feel all imaginable pleasure ... I am only a little bit angry that it caused you pain. You should know me well enough my very dear Caroline to believe that everything that concerns you is infinitely precious to me This new token of your love attaches me the more deeply to you and I assure you dear heart that I love the baby without having seen it ... Adieu my dearest heart, for God's sake take care of yourself and of the young family, particularly the new-born infant who at present has most need of care. The peace of my life depends upon knowing you in good health and upon the conviction of your continued affection for me. I shall endeavour to attract it by all imaginable passion and love and I shall never omit any way of showing you that no one could be more wholly yours dear Caroline than is your

George Augustus.[1]

This letter is dated 9 November 1709, when George Augustus, Electoral Prince of Hanover, was staying with his father in the hunting lodge of Gohrde to the north of his electorate. The two men were seldom together by choice but had decided to remove themselves from the action at home as the Prince's wife prepared for the birth of her second child. The sport was not good: a guest wrote, 'partridges invisible again, though the Elector bagged an owl';[2] and it was perhaps this fact which gave the Prince leisure to write a letter of tenderness and spontaneity which belies the image of George II as an irascible and pompous insensitive, only fractionally less boring than his father. Even the mockery of hindsight is impossible for the warmth and devotion it expresses was to last until Queen Caroline's death nearly thirty years later.

She had been born in Ansbach, a tiny state in present day Bavaria, one of about 300 independent territories which formed the complicated mosaic of the Holy Roman Empire; and although relatively rich from the royalties of the Harz mines it was an unlikely origin for one of the most intelligent and influential of English queen consorts. When she was orphaned at the age of thirteen she was placed in the guardianship of the Elector Frederick of Brandenburg (later the first King of Prussia) and his wife, Sophie Charlotte. This brought her to the heart of the brilliant court at Berlin, to one of the eight major German states whose rulers had the right to elect the Emperor, and for nine years Caroline lived in the enchanting pale yellow palace the Elector built for his wife just outside his capital. He loved display, and in a deliberate effort to emulate the court of Versailles, he spent freely on fine furniture, porcelain and paintings, which his ward was quick to appreciate and about which she was eager to learn. Sophie Charlotte's main interests were intellectual ones, and she presided over a salon of learned men from every country in Europe, where Jesuit and Huguenot theologians were encouraged to spar with philosophers and with each other, while scientists and freethinkers, however audacious, were given a sympathetic hearing. Everything and anything could be discussed without restraint; ethics were debated and religious beliefs questioned far into the night. Exhausted courtiers often had to stumble straight from her apartments into Frederick's lavish bedchamber, where he insisted on a royal levee at four in the morning, emerging, bright-eyed, from his sunken bath.

The most important of Sophie Charlotte's circle was Gottfried Wilhelm Leibniz, that rare being, according to a contemporary, 'a learned man who knew how to behave and did not stink.'[3] A political historian and a philosopher as well as the inventor of infinitesimal calculus, he would come to the court in his coffee-coloured coach painted with roses to discuss 'the why of the why' with anyone who was interested. Young Caroline was always interested, and she became absorbed in theological speculation and metaphysics; but also, before any but the smallest stage offered her a role, she developed a fascination for practical politics – its instruments and its personalities. Caroline surveyed the European scene and considered her options, which had been vastly increased by the high profile of her guardians. In 1701, when she was eighteen, the possibility was raised of her marriage with the Archduke Charles, son of the Emperor himself. The sixteen-year-old Archduke was enthusiastic, having heard glowing reports of Caroline's beauty and personality; but the Hapsburgs naturally insisted on a Catholic bride, and an eminent Jesuit arrived to instruct Caroline in the faith. Their disputations were long and complicated as, with the Bible on the table between them, Caroline fought him all the way, probably prompted by Leibniz, who helped her draft a final refusal of the match; all Europe was much impressed by the young Princess's 'pious firmness', and Caroline continued to enjoy life in Berlin.

But in the spring of 1705, Sophie Charlotte died of a tumour of the throat at the age of thirty-six while on a visit to her mother, the Electress Sophia of Hanover. As the doctors told her they could do nothing for her she merely smiled.

Do not pity me, I am going at last to satisfy my curiosity about the origin of things which even Leibniz could never explain to me, to understand infinity, space, being and nothingness; and as for the King my husband – well, I shall afford him the opportunity to give me a magnificent funeral and display all the pomp he loves so much.

The King had been furious over Caroline's refusal of the Austrian marriage, and only his wife's intervention had saved Caroline then. Now twenty-two, she was sent back to the dull provincialism and obscurity of Ansbach, which she had almost forgotten. Stoically, she devoted herself to good works and was rewarded some months later when a dapper little young man with bulging eyes calling himself M. de Busch arrived at her brother's court. He carried an introduction from Hanover, and was duly entertained to music, cards and elaborate suppers for several days. Having bid them a meaningful farewell, George Augustus rode hell for leather back home to announce to his father, the Elector, that he had fallen in love with the Princess of Ansbach and 'would not look at anyone else'.[4] His grandmother, Electress Sophia, had met Caroline many times in Berlin and though she had told him that this was the most agreeable Princess in Germany, an incognito visit of inspection had seemed advisable. Certainly, Caroline's blonde hair, very fair skin and what has been delicately described as 'a bosom of exemplary magnitude' attracted him, but since the Prince also praised her conversation she must have adjusted this to her audience; theology was not his line – he was later to dismiss the entire bench of English bishops as 'a parcel of black canting hypocritical knaves'.[5] His view on art and poetry was that he 'had hated all that stuff since his youth' and he hardly had a philosophical thought in his life. George Augustus's play-acting would not have deceived Caroline, who knew exactly who he was and the brilliant political future that was likely for his wife.

The marriage took place in the autumn, and the bridegroom, true to his principles, slept through the wedding sermon. Sophia, reporting this fact to her ebullient niece, the Duchess of Orleans, known as Liselotte, received the reply, 'what good news for the bride that he should be well rested'. The Duchess always expressed herself frankly, 'good natured behaviour, not kissing and slobbering is what makes a good marriage'.[6] The Duchess had been married as a brusque, sharp-tongued, strapping German princess to the dainty homosexual brother of Louis XIV, and after his death she remained in France as a clear-eyed and humorous observer of social mores. 'I could write books on the subject [of homosexuality],' she wrote to a prim relative, recalling how William III and the Duke of Albemarle would frequently kiss passionately before the Court. '[The French] think it is a polite accomplishment and say that God has not punished anyone for it since Sodom and Gomorrah … If people like these make you shudder, my dear Amelisa, you must see very few people.' Amelisa was her unmarried half-sister, and Liselotte delighted in upsetting her: '[William III] went to bed in woollen drawers on his wedding night. When [Charles II] suggested he might care to take them off, he replied that since he and his wife would have to live together for a long time she would have to get used to his habits.'[7]

George Augustus and Caroline moved into the electoral palace on the edge of the still largely medieval town of Hanover. It was a rambling complex overlooking the River Leine with splendid staterooms and a baroque opera house seating 2,000 that was the finest in northern Europe. It was also an object lesson in communal living, since the palace was shared with the Dowager Electress and George Augustus' unmarried sister, as well as his father, George Louis, and the latter's assorted favourites. All of them settled down to keep a sharp eye on Caroline's waistline. Six months after the wedding her pregnancy was announced and everyone awaited an autumn baby. But it was not until 3 February 1707 that the English envoy to Hanover reported,

> the court having for some time past almost despaired of the Princess Electoral being brought to bed, and most people apprehensive that her bigness which has continued for so long was rather an effect of distemper than that she was with child, Her Highness was taken ill last Friday at dinner and last night she was delivered of a son.[8]

The baby, baptised Frederick Louis, secured the succession of the dynasty to the third generation, though he himself is remembered to posterity simply as 'poor Fred'. Two and a half years later, the first of his sisters – Anne – joined him, her birth being the occasion of the Prince's loving letter to his wife. The two children were cordially to detest each other for much of their lives.

They and their two younger sisters – Amelia and Caroline – were born into another of the principal courts of Germany. Hanover had been raised to the rank of Electorate twenty years before, the Emperor being influenced, it was said, by a gift from the ruling prince, Ernst August, of twelve 'Hanoverian creams' – the grey horses prized throughout Europe for their strength and spirit. Ernst's widow, Sophia, the children's great-grandmother was already well into her seventies but still a formidable presence, tall and erect 'with not one wrinkle and all her own teeth'. She, like her daughter, Sophie Charlotte, studied philosophy and stitched fine embroidery (both without spectacles), enjoyed enormous meals during which she would frequently burst into song, walked for three hours a day and never stopped talking, often in two languages simultaneously. The children were required to accompany her as she bustled through her aviaries filled with canaries, she gave fancy dress parties for them and taught them how to dance, and they were introduced to the many exotic guests – Chinese doctors and uncouth Russian princes – whom she welcomed to her court.

Caroline became Sophia's confidante, genuinely enjoying the tales of her youth:

> The beautiful portraits of Van Dyck had given me so lovely a conception that I was surprised to find that the Queen [Henrietta Maria] was a small woman with long lean arms, shoulders out of proportion and possessed of a row of teeth which protruded like a line of defence from her mouth.

But Sophia's personal influence on her family was far outweighed by her political importance to it. Her mother was Elizabeth, daughter of James I of England and VI of Scotland, whose Protestant husband, Frederick the Elector Palatine, was defeated at the Battle of the White Mountain in 1620, barely a year after he had accepted Bohemia's offer of the crown in its rebellion against the Catholic Hapsburgs. Known as 'the Winter King and Queen' (in fulfilment of the prophecy that they would be gone with the melting snow) they and their many children were offered refuge and a generous subsidy by the Dutch government because Frederick was a grandson of William the Silent. One of Sophia's languages was therefore Dutch, and she was always very attached to the country, though she was also inordinately proud of her Stuart blood. However, she was the youngest surviving child of thirteen and when she was hurriedly married off at the age of twenty-eight (after titillating rumours of incest with her brother) to an insignificant German Prince, her family origins seemed unimportant.

After 1701, however, she became Heiress of England, when the last of the Stuart monarchs, Queen Anne, buried the one pathetic survivor of her seventeen children. Religious affiliation played an even greater part than personal tragedy in Sophia's progression through the ranks, for there were no less than fifty-seven Catholics with stronger hereditary claims than hers; but for most Englishmen, hatred of Catholicism was a tenet of faith. Lord Douglas was once asked by the exiled James II what he must do to regain his throne. 'Set sail from France taking a dozen Jesuits with you,' was the reply, 'and as soon as you arrive, have them publicly hanged – nothing will charm the English more.'[9]

The Act of Settlement of 1701 recognised Sophia 'and the heirs of her body, being Protestant' as Anne's successors on the English throne, and through the early years of the eighteenth century Hanover was increasingly drawn into English politics as diplomats, place-seekers and the merely curious arrived each year 'with the swallows' – that is, when the weather allowed that island race to cross the North Sea without being too ill. Neither Anne nor Sophia heeded those who proclaimed the illegitimacy of the former's half-brother (recognised by Louis XIV on the death of his father as King James III and maintained by the French in some style in Saint-Germain) – the point at issue was purely a religious one, and both knew he was as much a Stuart as they were. The arrogant and pompous envoy, Lord Halifax, was once proclaiming a set speech to Sophia in her private apartments when the old Electress leapt to her feet, backed against a wall and stood there as if transfixed before abruptly dismissing him. The offended Halifax later discovered that she was concealing a portrait of James, which she had forgotten to take down before his arrival.

Sophia's son, the Elector George Louis, considered her (with some justification) a political liability. Her triumphant excitement about the English succession, 'I care not when I die if on my tomb it be written that I was Queen of England', and her misunderstanding of English affairs – which led her to attempt to style herself Princess of Wales – greatly irritated him. His own enthusiasm for the inheritance was limited. England's reputation in Europe was for, at best, volatility and, at worst, violence and treachery. Here was a country which within forty years had executed one king and established a republic, welcomed back his son with wild rejoicing, and driven a third into exile. George himself had visited London in 1680 and watched Charles II, twenty years after his triumphant return, fighting for his very survival as the violent mob and hardly less mercurial Lords and Commons turned on their King – and anyone, however innocent, who stood in their way: 'They cut off the head of Lord Stafford yesterday,' George had written, 'and made no more ado about it than if they had chopped off the head of a pullet.'[10]

So he trod very softly twenty-five years later as political control in England swung between the pro-Hanoverian Whigs and possibly Jacobite Tories. Many supporters of James were as anti-Catholic as the rest of the nation, and all their efforts were devoted to encouraging him to renounce the religion which was recognised as the only bar to his succession. Certainly, England had become accustomed to the Stuart face. George was perceived (and considered himself to be) far more a German than a Stuart, and the choice of the House of Hanover could be presented as a dangerous leap into the unknown. In addition, European gossip about George's private life was not encouraging: it was whispered that one of his mistresses was his half-sister, while he had divorced his wife and kept her imprisoned after murdering her lover with his bare hands… The truth was slightly less dramatic. He had been twenty-two when his parents arranged his marriage with the sixteen-year-old Sophia Dorothea of Celle, who was pretty but flighty and spoilt, soon tiring of her phlegmatic husband. He was later described as a man whose idea of an enjoyable evening was 'a quiet game of cards for low stakes after a heavy supper' – hardly the ideal match for a flirtatious and high-spirited romantic.

The proprieties were observed until two children had been born, but Sophia Dorothea then fell in love with Philip Christoff von Königsmarck, a

Swedish count serving in the Hanoverian army, and they conducted their affair with the most extraordinary abandon. Letters flew between the pair, Königsmarck writing: 'Ye gods, what a night I spent – why cannot I now take wings like my desire. I should at this moment be in your lovely arms tasting the sweet delights of your lips as I did then.'[11]

The clichés were dynamite when George intercepted them, and further read of his wife's desire for his death in battle and her frank criticism of his sexual prowess. As it became clear that his wife (though probably not her lover) planned an elopement, drastic measures were needed: George left for Berlin to visit his sister, Sophie Charlotte, and her husband, while the errant pair were closely watched. One summer evening Königsmarck slipped into the Leine Palace as usual by a private path from one of the river islands and made his way to Sophia Dorothea's apartments. He was killed that night and either weighted with stones and tossed into the river or plastered into a niche in the wall. If the latter story is true, an extra frisson is added by the fact that these were the apartments later allocated to her son George Augustus and Caroline after their marriage.

George was innocent of actual murder but obviously colluded in it. He divorced his wife for refusal to cohabit with him and committed her to house arrest in the castle of Ahlden until her death thirty-one years later. It was reported that George 'froze' at any mention of his wife, and forever afterwards feared her as a potential focus for intrigue. The nine-year-old prince never saw his mother again. All portraits of her were removed, and as he grew up alternately bullied and ignored by his father, his semi-hysterical rages became familiar to his family and his court. He was a man, as his grandmother observed, who would be 'made by his wife', and so indeed it proved.

The effect on George himself, personally and politically, was that an already solitary and unemotional man became even more reserved – Liselotte wrote of him that he was 'so cold that he turns everything to ice'. Alexander Pope remembered a visit to Hampton Court. 'I walked there the other day by the moon and saw no creature of any quality except the King who was giving audience all alone to the birds under the garden wall.'[12] This determination to keep his own counsel was an advantage in the sensitive negotiations with different factions in London as Queen Anne, bloated with dropsy and possibly suffering from dementia, although only forty-nine, eked out her miserable life.

Notes

[1] Quoted in R L Arkell, *Caroline of Ansbach*, 1939, p.45. Biographies of Caroline (of which, astonishingly, this is the most recent) do not offer source references
[2] Maria Kroll, *Sophie, Electress of Hanover*, 1973, p.264
[3] Maria Kroll, [ed.] *Letters from Liselotte*, 1975, p.120

[4] Maria Kroll, op. cit., p.243
[5] MSS of Earl of Egmont HMC, 1920, 304
[6] Maria Kroll, *Liselotte*, p.245
[7] Maria Kroll, *Liselotte*, p.37
[8] Letter from Ambassador Howe, quoted in W H Wilkins, *Caroline the Illustrious*, 1901, pp.88–9
[9] Recounted by Liselotte to Caroline in a letter dated 14 November 1715. G S Stevenson, [trans.] *Letters of Madame*, 1924. 'Madame' was her French title as the wife of the King's younger brother.
[10] Quoted in J D Griffith Davies, *A King in Toils*, 1938, p.9
[11] A W Ward, *The Electress Sophia and the Hanoverian Succession*, 1903, p.214
[12] J W Croker, [ed.] *Letters of Alexander Pope*, 1886, p.395

Chapter Two

George Augustus and Caroline had chosen the name Anne for their eldest daughter, with an eye to the English succession. The Queen was invited to be godmother, but several more or less tactful reminders were needed before she sent a christening gift of her portrait set in diamonds. She had obviously tried to please: 'I beleeve ye stones are very good,'[1] she wrote, though Sophia ungraciously dismissed it as 'the sort one gives to ambassadors'. Her agitated concern with English politics made her vulnerable to every imagined slight or rumour as the two-party system swung this way and that; many English politicians too were spreading their bets The Earl of Oxford was taking the chief part in secret negotiations with the exiled James Stuart while visiting Hanover with State documents 'painted all round with flowers as though from Persia'.[2] (This was an English speciality. Sir Thomas Brand was employed to embellish letters to foreign princes, though he himself was completely illiterate.)

While their elders strained to follow the ebb and flow of popular feeling and political intrigue in England, the children divided their time between the Leine Palace and the summer residence of the Electors at Herrenhausen. Here, ambitious garden works extending over 120 acres were under way during the early years of the century. Religious scruples seldom applied to the arts in Germany – an Italian landscape architect built the largest orangery ever seen, and a Frenchman laid out the geometric hornbeam maze and parterres punctuated by classical statues and fountains. On three sides the garden was bordered by canals on which floated replicas of Venetian gondolas. However, Dutch craftsmen were called upon for the tapestries, furniture and internal decoration of Herrenhausen. George's links with the United Provinces of the Dutch Republic were strong, due to his mother's influence and to the fact that he himself had taken an active part in William of Orange's campaigns in the 1680s against the French.

The Elector's patronage of the arts lightens his stolid image. It was he who chose the young George Frederick Handel as his Kapellmeister in 1710 and he built a theatre at his hunting lodge in Celle. Masques and operas were the most important feature of the pre-Lenten carnival which was the highlight of Hanover's social year, when fancy dress balls spilled over into the streets and fireworks and torchlight processions often revealed members of the electoral family in open carriages drawn by the Hanoverian creams, richly caparisoned in velvet and controlled (barely) by reins of twisted silk. Everyone went masked so the behaviour often shocked foreign observers and there could be sinister happenings too: once four men carried a sedan chair into a courtyard, set it down and withdrew. When the robed figure inside did not alight or respond to the host's polite welcome, his servants removed the mask to reveal a decaying corpse.[3]

The carnival of 1714 followed its usual boisterous course, but everyone knew that events in England were moving towards a climax. The Queen was clearly dying, and rumours flew that James was planning to seize the initiative and land in England to claim his own with her consent; the Duchess of Orleans thoroughly alarmed her aunt by the opinion that 'Queen Anne must be well aware in her heart of hearts that our young king is her brother. I feel certain that before her death she will do justice to him'.[4] A debate in the House of Commons years before had voiced the warning 'throughout our whole history, whosoever came first to England had always taken it'. Harold Hardrada was forgotten, but Henry VII and William III showed that speed and daring could be rewarded. James's base at Saint-Germain would involve a journey of perhaps three days to London if winds were favourable, while the trip from Hanover could last over a week. The Elector moved at last: he deputed that arch time-server, the Duke of Marlborough, to have full powers from him to defend the succession if James should land, and he entrusted to his envoy in London a list of his nominations for a Regency council.

The Electress Sophia missed being Queen of England by two months. In early June she was taking her customary evening walk in the Herrenhausen gardens with Caroline and a lady-in-waiting. Talking hard as usual, she became agitated at some supposed insult from Queen Anne, and collapsed while hurrying to one of the pavilions to shelter from a sudden storm. Her lifelong wish was granted her: 'that I may die without doctor or priest.'[5] In one faraway corner of Europe the news was greeted with relief. The impoverished province of Friesland had bestowed an annuity at her christening which they could hardly have envisaged paying for eighty-four years. Twenty years after her death, almost to the day, one of her great-granddaughters would enter that province as wife of its ruling prince.

At the end of July, Queen Anne presided over a council of her ministers that lasted from nine at night until two in the morning discussing the succession. The supporters of George and James raged at each other and almost came to blows until the Queen first rose trembling to her feet and then fell senseless with a massive stroke. As she lay in the coma, the Jacobite Bishop of Rochester offered to don full pontificals and proclaim King James at Charing Cross, but the others lost their nerve; the Duke of Ormonde said he could only answer for the army if Anne named her brother as her successor. But with the Queen unconscious nothing could be done. It was the Whigs and the pro-Hanoverian Tories on George's secret Regency Council who acted decisively, concentrating several regiments around London, taking control of the ports to prevent invasion and, on Anne's death three days later, ensuring a peaceful acceptance of the heralds' proclamation of 'the High and Mighty Prince George, Elector of Brunswick-Lüneberg [as] our lawful and rightful Liege Lord by the Grace of God King of Great Britain, France and Ireland'.[6]

George I and his son landed at Greenwich late on the evening of 30 September 1714. A thick fog swirled round the flares illuminating Wren's buildings as everyone who mattered in London decked themselves in their best clothes and hurried out to inspect their King. Many were distinctly disappointed with what they saw: a small man with a dark weather-beaten skin (his mother said he could have passed for a Spaniard), slack-jawed and with hard, blue, almost expressionless, eyes. He was very simply dressed which caused the artist James Thornhill some difficulty when he was later commissioned to paint the scene for the Upper Hall at Greenwich: how should he show the King, whose dress had not been 'graceful nor enough worthy of him to be transmitted to posterity'?[7] He solved the problem by putting George in armour.

George's characteristic reserve was noticeable on the ceremonial drive into London the next day: with his hand on his breast he bowed occasionally but never smiled. George Augustus, beside him, was unable to contain his excitement at his elevation to Prince of Wales, and never stopped beaming, though he had been commanded by his father not to infringe on the royal prerogative by bowing himself. The lack of warmth between ruler and heir was manifest to the curious crowds.

Three weeks later there was a much jollier entry into London as the Prince escorted his wife and two of his daughters; the baby Caroline was ill and joined them later, but Anne and Amelia attracted interest as they bobbed up and down in the carriage and waved to the jostling crowds. There had been no royal nursery for over eighty years, only one of Queen Anne's brood having reached the age of two, so all their outings were noted and the small girls were admired 'for the excellent behaviour they showed much above what their age could promise'.[8]

They saw their father take his seat in the House of Lords, and watched the Lord Mayor's Show that November with the rest of the royal family from a crimson-canopied balcony built out from a house near Bow church. The King was delighted with the procession, and he tried to knight the owner of the house for his hospitality; however, the man was a Quaker and refused the honour, greatly surprising George, who had long experience of English greed. Venality was an English characteristic, with the added dimension, as a foreign diplomat once lamented, that its people simply would not stay bribed. Left behind permanently in Hanover was the seven-year-old Frederick who, by order of his grandfather, was to represent the family in the Electorate, and if his parents objected to this they never showed it. It would be a full fifteen years before they met again, for neither of them ever visited or – it seems – even corresponded with him. Surprisingly, the English also seem to have accepted it without complaint. The boy was after all second in line to the throne, and sensitivity about the influence of the Electorate was a standard grouse.

George I's coronation took place at the end of October. Since few people in England spoke German or even French, and George was careful to conceal his fair understanding of English, the ceremonies were explained to him in dog Latin. All the Jacobites were there, still wondering how they had been outmanoeuvred: 'They were very peevish with Everybody who spoke to them' but dared not absent themselves.[9] Lady Nottingham (the mother, incidentally, of thirty children) felt moved to bolster her husband's shaky commitment by pushing her way to the front when the Litany was being sung, falling on her knees in front of the King to proclaim the words. 'Everyone stared at her [thinking] she overdid her High Church part.'[10] Lady Dorchester, who had been James II's mistress, snorted audibly when the Archbishop of Canterbury asked for the people's consent. 'Does the old fool think anyone here will say no to his question when there are so many drawn swords?' She was joined at court by the Duchess of Portsmouth and Lady Orkney, respectively the mistresses of Charles II and William III. 'Who would have thought we three old whores would have met together here?'[11]

According to tradition, George was crowned as King of France, with two actors paying homage to him as the Dukes of Picardy and Normandy – Louis XIV had grudgingly accepted his accession in England, being as dumbfounded as most of Europe at the ease and smoothness of the regime change, which had long been expected to plunge England into chaos. The Dutch representatives were especially honoured guests, George spoke Dutch far better than he ever spoke English and was thoroughly at ease with them. In return, their address of welcome (in an unusual lapse of the Dutch critical spirit) hailed him as 'the happy genius of the British Isle' and 'prop of empire and the world's delight'.[12]

A highlight of the coronation festivities at the King's special request was Handel's opera *Rinaldo*. His granddaughters accompanied him, thus beginning at an early age their association with the German composer who was to dominate English music. He was appointed their music master at a salary of £200 a year – this was the same as their laundress, and at first he sulked – but when he discovered the aptitude of his eldest pupil he changed his mind. 'Since I left Hamburg nothing on earth could make me teach music, I make the only exception for Anne, flower of princesses.'[13] She already showed promise on the harpsichord, and under Handel's guidance she became a skilled musician and singer, and eventually one of his most valued advisers as well as his lifelong friend.

Caroline ensured that her daughters were highly educated: their native language of German and the official one of French were augmented by English, Latin and Greek, and for the quick and intelligent Anne, Italian also: she was described by one of her mother's friends: 'Princess Anne speaks, reads and writes German and French to Perfection, knows a great deal of History and Geography, speaks English very prettily and dances very well.'[14] She was just five years old. Their grandfather would often summon them to dance or play at the private supper parties he preferred to court ceremonial. It was Caroline who was left to show the flag at court, and she seized it with enthusiasm. Dean Swift had described the giddy excitement of one of Queen Anne's drawing room receptions: [She] 'looked at us with her fan in her mouth and once a minute said about three words to someone who was near her. Then she was told dinner was ready and went out.'[15]

Caroline made a point of speaking to all and charming most, though the Duchess of Marlborough noted a characteristic which was tactfully glossed over by the genteel Victorian biographers. She 'was never half an hour without saying something shocking to somebody and generally very improper discourse for a public room'.[16] The coarseness of her language was not unusual for the time and delighted her husband, but it was to make her some enemies. The Princess was a keen card player for high stakes, 'no one sits down to table with less than two hundred guineas'[17] (this at a time when a country parson could live very comfortably on an annual income of one hundred) and one of the Duchess's daughters once won six hundred on a single throw of the dice. Sometimes guests would be diverted by the presence of a 'wild man', found naked in a German forest and sent to the King as a curiosity.[18] He would stand like a statue against the wall with his dark unwavering stare fixed on Caroline: when one evening she was wearing a black velvet dress trimmed with diamonds and a little gold watch he would run up to admire it as it chimed the quarters, though after a while he had to be ushered away since he was not house-trained. The quality of food at these supper parties was much appreciated: superb goose pies and cold meats dressed in the simpler English style:

> French soups we do despise,
> They suiteth not our blood,
> Brown beer and good roast beef
> Is wholesome British food.

French food was held to be 'dressed in Masquerade, seasoned with slow Poisons and every dish pregnant with the seeds of Diseases both chronic and acute'[19] and since decoration could mask decay, a contemporary book of etiquette reassured people that with simply prepared food there was no need to smell the meat when it was raised on the fork. The King himself had caused great distress in the royal kitchens by complaining that the Colchester oysters they served had no flavour. Someone eventually realised that since Hanover was so far from the sea George had never had fresh ones before – they were kept a few days and then met with royal approval.

St James's Palace was the focus for court ceremonial, but it also had to provide living quarters for the whole royal family. The former hunting lodge was thus hardly less crowded than the Leine had been: a rickety and unimpressive warren of small apartments which twenty years later could still prompt the remark, "tis at once the contempt of foreign nations and the disgrace of our own, our beggars are housed [at Greenwich and the Chelsea Hospital] better than our King'.[20] A twenty-foot whale skeleton, clamped for some reason to the wall of one of the courtyards, diverted the children. George and his mistress, Melusine von den Schulenberg, formed one family unit with their three teenage daughters (carefully referred to as her 'nieces'). Another set of apartments housed Sophie Charlotte von Kielmansegge, certainly George's illegitimate half-sister though not his mistress, and a third was allocated to the Prince of Wales and his young family. The Hanoverian women were a strange pair: Melusine extremely tall and thin, atrociously dressed and affecting a flaming red wig, and Sophie Charlotte, vividly described by the young Horace Walpole thus:

Two fierce black eyes large and rolling below two lofty arched eyebrows, two acres of cheek spread with crimson, an ocean of neck that overflowed and was not distinguished from the lower part of her body and in no way restrained by stays.[21]

The English mocked – they were well used to favourites, of course, but the Stuart taste had run to beauties and these two were dubbed 'the Elephant and the Maypole', while George's two Turkish servants, Mehemet and Mustapha, added to the perception of a thoroughly alien court:

Hither he brought his dear Illustrious House
That is, himself, his pipe, close stool and louse;
Two Turks, two Whores, and half a dozen nurses,
Five hundred Germans, all with empty purses.[22]

George's Hanoverians were bitterly attacked for their supposed greed and corruption. A probably apocryphal story much enjoyed in the coffee houses had Melusine and Sophie Charlotte's carriage stopped by an angry mob, their plea, 'Good people, what for you abuse us, we have come for your goods,' was answered, 'Yes, damn you, and for our chattels too!'[23] There were tensions at court also. The introduction of the Hanoverian tradition of all-night masquerades was deplored as 'the corruption of our youth and a scandal to the nation'. One of the German entourage told Lady Deloraine that the English were not quality because they hung their heads, while foreign ladies held theirs up in a noble way; the Countess in one of her comparatively rare sober moments was able to retort, 'We show our quality by our Birth and Titles, Madam, not by sticking out our Bosoms.'[24] Court positions were bought and sold all over Europe as part of the social system – those in power had to provide for their old age. The Hanoverians who came to England with George had relatives and estates at home to support and they found the cost of living in London was four times higher than in the Electorate. Friedrich Wilhelm von Gortz, the King's most trusted minister and financial expert, assumed he would be given a London house and was horrified to be told by Sir John Vanbrugh of the Office of Works that he must buy his own like the English ministers did. In reality, of course, this was done with the proceeds of patronage, but the Act of Settlement was interpreted as barring any encroachment in British affairs by those who were not British-born. Therefore no Hanoverian could receive land or office from public funds, nor could they exercise the patronage which was the key to political power. They relied solely for the spoils of office on the King's bounty or on bribes of doubtful legitimacy – neither of which endeared them to the native population.

Notes

[1] Portland MSS 111, Longleat, f.29
[2] Quoted in Michael De-la-Noy, *The King Who Never Was*, 1996, p.29
[3] Letter of Liselotte to Caroline, 27 February 1721, Stevenson, op. cit.
[4] Quoted in Wilkins, op. cit., p.90
[5] Kroll, *Liselotte*, p.178
[6] Coronation formula from R Hatton, *George I*, 1978, p.110
[7] N Pevsner, *The Englishness of English Art*, 1964, p.30
[8] *Daily Courant*, 19 October 1714
[9] C Spencer Cowper, [ed.] *Diary of Mary, Countess Cowper 1714–20*, 1864 p.5
[10] Charles Chenevix Trench, *George II*, 1973, p.41
[11] Quoted by Trench, ibid., p.57. Original source Cowper p.5
[12] *Saturday Evening Post*, 23 September 1714
[13] Jacob Lustig reporting a conversation with Handel in 1734, quoted by O E Deutsch, *Handel, a Documentary Biography*, 1955, p.360
[14] Cowper, op. cit., p.38
[15] Quoted in Wilkins, op. cit., p.175

[16] John Walters, *The Royal Griffin*, 1972, p.171

[17] Wilkins, op. cit., p.174

[18] *Brice's Weekly Journal*, 8 April 1725

[19] R Campbell, *The London Tradesman*, 1748

[20] James Ralph, *A Critical Review of the Public Buildings In and About London and Westminster*, 1734, p.48

[21] Horace Walpole, *Reminiscences*, [ed.] Paget Toynbee, 1924, pp.29–30

[22] Trench, op. cit., p.119

[23] Ibid., p.53

[24] Wilkins, op. cit., p.259

Chapter Three

By the late spring of 1715, pamphlets began to circulate referring to 'this flight of hungry Hanoverians like so many famished vultures falling with keen eyes and beaded talons upon the fruitful soil of England'. Opposition was growing because the Whigs had won an overwhelming victory in the March elections and were depriving Tories of even minor office, while impeachment processes were begun against the great Tory Lords, Ormonde and Bolingbroke. The latter fled to France and became James's secretary of state, bringing to Jacobite service a highly intelligent and cunning politician with the unrivalled experience of English affairs it sorely needed. But it was not only the known Jacobites who went into opposition – the perceived Whig tactics of revenge alienated many who had never contemplated rebellion, while the Duke of Marlborough, ever a reliable barometer of English attitudes, was, in Thackeray's memorable phrase, deep into 'dark doubling and tacking' and secretly sending money to James in France.[1] There had been Jacobite riots in several provincial cities on coronation day, and now the volatile and dangerous London mob which had then cheered King George began to change its tune: his assurance to his mistress about the move to England, that the king-killers were all on his side, began to look rather hollow. Openly, Jacobite gangs roamed the streets burning Hanoverian effigies and breaking the windows of any householder who would not join them; these disturbances may have been orchestrated, since ministers received intelligence reports that after the mob had proclaimed James, 'persons of distinction' were to appear at its head to direct it further. It was certainly the case that many of the welcoming committee at Greenwich had strong Jacobite sympathies, and enough of those now threw in their lot with James to cause the artist Thornhill more problems as he strove to complete his painting of George's arrival.

News came from Scotland that the clans were gathering, and an army of 5,000 marched to Perth, which they entered on 16 September 1715, expecting to find their leader. The English, too, had expected James to land in Scotland long before, the plans having been passed on to them by the English ambassador in Paris, who seems to have had access – of whatever kind – to Bolingbroke's French mistress. Poor security was always the Jacobites' Achilles heel: lines of communication stretching from Lorraine and Saint-Germain to the west of England and the Scottish Highlands were all too easy to tap into.

Five clerks and four codebreakers beavered away at the intercepted correspondence, one hundred volumes of which are held by the Public Records Office; but even these dedicated Crown servants may have had a problem with the message to James in June 1714 from George Lockhart of Carnwath, his main agent in Lowland Scotland, which reads thus:

> Frog first mentioned it in Councell and Frog was put onto it by Rabbit... Tyger came to Orange and told him he was Gooseberry's darling, and Gooseberry would stand by him and enable him to get the better of Haddock if Gooseberry was convinced he was not a Hound but a friend to Baker.[2]

No doubt this was a masterly summing-up of the English political situation shortly before Queen Anne's death, but James can hardly be blamed for his confusion. However, he is culpable, together with his political advisers and military commanders, for the inept leadership which doomed the Jacobite Rising of 1715 – the year when historically and politically much was in their favour.

It could even be said that he at least refuted any rumours about his illegitimacy by displaying all the family failings of indecision, ineffectuality and faithlessness. Two major battles had been fought by the Jacobites, coincidentally on the same day in Scotland at Sheriffmuir and at Preston in England, before he finally arrived in Perth in December and revealed a further sad truth: that the legendary Stuart charm had passed him by. He was as wooden in his demeanour as the Hanoverian he sought to displace: 'We were not at all animated by his presence,' wrote one Jacobite officer, 'we saw nothing in him that looked like spirit. He never appeared with cheerfulness and vigour ... his countenance looked extremely heavy and he cared not to go abroad among us to see us handle arms.'[3]

To the men who were risking everything for him, James's fatalism and pessimism were dispiriting. 'My whole life,' he told them, 'even from the cradle has shown constant series of misfortunes and I am prepared, so it please God, to suffer the threats of my enemies and yours.'[4]

It was hardly an inspiring invitation, and many Scots faded back into the heather. Few English Jacobites had ever joined them – 'their love for the Pretender [not going] so far as to make them lie three nights under a hedge in November'. The flare of rebellion sputtered out and 'Jamie the Rover' slipped back to the continent and fifty years of exile, leaving his higher profile followers to English retribution.

Petitions begged the Princess of Wales to mediate for many of the prisoners who had 'the misfortune to engage in unnatural rebellion against their rightful and lawful sovereign... and now have an unfeigned sorrow and abhorrence for so Unnatural an Attempt'.[5] Anne, Dowager Countess of Home, wrote a pathetic letter on behalf of her son, 'who hath been all along so weak in understanding that he was always under the care and management of others till he made his Escape from them and falling in with a Party of Rebels followed them to Preston'.[6]

Caroline showed much sympathy and asked for clemency even as Government ministers howled for blood in the House of Commons, attacking 'the unworthy members of this great body [the Tory opposition] who can without blushing open their mouths in favour of rebels and parasites'. There was further outrage when it was discovered that the Jacobite peers being tried in Westminster Hall were allowed to break their journey back to the Tower each day at a tavern in the Strand, and after a good dinner of roast beef, visit the shop next door to replenish their snuff-boxes. Many petitions were granted, as George showed a leniency which was as wise as it was unprecedented. Some Scottish prisoners were allowed to escape, and for those English rank and file who came to trial the punishment was deportation to West Indian plantations rather than death; on one of these journeys the prisoners overpowered their guards, took over the ship and sailed to France, where they sold it and settled in various trades and lived happily ever after.

The Scottish peers were pardoned; one because he had been at Eton with the Secretary of State for Northern Affairs, and only the two English earls – Derwentwater and Kenmuir – were executed. The former was only twenty-seven, a devoted family man who had joined the rebellion reluctantly, and only after a warrant was issued for his arrest as someone who might be expected to be against the government; it was recounted that he was 'greatly dismay'd' on the scaffold but quickly recovered himself, replying to those who offered a reprieve if he would forswear his Catholicism that 'life on those terms would be too dear a purchase'[7]. Kenmuir was Protestant but had remained loyal to the Stuarts all his life, and although 'a total stranger to military matters and singularly unfitted to command troops'[8] had accepted a commission to lead a small company of mounted soldiers. He was supported on the scaffold by his eldest son and two Church of England clerics, and waved aside an invitation to address the crowds: 'I come to dye not to make speeches.'

In a gesture which politicians in another age might well study, the King specifically directed that up to £20,000 of the annual income from forfeited Jacobite estates should be allocated to provide schools in the Highlands. Jacobitism was never in itself a bar to positions in the royal household – the Chief Confectioner made no secret of his support for the Pretender, but he was only dismissed when 'he used such indecent expressions concerning the King and Madame Kielmansegge as are not fit to be recorded'. These probably referred to the incest issue, but even then George refused to punish him further because he was such a skilled pastry cook. The French ambassador hopefully reported that George considered England a temporary possession, and at a masked ball when a woman challenged him to drink 'King James's health' the King laughed and complied. 'I drink with all my heart to the health of any unfortunate prince.'[9] Like William III, who had gained the throne in ambiguous circumstances he refused ever to touch for the king's evil – or maybe these monarchs were just more squeamish or less sacramentally aware than those they replaced.

Whether his sensitivity was personal or political, George was by no means the stupid and stolid boor he has been proclaimed. The Hanoverian had been shown as the better of two fairly unsatisfactory alternatives, and his family was safe until memories faded again and a new generation returned to old dreams. An extraordinary display of the Northern Lights on the night news was received of James's flight to France convinced the superstitious that right had triumphed – 'a huge body of light seemed to dispose itself into columns or pillars of flame... interspersed with green, blue, red and yellow'[10] so illuminating London that at one in the morning people walked on Lincoln's Inn Fields as if it were broad daylight, and a lady returning from court in a sedan had alternately to bully and coax her terrified chair-bearers.

George could now unpack the bags he had reputedly left ready for a quick getaway and, to relieve the pressure on St James's, he began an ambitious restoration of Kensington Palace, which was completely remodelled and extended. After the major architectural alterations, James Thornhill was commissioned to decorate the State Apartments, but William Kent slipped in an estimate for less than half the price and thereafter was allowed free rein, though his painted Etruscan ceilings were criticised by the conservative Board of Works, who protested they had seen 'very few worse for such a place'. In a further frugal touch, the blue curtains and hangings which had set off William and Mary's collection of Delft porcelain were dyed green and reused. The King also took a great interest in the design of his garden there, constructing the Round Pond, then called the Basin, and the Grand Walk. George was as enthusiastic a walker as his mother had been, and Caroline, and often the young princesses as well, would join him on his tours of inspection.

Kensington offered a more private environment than St James's Park, where they had been accustomed to walk along the canals and tree-lined paths. But the jostling staring crowds had become tiresome, and enterprising countrywomen would drive their animals into the park and offer cups of milk straight from the cow, thus 'offending and disturbing the persons of quality'.[11] Kensington had more exciting beasts for the children to marvel at when its collection of snails and tropical birds was expanded to include civet cats, tigers and leopards. Twenty stone of beef was delivered for them each week – at a cost of 16s 8d – by a local butcher, who once submitted a pathetic plea to the Treasury that he had not been paid for eighteen months.

For Caroline, the excitement of her life in England was made all the greater by the access it gave her to new intellectual and political circles: she warmly welcomed Sir Isaac Newton, whom she had first met in Sophie Charlotte's salon, read Bacon's complete works, held weekly meetings of learned theologians, and developed a close friendship with Robert Walpole. Her Lady of the Bedchamber, Mrs Clayton, remarked waspishly that the Princess might be better employed correcting her children's faults than in 'settling points of controversial divinity' – Anne in particular was 'displaying a most ambitious temper'.[12] On the other hand, Sarah, Duchess of Marlborough found herself comforting a screaming princess after Caroline had personally given her a whipping.

The children led a highly regimented life: they rose at seven and after 'prayer, coiffe and breakfast' walked in the park from eight until nine before the crowds arrived. Lessons lasted all morning, and their main meal at one consisted of low quality roasts with no spices or dressings; in the afternoon they walked again or, if the weather was bad, 'talked of sensible things'.[13] For the rest of the day, lessons in dancing, riding, painting and music alternated with games of shuttlecock, until they took their embroidery into their mother's apartments for an hour before bed.

Caroline's household assumed great significance in the absence of a queen consort, and she appointed a bevy of teenage maids of honour – well-born, witty and beautiful – who alternately delighted and scandalised the Court. Sophia Howe, granddaughter of Charles I's general, Rupert of the Rhine, when reproved by a solemn duchess for giggling during divine service at the Chapel Royal and told she could not do a worse thing, answered, 'I beg your Grace's pardon, I can do a great many worse things';[14] which she duly did, staging her public elopement with a notorious rake who then refused to marry her. The beauty of Molly Lepel attracted even the King's eye, a fact which was celebrated just after the Fifteen by the Earl of Chesterfield with his customary delicate phrasing:

> Heaven keep our good King from a rising,
> But that rising who's fitter to quell,
> Than some lady with beauty surprising,
> And who should that be but Lepel?
>
> O now I am King of Great Britain
> To choose a minister well
> And support the throne that I sit on,
> I'd have under me Molly Lepel.[15]

The Jacobite threat had come from parts of their kingdom which George and his son would never even visit. Apart from rare visits to Newmarket for the racing or to Oxford and Cambridge for ingratiation, only the narrow corridors to Harwich or Gravesend for journeys to the Electorate or unusually energetic hunted animals took them outside their capital and its surrounding arc of Kensington, Windsor and Hampton Court.

In London, a population of nearly three-quarters of a million divided itself between the business area of the City, political Whitehall and royal St James's, with areas of wasteland in between. Buckingham House, on the edge of St James's Park, stood in 'a little wilderness of blackbirds and nightingales', while Lord Burlington had chosen his house on rural Piccadilly so that he would be safe from anyone building beyond him. Within the densely populated areas, away from the stately squares with their central gardens, it was the sheer variety of London which struck foreign visitors:

> Here lives a Person of high Distinction; next door a Butcher with his stinking Shambles! A Tallow Chandler shall front my Lord's nice Venetian window and two or three brawny naked Curriers in their Pit shall face a fine Lady in her back closet and disturb her spiritual Thoughts.

Samuel Johnson took up this train of thought in an early poem:

> Here malice, rapine, accident, conspire,
> And now a rabble rages, now a fire.
> Their ambush here relentless ruffians lay,
> And here the fell attorney prowls for prey,
> Here falling houses thunder on your head
> And there a female Atheist talks you dead.[16]

The noise in narrow streets was bewildering, as carts and coaches rumbled by incessantly, street vendors bawled out their wares, bells clanged from dozens of city churches and yelling crowds could gather in a moment, for 'King Mob might at any time resume his reign after the briefest interregnum'.[17] 'The Mob' was feared by all – a powerful entity in any town, whether corporally to intimidate and manipulate, or in the abstract as a tool of politicians. All manner of dangers might await the weak, the vulnerable or the inexperienced. A newspaper advertised for:

> A Lost Gentleman, aged one and twenty, of a fair complexion, having on a flaxen tie-wig, a light cinnamon suit of fine cloth, the coat buttoned with yellow mettle, black silk stockings, wrought silver shoe buckles, a silver hilted sword and gold buttons to his shirt sleeves. If he is living he is desired to return to his

friends in London, or if he be dead the Person who gives any account of him shall receive ten guineas reward.

So travel through the rutted streets jostled by who knew whom, or over the wild heath of Hyde Park, was too risky for wealthy citizens or fashionable society, and the Thames had long been the great highway. It was estimated that 15,000 craft of all kinds plied the river. The multi-oared decorative barges owned by the nobility were prominent, and it was the custom that anyone could 'call out whatever he pleased to other occupants of boats, even though it were the King himself, and no one has the right to be shocked'.[18] On summer evenings parties and picnics would be held on the river, the Duke of Newcastle once offering his guests a feast of eighty cold dishes, and accompanying boats ferried groups of musicians – Handel's 'Water Music' was composed for such a festivity, George liking it so much that he ordered it to be played three times over. It was one of the rare public occasions when he was seen to enjoy himself. His natural reserve, his difficulty with the language and the obvious lack of enthusiasm for his new country, however well he governed it, led to a sense of detachment.

The Prince and Princess of Wales, on the other hand, deliberately set out to please: their English was fluent, if heavily accented, and 'they were civil and kind to Everybody and applied [themselves] to understand the State of the Nation'.[19] They revelled in those obligations of royalty – the 'public days' of levees, open table and evening receptions – which the King so disliked. Such gatherings inevitably assumed a political slant, and the Prince began to build up an interest of his own in Parliament independent of the King's – something no monarch could tolerate in his heir. Caroline enjoyed the influence this brought her, but she was also astute enough to mediate when possible between her choleric husband and his suspicious father.

A year after the birth of a stillborn son in November 1716, which had nearly killed her, Caroline went into labour again at St James's. Present in the room were her husband, the Archbishop of Canterbury, four Duchesses and five Countesses, though probably of more use to her were two male physicians, marking her rejection of the German tradition, whereby only women attended a birth. Fireworks and a cannon salute celebrated the arrival of the first Hanoverian prince to be born on English soil. But an open quarrel erupted at the child's christening as simmering ill-feeling was exacerbated by the usual family arguments over names and godparents. The Prince, shaking with rage, said something to the Duke of Newcastle which that ever timid gentleman interpreted as a challenge to a duel, and he scuttled off to tell tales to the King. There is evidence that government ministers, fearful of the opposition's increasing power in the Commons, propelled the King into an uncharacteristic overreaction. George first put his son under close arrest at St James's and then ordered him to leave the palace, expecting the family to remain behind. But Caroline made an instant choice, leapt from her bed, supervised the packing, left her newborn baby, kissed the three weeping little princesses and, at seven o'clock on a November evening, she and her husband walked up St James's Street in front of a hastily summoned sympathetic crowd to the house of the Prince's chamberlain. The drama of the occasion was further heightened by an irrepressible maid of honour who cheered 'their flight into the wilderness with a spirited rendering of "Over the Hills and Far Away"'.

> But Bellenden we needs must praise
> Who as down stairs she jumps
> Sings 'O'er the hills and far away'
> Despising doleful dumps.[20]

(This was Mary Bellenden, who was also a lively correspondent, referring in a letter to a clothes-bill 'as long as my arm and as broad as my ass.')[21]

The royal couple moved to Leicester House in an ill-lit dangerous slum, which is now known as Leicester Square. This quickly became a rival court – 'a pouting place of princes'.[22] The actual house was large and spacious. It had been used by Peter the Great on his visit to England and George Augustus' great-grandmother, Elizabeth of Bohemia, had died there while in London for the coronation of her nephew, Charles II. Its handsome reception rooms now became the focus for a far more brilliant court than St James's, despite the household being controlled by the Earl of Grantham, described by Lord Hervey as having 'the animal gift of reasoning in so small a proportion that his existence was barely distinguished from a vegetable'.[23]

Caroline continued her manipulation of public opinion by publishing the emollient letters she made her husband write to the King. The overtures were ignored as George's attitude hardened: Caroline alone was allowed to visit the children for an hour a day, forced to hide in another room if the King approached, and was totally helpless as she watched the increasing weakness of her baby son. He died at four months old, and despite a post-mortem revealing congenital heart disease, George's already shaky reputation was further undermined when the pamphleteers accused him of neglect, or worse. 'There must be something at the bottom of all this,' the Duchess of Orleans speculated wildly, 'perhaps the King is in love with the Princess.'[24] He certainly admired her spirit; she had always been able to say things to him which no one else would dare. He called her 'that she-devil' and was finding she was a more formidable enemy than his son.[25]

The three princesses, aged between eight and four, must have been totally bewildered. Anne once burst out, 'We have a good father and a good mother and yet we are as charity children.'[26] She sent frequent notes to Caroline assuring her of their well-being, and after they were moved to Kensington she picked a basket of fruit from the glasshouse, without the King's knowledge, and sent it to her parents. Even such notes and gifts had to be smuggled out in a cloak-and-dagger operation: a lady-in-waiting allowed contact with the children but not with Caroline came secretly by river to Hampton Court early in the morning on instruction to leave her message 'in the garden-house at the end of the terrace that nobody may see you'.[27] George ordered his granddaughters to preside at formal receptions instead of their parents, and at the end of May the Council went to Kensington to compliment the princesses on the occasion of the King's birthday, though it is recorded that they went in by twos and threes to avoid frightening the children. This separation and the scandal it caused dragged on for many months; public quarrels do a royal family no good, and this one was fuelled by the vindictiveness of ministers such as Lord Stanhope, who wrote to the King urging the Prince's banishment to plantations overseas: 'it is true that he is your son, but the Son of God himself was sacrificed for the good of mankind.'[28]

Anne herself eventually provided the opportunity for reconciliation without either side losing face. She fell ill with smallpox and George panicked at the thought of losing another grandchild while under his protection. Caroline was allowed to move in with her daughter, the King came to visit them once Anne was out of danger, and they met in her apartments while anxious courtiers waited outside. The Turk Mehemet entertained them with his reminiscences about the Queen of Prussia's post-mortem – 'when she was opened her stomach was so worn that you could thrust your fingers through at any place' – and he himself had had the honour of doing so.[29] In private George railed at Caroline, but she came out and diplomatically told everyone including her husband how kind he had been. Next day there was a formal reception where King and Prince appeared together for the first time for two years. 'The whole Thing,' wrote a witness, 'looked like two Armies drawn up in battle array,'[30] though in front of a large crowd of curious onlookers it marked a reconciliation of a sort. However, George retained care and control of his three granddaughters, who remained apart from their parents and under his roof for the rest of his life. He seems to have managed to keep their affection; among Anne's papers at her death fifty years later was an obviously treasured letter from him:

...since I do not doubt your continued good conduct I do not recommend it to you, all that I wish my dear granddaughter is that you further nurture your friendship towards me. Embrace your two sisters for me and always be assured of my devotion.[31]

Caroline was now allowed responsibility for their health, and with Anne badly scarred by smallpox, she made the courageous decision to have Amelia and Caroline inoculated against the disease. Smallpox could be anything or nothing; their father had escaped with only 'a few flea-bites', but more often 'it came forth like a destroying Angel' which caused problems after death. Lord Dalkeith was ill for only two days, but putrefaction set in so fast that his limbs fell off as he was being placed in his coffin.

The intrepid explorer, Lady Mary Wortley Montagu, had brought back serum from Turkey where, she assured everybody, 'thousands undergo this operation and the French ambassador says pleasantly that they take the small-pox here by way of diversion as they take the waters in other countries'.

The Duchess of Orleans was appalled.

> I worry a great deal about the dear Princess of Wales and the two little princesses – I am not so brave and could not possibly steel myself to make my children ill when they were quite well. My doctor doesn't think it safe.

The children flourished and the Duchess died a few months later at the age of seventy, her doctor having ordered eighty purges in eight days.[32]

Notes

[1] W M Thackeray, *The Four Georges*, 1861, p.45
[2] Daniel Szechi [ed.], *Letters of George Lockhart of Carnwath*, 1988, p.108
[3] *A True Account of the Proceedings at Perth by a Rebel*, 1716. This pamphlet's title alerts one that it may have been a propaganda exercise to discredit James, but it is certainly true that he had none of his son's charisma.
[4] Fitzroy MacLean, *Bonnie Prince Charlie*, 1998, p.6
[5] Stuart Papers 35/77
[6] Ibid.
[7] Oxford Dictionary of National Biography, 2005
[8] Robert Patten, *History of the Late Rebellion*, 1717, p.51
[9] Wilkins, op. cit., p.144
[10] Christopher Sinclair-Stevenson, *Inglorious Rebellion*, 1972, p.152
[11] Drummond and Wilbraham, The *Englishman's Food*, 1957, p.194
[12] K Thomson [ed.], *Memoirs of Viscountess Sundon*, 1847, p.287. Mrs Charlotte Clayton became Lady Sundon in 1735
[13] Egerton MSS 1717, f.78
[14] W Michael, *Beginnings of the Hanoverian Dynasty*, 1936, p.53
[15] Chesterfield, *Miscellaneous Works*, 1778, p.53
[16] S Johnson, *London*, 1738
[17] F MacLean, op. cit., p.129
[18] C de Saussure, *A Foreign View of England in the Reigns of George I and George II*, pp.151–2
[19] Davies, op. cit., p.49
[20] Egerton MSS, 1717
[21] J W Croker [ed.], *Letters to and from Lady Henrietta Howard, Countess of Suffolk*, 1824, p.105
[22] Thomas Pennant, *Account of London*, 1813, p.163

[23] Romney Sedgwick [ed.], *Some Materials towards Memoirs of the Reign of King George II* by John Lord Hervey, 1931, p.345

[24] Quoted by Davies, op. cit., p.68

[25] Cowper, op. cit., p.79

[26] W. Michael [ed.], *Engelische Geschichte im 18 Jahrhundert*, 1896–1955

[27] Sundon, op. cit., p.123

[28] Hervey, op. cit., p.849

[29] P Quennell, *Caroline of England*, 1939, p.82

[30] Arkell, op. cit., p.123

[31] Koninklijk Huisarchief, s'Gravenhage, (henceforth KHA) Anna van Hannover 430

[32] Kroll, *Liselotte*, p.264

Chapter Four

Deprived for various reasons of their six eldest children, George Augustus and Caroline began a second family. Two more daughters, Mary and Louisa followed a son who became the favourite of both his parents. The doctor in attendance on him was a known Jacobite and he may have lived to regret his skill as William Duke of Cumberland marched to Culloden in 1746. The three elder girls meanwhile drew together in a close and supportive relationship that was to last all their lives. Anne was the leader in everything – her intellect was formidable, since she became as involved in philosophy and theology as her mother could have wished. She was an exceptionally graceful dancer and her musical gifts, both as composer and performer on the harpsichord, were developing to a near professional level. Her accomplishments were greatly admired, not least by Anne herself. Her 'ambitious temper' had developed into arrogance as, with Frederick still in Hanover, she thoroughly enjoyed her pre-eminence, taking her place as the eldest with the enthusiasm that only a second child can know. The young Amelia made her way in the world by charm; as blonde as her elder sister but with a flawless complexion, she was witty and sociable, showing few signs of the determined eccentric she would become. Caroline, was the prettiest of the three, as dark as they were fair, and ever the peacemaker in any quarrel; but her mother worried about her indolence which, as she put it, 'prevents you from expressing your pretty thoughts and makes you act as if you had neither feeling nor reason'.[1] Caroline's lethargy probably came from her ill health, and her childhood was no doubt blighted as much by the medical treatments she endured as by the illnesses themselves.

Enemas, whether of chicory water and rhubarb or the new 'English medicine' of Epsom salts, were heavily relied upon. Enormous doses of opium mixed with alcohol were used for pain relief; while letting blood, carefully measured by the ounce, was the remedy for every ill. What was left might be purified by drinking ass's milk mixed with powder of crabs' eyes and oyster-shells. Louis XIV's gangrene was treated by swaddling the limbs with feather pillows and imposing a diet of overripe figs, melons and mulberries.[2] Physicians were beginning to experiment with electrical treatment, drawing sparks off the patient's tongue; John Wesley was an especial enthusiast, setting up three clinics for 'this surprising medicine… the most efficacious in nervous disorders of every kind which has ever yet been discovered'.[3] A much promoted cure for consumption involved a mixture of ale and herbs containing a peck of garden snails roasted 'till they leave off making a noise',[4] while a rather pleasanter treatment for the Bloody Flux recommended a little cochineal boiled in spring water with loaf sugar and cinnamon. The surgeon William Cheseldon spent the 1720s refining his technique of cutting out kidney stones until he could do it in thirty seconds instead of fifty-four; those who could not endure the knife opted for the many remedies advertised in the newspapers. An invitation for progress reports after taking Mrs Stephens' Medicine produced a reply from Joseph Burrows of Clerkenwell who, after taking it, passed eighteen stones in a fortnight, one of which, he was sure she would be interested to know, was a perfect oval shape, one and a half inches by one inch.[5] Surgeons showed much ingenuity in their treatments: it was reported that when a boy swallowed a fishing hook, they 'made a hole through a leaden Bullet, threaded it with a line and when the Boy swallowed the Bullet [it ran] down the line and by its weight loosing the Hook, both were drawn up with Ease'.

The sisters appeared at all formal royal occasions when the King was present, at a ball in 1725 to celebrate his birthday they were closely observed by a young Swiss, César de Saussure. Entry to such occasions was open to anyone who was dressed appropriately – footmen acted as rather inconsistent bouncers but were always helpful if a shilling was pressed into their hands. De Saussure watched George greeting his guests, noting that he kissed pretty women on the cheek and the prettiest on the lips. An old man pressed forward with a bunch of flowers, saying, 'I do not know how old I am, but I first bore arms in the Civil War, served Cromwell and Charles, James, William and Anne.'[6] The princesses, César thought, were beautifully dressed – their wardrobe accounts show five court dresses a year – either richly embroidered velvet or multicoloured silk worn looped back to reveal petticoats trimmed in gold or silver. Dean Swift was once asked by their governess to procure some Irish plaid for them in purple, yellow and white at 8s. 3d a yard, and, the Court having much enjoyed *Gulliver's Travels*, a second order was submitted with the measurements stipulated as 'the height of a Brobdingnag dwarf multiplied by two and a half.'[7]

The cost of appearing at Court was enormous, not many people agreeing with the pious Lady Cowper who made it 'my study to adorn my mind [rather] than set off a vile body of Dust and Ashes'.[8] Her brother-in-law, Spencer Cowper, an eminent but impoverished lawyer had to refuse his disconsolate only daughter permission to attend a birthday ball: 'I think it better not to attempt without doing it as it ought to be.' The men were as fine as the women – 'Lord Essex wore a silver tissue coat and pink colour lustring wastcote'.[9] But however costly, such clothes could only have been worn once, judging by the graphic descriptions of social occasions. 'The sweating and stinking' was barely concealed by lavish applications of ambergris and musk, and as white powder replaced grey the hair was stiffened to hold it: 'My Lady Baltimore looked like a frightened owl, her locks strutted out, greased, gummed and powdered.' One guest found that for a supper of cold chicken, tongue and jelly there were neither knives nor plates; since he 'did not think it looked good to be pulling greasy bones about in a room full of princesses' he ate nothing and watched with distaste as the bones were tossed out of the window. This was Peter Wentworth, first equerry to George, later secretary to Caroline who, as he wrote to his cousin, was always careful to place himself in sight of the King 'well powdered, but [I] have no money yet'.[10] The Vice-Chamberlain reported after another entertainment that the room was so stained with claret that 'it was necessary to provide saylcloth against another ball'.[11] Heavy drinking was customary at court: some years later the Duke of Newcastle was 'most excessively drunk' when deep in conversation with Anne, and as he apologised for his condition the next day she assured him that he had been charming and she had never found him so entertaining.

Sober, Newcastle was a timorous and pedantic fusspot: 'his Mind can never be composed, his Spirits are always agitated.'[12] He was nicknamed *Permis* by the princesses for his habit of beginning every sentence with '*Est-il permis?*', and since he was 'unwilling to displease any man by a plain Negative [he] frequently does not recollect that he is under the same Engagements to at least ten Competitors'.[13] He never took an initiative in his life, but he served in the Cabinet for thirty-six years between 1724 and 1762 where his tireless attention to detail and understanding of European politics made him an invaluable minister.

De Saussure was a fascinated observer of English life and the English character. He describes an equestrian statue of Charles I, which had been greatly admired, but at the unveiling the sculptor noticed that he had omitted the saddle's girths, and hanged himself in shame. 'The man was without doubt an Englishman, this trait depicts his energetic character.'[14] He soon learnt that wearing a plume in his hat or his hair tied in a bow in the street encouraged the London mob to throw 'playthings' (usually dead cats) at 'the French dog'. He ventured into *The Folly*, a large boat moored opposite Somerset House. On the first deck a large room decorated with interesting murals offered splendid food and wine, while above were a few small apartments where 'nymphs, tired of the world, retire and for fear of being lonely, invite a friend to amuse them'.[15] He also watched, entranced, several of the public hangings which took place every six weeks or so. Friends of the victim would tug at his feet so that he would die quicker and then there were 'most amusing scenes between messengers sent by the surgeons and people who do not like bodies to be cut up'.[16] He spent much time in the coffee houses where wine, brandy, chocolate and punch were also served, gossip exchanged and newspapers studied, though he no doubt agreed with another continental visitor who complained that, however instructed, all the English could produce from half an ounce of coffee was 'a prodigious amount of brown water'. He read the accounts of Mary Toft of Godalming who 'in the presence of an eminent surgeon' had given birth to four rabbits; pamphlets were written about her and more rabbits appeared; the King sent his own doctor, who arrived just in time to deliver another, but fraud was suspected.[17]

He was interested in the English passion for smuggling but it did not surprise him, for the duty paid on a cask of wine equalled the cost of both the wine and the journey from France. He had himself crossed by packet boat from Rotterdam, and between Gravesend and the Pool of London five different sets of excise men had boarded and searched the passengers, only leaving when offered gifts of wine and eau de vie. He had been shocked when one group put their hands up the ladies' skirts, but realised they knew their business when several pieces of Flemish lace were found.[18] Avoidance of duty was the national game – Swift was warned to send the princesses' plaid in a plain wrapper 'so it is not seized for duty'; and even the Prime Minister, Robert Walpole, when at his Houghton estate took delivery of contraband wines and linens, run ashore on the isolated Norfolk coast, and proceeded to bring them up to London by Admiralty barge.[19]

The enormously high cost of living in England, about which all visiting foreigners complained, and the strain of maintaining a position at Court encouraged the nobility, Hanoverian and English alike, to embrace in 1720 a method of money-making which seemed to offer all the excitement of gambling without the slightest risk. Traditional methods of finance could not support the explosion of expenditure which marked the early years of the eighteenth century. Land was being enclosed and the great families were building or modernising houses both in town and the country, but conspicuous display was no longer the prerogative of the nobility. Wealth was more a key to power and influence than class, and the desperate scramble for it led to the phenomenon of the South Sea Bubble, which affected every stratum of society.

The English were a nation of gamblers; huge amounts were won and lost on card games or horse races, on whether Lord X would marry Lady Y, or what date a foreign siege would end. A man once collapsed in the street outside White's Club and bets were laid as to whether he were dead or not. When a Good Samaritan went to his assistance there were howls of fury since this would affect the payout. Men were also fascinated by the idea of the Spanish Main – a land of gold and silver where English buccaneers had always made their fortunes. So, when the South Sea Company took over the National Debt, which it converted into publicly owned stock with rocketing values, 'the ghosts of Drake and Raleigh seemed to hover round the Royal Exchange', and near hysteria gripped the country. The Chancellor of the Exchequer himself commended the scheme to the House of Commons as a prudent one. Courtiers, politicians and royal mistresses received sweeteners worth up to one and a half million in today's money, and people of every class poured all their savings into the venture. George invested a large sum from the Civil List, and women were among the foremost speculators because for the first time a thoroughly respectable and government-approved enterprise seemed to offer them the hope of financial independence.

> Our greatest ladies hither come
> And ply in chariots daily,
> Oft pawn their jewels for a sum
> To venture in the Alley.
> Young harlots too from Drury Lane
> Approach the 'Change in coaches
> To fool away the gold they gain
> By their impure debauches.[20]

Such success led the directors of the Company to offer new issues through the spring and summer of 1720, and as each were fully subscribed, the stock value rose from 100 to 1,000. Such frenzy to invest led other 'bubbles' to be floated. 800 per cent was promised for subscribers to a proposal for 'effecting the Transmutation of fluid Mercury or Quicksilver into a solid and malleable body so that 'twill spread under the hammer and be of equal Use, Beauty and Value with the purest standard Silver'.[21] Another investment opportunity was Puckle's machine gun, which would fire round bullets against Christians and square ones against the Turk. One enterprising gentleman absconded after scooping £1,000 in one morning by offering two-guinea shares for stock in 'an undertaking which shall in due time be revealed'.[22]

At the heart of the main scheme was John Blount, a middle-class tradesman who had been a director of the South Sea Company since its modest beginnings as a small finance company in 1711. His many contacts abroad and his own financial acumen had prompted speculative ventures in the past, but the scale this one achieved shook him and he was one of the first to jump ship. Having received a baronetcy in April for his 'services to the Crown', he moved in June to Tunbridge Wells 'writing every Post to his Brokers' to sell his stock.[23] Others also sniffed the wind and quietly sold; the Duchess of Marlborough made a profit of about £100,000 (£7 million by today's values), and Thomas Guy was able to finance the hospital which bore his name. The secret sales weakened the market, creating its own momentum of panic, and by

September the stock had lost 90 per cent of its value. Sir Isaac Newton lost one and a half million: 'I can measure the motions of bodies,' he lamented, 'but I cannot measure human folly.' A London newspaper reported it was painful to convene in public places and a torment to visit private houses, as 'not a few ancient and honourable families are entirely ruined and multitudes of unwary but covetous persons unfortunately crushed'.[24] Speculators blew out their brains or cut their throats, madhouses were forced to shut their doors to further patients, and the ruined cried out for vengeance. One MP suggested the Company's directors should be sewn up in sacks and thrown alive into the Thames. It was recommended that at the public inquiry honest men should not be allowed near the directors for fear of accidents, since 'several people went with pocket pistols and a desire to use them'.[25] The latter were committed to the Tower, whence their depositions variously argued that they had been absent from crucial meetings, no one told them stocks could fall as well as rise, and anyway they were not responsible for human cupidity. Their estates were forfeit down to the last thousand pounds which, Blount vainly pleaded, left him 'without necessary support or a Bed to lye on' for his eighteen children.

The collapse appeared a threat to social order and cohesion, with wild rumours of revolution in favour of the Stuarts, but George's steady nerve calmed the hysteria just as he had ridden out the turbulent family quarrels and the threat of the Fifteen. He allowed a select committee to apportion blame, but deprived it of its most wanted witness. Robert Knight, the chief cashier, knew better than anyone else the often corrupt involvement of government and Court – and when he escaped to France George privately asked the Regent to refuse the British Ambassador's request for forcible extradition.

After 1721 George's kingdom and his family settled down to more tranquil times. The rhythm of Court life was dully predictable as he moved between Kensington, St James's and Hampton Court with his granddaughters in tow, and his devotion to them was always apparent. The twelve-year-old Anne was specifically included in the granting of a royal lease to her parents on Richmond Lodge, which was described by a contemporary as 'a perfect Trianon, very neat, very pretty'. It stood in the midst of woods through which walks, marked by iron balustrades, meandered to the river. Formerly owned by Lord Ormonde, the house had stood empty since his disgrace in 1715 and had been colonised by undesirables: 'One John Humphries, a famous rat physician, was sent for from Dorsetshire by the Princess [and] collected together five hundred rats in his Royal Highness's palace which he brought alive to Leicester House as a proof of his art in that way.'[26]

George would never visit his son – indeed he was seldom seen to address a word to him – but he often went to Richmond where his first minister, Robert

Walpole, had a hunting lodge. They would discuss politics over a pipe and large bowls of punch, usually in Latin, which was the only language in which both were at ease. Walpole was an invaluable ally in controlling the Commons and steadying the country; and within a year or so Voltaire was astounded to see so many loyal subjects lining the banks of the Thames roaring appreciation of their foreign King. The Frenchman was in London to meet the intellectuals and literary men who adorned the London scene – Newton, Swift and Pope. At a dinner party in Pope's Twickenham home, the poet's 76-year-old mother presided, and was concerned about the young man's poor physique and lack of appetite. Voltaire gave her 'so indelicate and brutal an account of the occasion of his disorder contracted in Italy' that she had to be helped, swooning, from the table.

Many writers such as Pope and John Gay attacked political corruption and so, by implication, the ruling establishment, thus finding a ready welcome with the rival court of the Prince and Princess of Wales. Gay, who had lost a fortune in the Bubble, became one of Caroline's 'led captains' and wrote a book of fables for the young Cumberland. He had first met Caroline in Hanover, where he had ingratiated himself, as he wrote to Jonathan Swift, by dressing in blue and silver 'bowing profoundly, speaking deliberately and wearing both sides of my long periwig before'.[27] Swift himself was summoned to Caroline's presence with the assurance that she enjoyed odd people and was anxious to meet the wild Dean from Ireland. She was always delighted to receive the aged (and impoverished) Newton and one of his closest friends, Dr Samuel Clarke – the latter being set by her, first against Leibniz to discuss the existence of time and space, and then against sundry Roman Catholics to anatomise Trinitarianism.

The King was as little interested in philosophy and metaphysics as his son, but literary men did not benefit from his patronage either. His lack of facility in English made their intricate wit difficult for him to follow; but he was a founder member of the Royal Academy of Music, which revived opera on the London stage under the direction of Handel, and imported the best continental musicians to perform there. George would often attend to applaud such singers as Francesca Cuzzoni – 'ugly but with a nest of nightingales in her belly',[28] and he announced the news of Cumberland's birth in April 1721 at the first performance of Handel's *Muzio Scaevola*. The operas were more refined in style than other public entertainments on offer: a gladiator show staged two scantily clad women wielding two-handled three-foot swords with razor-sharp tips, and to add to the excitement their wounds were sewn up on stage. Moralists attacked the theatres as dangerous places encouraging loose living and crime, and quoted with glee the occasion when a cleric knocked on the door of a box and asked the assembled ladies if 'the count', a beautiful little boy, could watch the performance with them. Much petted and kissed, he then begged permission to sleep on the floor, from where he cut off all their jewelled shoe-buckles and made his escape.

By the mid-1720s the marriage prospects of his elder grandchildren began to preoccupy the King. Anne's name was on a shortlist of possible brides for Louis XV – a prospect which would have pleased her. She was once heard to wish she had no brothers so that she could become Queen, and when re-proved, rapped back, 'I would die tomorrow to be a queen today.'[29] She was indeed to wield more power in a foreign country than any English princess before or since, but not through a Catholic marriage. The House of Hanover had gained the throne purely because of its religion and would be seriously compromised by any Catholic connection; until her brothers married only two lives stood between Anne and the Crown she craved. Anyway, George had an impeccably Protestant royal connection in mind. His sister and daughter had married successive Electors, now Kings, of Prussia, and he planned to continue the tradition into the third generation with a double marriage between his niece Wilhelmine and Frederick, still languishing in Hanover, while Anne could have Crown Prince Frederick of Prussia. An announcement of the marriage was planned for 1727 when the King was due in Hanover for his regular summer visit, and the eighteen-year-old Anne prepared for a life in Berlin.

King George left London in June, two weeks after his sixty-seventh birth-day, in excellent spirits as always at the prospect of seeing his Electorate again. He looked forward to seeing how his plan for a great avenue of lime trees between Hanover and Herrenhausen was progressing. He enjoyed the com-pany of his grandson, Frederick; and his daughter, the Queen of Prussia, to whom he was very close, planned a prolonged visit to finalise the marriage arrangements. However he was reported to be more emotional than usual in parting with his granddaughters and a certain Miss Brett, who was reputed to be his latest mistress. She was promised the title of Duchess on his return and meanwhile given rooms at St James's adjoining those of the princesses. According to Horace Walpole, an assiduous collector of gossip, Miss Brett ordered the door between the apartments to be taken down, whereupon Anne and Amelia fell into a rage and had it blocked up again.

The crossing from Gravesend was smooth and speedy, and, escorted by a courtesy guard of Dutch cavalry, George's carriage pressed on at the furious pace he always demanded. At the German border he stopped for a supper of strawberries, oranges and watermelon; and here, it was reported, a letter was handed to him from his wife, Sophia Dorothea, who had died eight months before, in which she prophesied that he would die within a year of her own death. He insisted on resuming his journey in the small hours of the morning but after an hour or so he suffered a stroke. He was lifted from the carriage and laid on the ground while the accompanying surgeon bled him, whereupon he partly regained consciousness and indicated firmly that the journey should continue. On arrival at the palace in Osnabrück where he had been born, he courteously removed his hat in greeting his chamberlain and died.

Notes

[1] Hervey, op. cit., p.272
[2] Kroll, *Liselotte*, p.189
[3] John Wesley, *Journal*, 1827
[4] Thomas Newin, *The Butler's Recept Book*, 1719
[5] *Gentleman's Magazine*, March 1738
[6] de Saussure, op. cit., p.151
[7] Arkell, op. cit., p.137
[8] Cowper, op. cit., p.76
[9] E Osborn [ed.], *Political and Social Letters of a Lady of the Eighteenth Century*, 1891, p.23
[10] J J Cartwright [ed.], *Letters to Lord Strafford*, 1883, p.459
[11] Public Records Office, Lord Steward's Department, MSS 13/15, f.97
[12] Lord Holland [ed.], *Memoirs of James, Lord Waldegrave*, 1821, p.150
[13] Ibid., p.151
[14] de Saussure, op. cit., p.67
[15] Ibid., p.95
[16] Ibid., p.125
[17] Elizabeth Burton, *The Georgians at Home*, 1967, p.254
[18] de Saussure, op. cit., pp.32–4
[19] Trench, op. cit., p.163
[20] Wilkins, op. cit., p.346
[21] Trench, op. cit., p.101
[22] W T Laprade, *Public Opinion and Politics in Eighteenth Century England*, 1936, p.237
[23] Ibid.
[24] *Freethinker*, quoted by Trench, op. cit., p.103
[25] HMC XV, 6, 26
[26] Wilkins, op. cit., p.312
[27] Ibid., p.298
[28] de Saussure, op. cit., p.272
[29] Sundon, op. cit., p.287

Chapter Five

The first casualty of the new reign was Anne's marriage. George Augustus, delighted to be in a position at last to frustrate a plan of his father's, made the affable remark that 'grafting my half-witted son upon a madwoman would not improve the breed'[1] and Anne's match foundered as well. Had she married the future Frederick the Great, they would have been a formidable pair. He once said he would rather be cuckolded by a clever woman than married to a fool, and he would have had to treat the forceful and intelligent Anne better than the self-effacing and masochistic princess he eventually married. As it was, Anne remained personally close and politically useful to him all their lives. The disappointment was probably fleeting as, newly created Princess Royal, she exploited her position to the full: with Frederick still out of the competition and as the strongest character in the family after her mother, she was dominant. She was her father's favourite daughter, and only rarely provoked the furious bouts of temper which were the daily burden of everyone else, including Caroline. An observer wrote of a five-minute visit to his family when he:

> snubbed the Queen who was drinking chocolate for being always stuffing, the Princess Amelia for not hearing him, the Princess Caroline for having grown fat, the Duke for standing awkwardly… and then carried the Queen to walk and be re-snubbed in the garden.[2]

This observer was Lord Hervey, a minor politician appointed Vice-Chamberlain to the Royal Household, whose sharp eye and biting wit ensured little privacy and less dignity for George II's family. Hervey's 'fine set of Egyptian pebble teeth'[3] (actually agates) were much admired, but his lavish use of cosmetics and taste for delicate silks and young men led to the saying that there were three sexes – men, women and Herveys. His merciless pen brings to life the three elder daughters as they reached adulthood. The youngest, Caroline, conducted her life as a desperate attempt to remain on good terms with everyone. Nursing a secret passion for Hervey himself, of which he was well aware, she comforted herself by indulging her sweet tooth and growing ever fatter and more depressed. Amelia was changing, becoming – to put it politely – an original. She was, Hervey says, 'glad of any back to lash and the sorer it was the gladder she was to strike'.[4] She made enemies wherever she went, insulting people to their face with her forthrightness, and spreading poisonous tales about them behind their back.

Her own relationship with the Lord Chamberlain, the Duke of Grafton, caused much gossip. He was a grandson of Charles II, twenty-eight years her senior, with five grown sons – a rollicking devotee of practical jokes and a mountain of a man; he usually, according to a contemporary, 'turned politics to ridicule, never applied himself to business and as to books was totally illiterate, yet from long observation and natural sagacity he became the ablest courtier of his time'.[5] He was one of the few men the King was devoted to, though George once remarked that he could not understand the Duke's pleasure in hunting since 'with your great corps of twenty stone weight no horse, I am sure, can carry you within hearing, much less within sight of your hounds'.[6] Hunting was Amelia's passion too. She was a brilliant horsewoman who always kept up with her father across country. Eight hundred people once pursued a stag from Windsor Great Park over the Thames, eventually killing it on the terrace of a nobleman's house in Surrey where, to cheer him up, George and Amelia invited themselves to a late breakfast. On another occasion, Grafton and Amelia allegedly lost their way in Windsor Forest, spending much of the night there in a woodman's cottage and riding back to the castle at dawn to a scandalised reception committee.

Hervey has much to say about Anne, confirming her intellectual gifts and social skills. 'She rose very early,' he says, 'was many hours alone and never unemployed,' and 'she had more command of her passions than people generally have whose passions are so strong.'[7] She could, however, be impatient – the drumming of her fingers as she waited for slower players to sort their cards terrified them – and her rank was all important to her. She made little secret of her lack of affection for her father: 'She was glad of opportunities to point out his faults and wherever these were small enough to admit of it, she would magnify them and deepen the colours without caution.'[8] Her scarred complexion was unfortunate in a person 'very ill-made, though not crooked, with a great propensity to fat'.

The two youngest daughters, Mary and Louisa, aged four and five, were still in the nursery at the time; but their brother William, created Duke of Cumberland by his grandfather in 1726, was, though only a couple of years older, allowed a major role in court ceremonial. At the age of four he had been made a member of the Order of the Bath – that decoration devised by Walpole 'who knew the persuasive value of a ribbon as well as a handful of silver'. That he was right was shown in a letter from Lord Bateman who, on receiving the Bath, 'solemnly promised and gave his great honour that he would always attend the House and vote as he should be directed.'[9] As an appointed grenadier in the 2nd Foot the six-year-old Cumberland was allowed to drill a muster of well-born infants in the courtyard of St James's. The partiality shown by both George and Caroline to their younger son was in sharp contrast to their attitude to the firstborn, Frederick, whom they had not even seen for fourteen years. Caroline's evident delight as her three eldest daughters returned to live under her roof on their grandfather's death did not extend to a desire to reunite the whole family, and Frederick remained in Hanover. There was no separate provision for him in the generous Civil List steered through Parliament by Walpole, though £100,000 was set for Caroline, since 'she hath merited and engaged herself to the inviolable affection of His Majesty'.[10]

George was as devoted to his wife as he had ever been, and those seeking preferment who approached his mistress of sixteen years, Henrietta Howard, Countess of Suffolk, mistook their man. 'No established mistress of a sovereign,' said Horace Walpole, 'ever received less brilliance from the situation than Lady Suffolk.' She received some financial benefit, though perhaps not enough to compensate for hours of tedium. George would stand, watch in hand, waiting for the precise moment of his daily visit to regale her with his reminiscences and opinions, but the ultimate humiliation must have been Caroline's active encouragement of the association long after George had tired of it. Knowing that her husband 'must have some woman for the world to think he lay with', she knew also that the lady had not the slightest influence over him.

The argument about how far George was ruled by his wife is still unresolved. The pamphleteers had no doubt:

You may strut, dapper George, but 'twill all be in vain,
We know 'tis Queen Caroline, not you that reign,
You govern no more than Don Philip of Spain.
So if you would have us bow down and adore you,
Lock up your fat spouse as your dad did before you.[11]

And Hervey asserted that she was 'the sole spring on which every movement turned'. 'Nobody,' he wrote, 'who had not tampered with our priestess ever received a favourable answer from our god; storm and thunder greeted every votary that entered the temple without her protection.'[12] But, generally speaking, the more Hervey's imagery took flight the further he moved from truth. Caroline undoubtedly influenced George's behaviour, once throwing herself between him and a politician bringing unwelcome news,[13] while her subtly offered advice on how to approach issues and personalities was often heeded; but the theory that she either instigated or even expedited policy is an unlikely one. George's monarchy does not change after Caroline's death. The German-born George was, in fact, as his only serious biographer has pointed out, 'the first King of England truly to understand the principle and accept the reality of constitutional monarchy',[14] and this was recognised in his own time by the 2nd Earl Waldegrave: 'In the Course of a long Reign, there has not been a single attempt to extend the Prerogative of the Crown beyond its proper Limits.'[15] George publicly grumbled that he was 'a King in toils', but he was shrewd enough to accept the limits with relatively good grace; his greatest gift was his ability to recognise good advisers, whether those were his father's ministers or his wife. The four leading men of the preceding reign were described by him as a rogue, a blockhead, a dirty scoundrel and an impertinent fool, but he acknowledged their worth and he kept them on. He seldom allowed his personal, and often openly expressed, dislike of ministers to cloud his acceptance of their sound advice.

George and Caroline's coronation was one of the grandest ever seen, 'it is impossible for me to make you understand and imagine [such] pomp and magnificence' wrote a foreign observer.[16] The new King had always been aware of the importance of court ceremonial and tradition: 'all the pageantry and splendour, badges and trappings of royalty' were to be embodied in the solemn liturgical ceremony hallowed by precedent but enhanced by modern music. The Queen wore gold and silver tissue brocaded with coloured flowers, and, Queen Anne's jewels having disappeared (mostly, it was assumed, to Hanover) Caroline was

> ...as fine as the accumulated riches of the city and the suburbs could make [her]... for she had on her head and shoulders all the pearls she could borrow of the ladies of quality at one end of town and on her petticoat all the diamonds she could hire of the Jews and jewellers at the other.[17]

She was attended by Anne, Amelia and Caroline in stiff-bodied dresses of silver with ermine-trimmed cloaks of purple velvet. The procession took two hours to cross a long wooden bridge erected between Westminster Hall and the Abbey. On several occasions everyone shuffled to a halt, and the aged Duchess of Marlborough seized a drum from one of the musicians to sit on.

During the ceremony instrumental music of every sort accompanied the soaring voices of thirty-five men and twelve boys for Handel's specially composed anthems, 'Zadok the Priest' and 'Let my hands be strengthened'. William III's mistress, Lady Orkney, was there again, somewhat affected by the passage of time:

> I should have thought her one of the largest things of God's making if my Lady St John had not displayed her charms in honour of the day [for] she exposed behind a mixture of fat and wrinkles and before a very considerable protuberance. Add to this the inimitable roll of her eyes and her grey hairs which by good fortune stood directly upright.[18]

George managed to control the twitches which too many bishops always provoked and bore himself with great dignity, possibly because he had commanded that no sermon should be preached. It was his habit to chat to his neighbours in German throughout sermons and a certain Dr Young had once burst into tears in the pulpit because the Defender of the Faith would not pay attention.

After the ceremony the royal family dined with the peers in Westminster Hall. Three-tiered tables were set with hot and cold meats, pyramids of fruit and sugared sweetmeats. As the light faded, forty suspended crowns of thirty-six wax candles each were lit simultaneously by an ingenious device of cords soaked in saltpetre and spirit. Lesser personages crowded the gallery to watch, as they gazed hungrily down some sympathetic guests wrapped food in napkins, which were hauled up on ropes of knotted garters. Once royalty left, the public fell on everything and within half an hour, food, pewter dishes and even the tables had been borne away, though Heidegger, the Swiss Master of the Revels, managed to save his crowns.[19]

George II thus began one of the longest reigns in English history, which has underestimated his achievements as much as those of his father. No longer the dashing young cavalryman who had plunged into the thick of the battle at Oudenarde when his horse was shot under him, he was now forty-four, his upright bearing compensating for small stature, and a ruddy complexion setting off protuberant blue eyes which would bulge even more alarmingly when a combination of piles and his low opinion of the human race caused near apoplexy. His only cerebral interests were a detailed knowledge of military history (especially his own) and of royal genealogy: Hervey was once roundly abused for not knowing the relationship between the Elector Palatine and the Prince of Sulzbach, and George was obsessed with deficiencies of birth. 'I cannot bear it when women of quality marry one don't know whom.'[20] He was certainly irascible, but only over trifles; Anne herself said of him that he was calm 'when great points were as he would not have them, but when he is in his worst humours and the devil to everyone who comes near him, it is always because one of his pages has powdered his periwig ill or a housemaid has set a chair where it does not use to stand.'[21] In moments of national – as opposed to personal – crisis, his calm self-control steadied his often panicky advisers. His intemperate language meant little to his contemporaries – if he called a statesman a stinking scoundrel 'it merely meant that His Majesty was displeased'; but it was this language which has played a major part in damning his elder son in the eyes of history.

Eighteen months into the new reign, recall of Frederick from Hanover could no longer be decently delayed and the family prepared to receive a figure who half of them could barely remember and the other half had never even met. The antipathy of his family to the newly created Prince of Wales has led to wild speculation about illegitimacy or substitution at birth (it did not help that one of George's favourite terms of abuse was 'changeling'), but a mixture of political and psychological factors may provide at least a partial explanation. It was reported in the *Daily Post* of 8 December 1728:

> His Royal Highness Prince Frederick came to Whitechapel about seven in the evening and proceeded then privately in a hackney coach to St James's [where] he walked down to the Queen's backstairs and was conducted to Their Majesties' apartment.

A more low-key arrival could hardly be imagined, nor a more uncomfortable meeting. Across a gap of fifteen years a family which had totally adapted itself to English society eyed a foreign prince of twenty-two; it felt itself complete, its private relationships established and its public roles familiar. The sudden arrival of the heir to the throne threatened each of them, but George and Anne most of all. The previous reign had shown only too clearly how the natural tensions between any ruler and his heir could be exploited within the English political system, as a Prince of Wales became the natural focus for opposition; and initial reactions can be seen hardening into set opinions which were – as always with George and Caroline – expressed in public and with intemperate force.

Frederick's further misfortune was that he was loathed by the two leading memoir writers of the age – Hervey and Horace Walpole – whose venom overwhelms other references to unpretentious friendliness and cultured tastes. His passion for music should have endeared him to his eldest sister at least, but Anne's loss of seniority after so long hit her hard. She dismissed his efforts on the cello as mere play-acting, and was contemptuous of (while not failing to publicise) his undignified escapades, such as losing his watch and seals to a prostitute in St James's Park and sending a Grenadier to retrieve them.

Let loose in an unfamiliar city while his father retained three quarters of the allowance Parliament voted for him, it was hardly surprising that Frederick turned to anyone who was ready to pay him attention, provide him with credit or offer him companionship. He disliked the country sports indulged in by the rest of the family – hunting in 'an infinite Mob, a cloud of dust with ground hard as flint',[22] or the parties in Richmond Park to shoot wild turkeys which had been fattened on acorns and barley until, at thirty pounds, they could barely move. His excitement came from joining a rowdy group of young noblemen breaking the Duchess of Buckingham's windows, and dodging the ensuing grapeshot from her guards. The King was also appalled to find that his heir had little interest in military affairs or royal genealogy, preferring instead to write poetry. Frederick wrote a play, too, which he offered for production at the Drury Lane Theatre: the actor manager John Wilkes remarked that 'if the last two acts which he had not seen were exceeding better than the first three which he had, the piece might last one night'.[23] In the event it managed four.

However, Frederick was more successful in other artistic fields. On borrowed money and as soon as he arrived in England he began a career as patron and collector which few other princes can match. Caroline's interest in art did constitute an early bond between mother and son, and while George was on a trip to Hanover they visited Cliveden together to inspect the fine collection of paintings and furniture. They obviously enjoyed themselves, since they did not return home until four the next morning, but their hostess feared it had been a social disaster. Writing a frantic letter of apology to the Queen's lady-in-waiting, she accused the Lord Chamberlain of overriding all her careful arrangements, rejecting her tablecloths and reorganising the courses. Her servants had consequently become so confused that the food had been kept too long before the fire so that the dressing was spoilt. The Duke of Grafton had made some extremely wounding remarks, though the Queen and Prince had been 'wonderfully gracious'.[24] Service of food in noble houses was gradually changing and she was obviously not up to date. Early in the century the whole meal was presented at the same time:

> …our table was covered with salmon at the top, fennel sauce to it, melted butter, lemon pickle and soy, at the bottom a loin of veal roasted with on the one side kidney beans and on the other peas, and in the middle a hot pigeon pie with ham and chicken… when everything was removed came a currant tart… then gooseberries and melon, wines and cider.[25]

However, now, fish and game birds appeared most often during a second course, and the elaborate sweet confections and fruits of the previous century were being served as a third course or dessert, although still accompanied by savoury dishes such as larks or monkfish. A typical first course would consist of the larger joints of meat – boiled mutton, turkey, goose and beef – along with the slow-cooked pies and soups, thus leaving the kitchen time while people were eating to prepare the quickly cooked small game birds, crabs, sweetbreads and egg fricassees of the second course. Breakfast consisted, in the royal household at least, of fruit with sour cream and hot chocolate. Dinner gradually moved from midday to three o'clock and would not end until after six, leaving just time to change for the evening's entertainment and a 'light' supper of cold meats and raised pies.

This absence of George in Hanover had deepened the difficulties between father and son, since Frederick could reasonably have expected some representation on the Regency Council. Instead Caroline was made sole Regent, as she was on three further occasions, and as Frederick was passed over (just as his father had been) he was driven further into the arms of opposition politicians. On the surface, the proprieties were observed: Frederick and Anne opened a court ball by dancing 'a minuet and several set dances with the quality', but it was noted that the Prince obviously preferred the less dignified country dances which he performed with great spirit.[26] He appeared with his family at a celebration of the King's birthday in mouse-coloured velvet, turned up with scarlet and embroidered with silver – a subtle combination compared with Amelia, who was advertising her eccentricity by trimming her gown of blazing orange brocade with masses of purple ribbon; and on the feast of the Epiphany, Prince and King offered the traditional gifts of gold, frankincense and myrrh at the Chapel Royal. But music was to offer him the opportunity to make his mark on the social scene. Handel had for some years directed opera at the King's Theatre in the Haymarket, but an unfortunate argument with one of his Italian singers led to their mass walkout and a rival theatre in Lincoln's Inn. Since his family, and especially Anne, supported Handel, the Prince of Wales would head the 'faction of fiddlers' at the other place. So many of the nobility followed him that Anne bitterly remarked that she 'soon expected to see half the House of Lords in their robes and coronets acting as the orchestra'.[27]

The Prince commissioned a splendid barge from William Kent, decorated with mermaids and dolphins, the Prince of Wales' feathers and a Garter star. It was rowed by twenty-four watermen in scarlet coats laced with gold to represent fish scales, and it was his especial pride that his barge was faster than the King's. He invited his mother and sisters to a musical party on board – his love of children ensuring that Mary and Louisa were included – though he was by this time barely on speaking terms with Anne, telling a friend she was 'false, designing and worthless'. Their mutual dislike was crucial in the deteriorating family relationships. Anne was usually far more guarded than George and Caroline; Hervey commented that her behaviour towards Frederick was one of the very few examples of her passions getting the better of self-interest: 'His friendship could have been of use to her hereafter and she ought in prudence to have behaved towards him in a manner that would have made it less irretrievable.' But, as 'the proudest of all her proud family' this she could not do.[28] She was by now well into her twenties, and she must marry better than the four younger sisters who jostled at her back. However, the German princely families that had provided bridegrooms for an elector's daughters were too insignificant for a connection with the Princess Royal of England, and the pressure on her was increased by the fact that the Prussian marriage was being discussed again, though this time for Amelia, not for her. Crown Prince Frederick imagined himself passionately in love with Amelia (whom he had never seen) and sent her a miniature of himself which she wore until the day she died; but it came to nothing and the Prussian was married against his will to the daughter of a minor German duke – he had, it was said, to be threatened 'to get him into the bridal bed, but didn't stay there for more than an hour'.[29]

One of the English royal physicians wrote to a friend, 'I have a very great respect for [Anne] and I am only sorry that there is no prince in Christendom at present who deserves her.'[30] He was a tactful man. There was only one prince in Europe who even wanted her, and he offered an unprepossessing personal appearance and a huge political gamble. In aristocratic society generally the strictly controlled arranged marriages of the previous century were giving way to a more relaxed attitude, and women were allowed more freedom of choice. One even wrote to a newspaper claiming her right to virginity, seeing 'no Encouragement to Matrimony' and reproving 'the Malaperts who ridicule Chastity'.[31] The Duke of Manchester, rejected twice by his chosen bride, locked himself in a room with two loaded pistols. The first carried away his right eye and part of his forehead while the second shattered his jaw, and as his servants broke in they found him, groping through the blood, trying to hang himself.[32] The lady's heart was touched and she married him, though sadly it brought her little good, since he died young, leaving her half a year's pin money and an old sedan chair!

The romantic idealism of the new century, combined with women's increasing self-assertion, could lead to scandal: the thirteen-year-old daughter of the Earl of Londonderry and her seventeen-year-old cousin ran away early one morning to marry two scholars of Westminster School: 'a Fleet parson did the office and between them four they could raise but seven shillings to pay him'.

Amelia's blatant intimacy with Grafton was a sign of changing royal attitudes, and Anne, too, may have had her moments; but Princesses were, before all else, important political commodities to be disposed of as King and government saw fit. There was no freedom of choice for them, but for Anne at least there was, unusually, an option to refuse. George broached the subject to his eldest daughter on a solitary walk in the gardens of Hampton Court in the spring of 1733. He told her frankly that the marriage he proposed for her was far from ideal but appeared the only one possible, and faced with the alternative of spinsterhood at her brother's court, Anne made the pragmatic decision to marry 'even if it was a baboon'.[33] There would be many in the future who would echo George's retort, 'Well, there is baboon enough for you.' But Anne herself never regretted her swift decision. The name of her Prince was at least one to conjure with – William of Orange – but he was in fact a hunchback and – far worse – politically discredited.

Notes

[1] Hervey, op. cit., p.814
[2] Ibid., p.490
[3] Wilkins, op. cit., p.293
[4] Hervey, op. cit., p.275
[5] J D Clark [ed.], *Memoirs of Lord Waldegrave*, 1988, p.199
[6] Hervey, op. cit., p.494
[7] Ibid., p.195
[8] Ibid., p.277
[9] House of Commons 1715–54, p.444
[10] Arkell, op. cit., p.148
[11] Hervey, op. cit., p.278
[12] Hervey, op. cit., p.69
[13] Lord Wharncliffe [ed.], *Mary Wortley Montagu: Letters and Works*, 1837, pp.393–4
[14] Trench, op. cit., p.225
[15] Waldegrave, op. cit., p.147
[16] de Saussure, op. cit., p.257
[17] Hervey, op. cit., p.66
[18] Letter of Lady Mary Wortley Montagu, dated 11/10/1727
[19] de Saussure, op. cit., p.262
[20] Wharncliffe, op. cit., p.73
[21] Hervey, op. cit., p.278
[22] V Baker-Smith, *Anne of Hanover*, 1995, p.26
[23] Sir G Young, *Poor Fred*, 1937, p.36
[24] Arkell, op. cit., p.172
[25] D Marshall, *English People in the Eighteenth Century*, 1956, p.128
[26] *Daily Advertiser*, 3 March 1731
[27] Walters, op. cit., p.97
[28] Hervey, op. cit., p.195
[29] Quoted by G MacDonough, *Frederick the Great*, 1999, p.99
[30] Henrietta Howard, op. cit., p.241
[31] *The Universal Spectator*, January 1731
[32] de Saussure, op. cit., p.199
[33] Quoted by Walters, op. cit., p.83

Chapter Six

The United Provinces of the Dutch Republic offered, with Sweden, Denmark and the German states, the only marriages possible at that time for a family determined to maintain its Protestant credentials. For Anne, the German states had been discounted; the King and Queen of Sweden were childless and the Crown Prince of Denmark was only ten years old. Twice in the last hundred years an English princess had married into the House of Orange, and for the English government a Dutch alliance represented the old diplomatic way. But the times were very different.

Before William III became King of England through his marriage to James II's daughter, Mary, he was *stathouder* of Holland. The term means literally 'keeper or upholder of the state' – almost in the sense of keeper of the ring – and describes an institution which was always the despair of foreign diplomats. The English inability to understand it, but blithe conviction that they did, would now make Anne's life a difficult one. The country was a union of seven provinces, of which Holland was by far the most important; but each one had the fiercely defended right to elect its own stathouder and appoint a captain-general of its army. The threat of outside invasion always concentrated the Dutch mind, and a strong prince of the House of Orange never had difficulty in claiming the military appointment in every province, but the civil power was far less willingly granted and did not automatically follow the other. A prince had to prove himself worthy of both and claim each through the laborious process of wooing each province separately. A man of special calibre was required – a military strategist and inspiring general with political flair and diplomatic skill. William III had triumphantly combined all these attributes, but even he was stathouder of only five of the provinces, and he failed in the further princely duty of producing an heir. His death in 1702 marked the end of the male line of William the Silent, and the House of Orange thereby lost its charisma as well as its authority.

His will left all his Dutch property to a fifteen-year-old distant cousin, Johan Willem Friso, who had been recognised as his heir since Mary's death in 1695. Friso was stathouder of Friesland, the most northerly of the provinces, and the title 'Prince of Orange' was henceforth held by descendants of a junior branch, a fact which would never be forgotten. Friso was descended in the female line from Frederick Henry – William the Silent's son, and a powerful figure whose military expertise and statesmanship guided the union for twenty years from 1625; but Friso's grandmother was Frederick's younger daughter, and since her elder sister had married the Elector of Brandenburg there was a legitimate grievance over the inheritance. The Electorate's recently acquired status as the Kingdom of Prussia kept it fully occupied at the time of William III's death, but the Prussians reserved their position and were to be an ever present threat for fifty years.

Friesland's physical inaccessibility and stubborn adherence to its own language made it largely irrelevant to the mainstream of political life in the Dutch Republic. Each province was ruled by a body of 'regents', partly drawn from noble families, partly from rich urban ones, and each sending representatives to the States-General in The Hague; without a stathouder, government was totally decentralised and all decisions of the States-General had, in principle, to be referred back to the infrequent meetings of politically inexperienced men in distant parts of the country. The system was the despair of foreign diplomats, one of whom wrote of 'the form of the government of this country which is such a shattered and divided thing'.[1] The Stathouder-King, William III, had known he had no power to influence the provinces to accept his personal heir as their stathouder, and since his own father had died just before he was born, there had been a minority before. Now it was left to the young Friso to bide his time and prove himself. He had inherited his cousin's courage and he flung himself enthusiastically into the continuing war against Louis XIV in which William had played such an important part. He was the only surviving son in a family of seven daughters and his ambitious mother, Amalia of Anhalt, was appalled that he risked his life over and over again; she begged him to marry, but Friso was having too much fun. Far from sharing his cousin's preference for men, he was continually writing home for more money, because tradesmen were refusing him credit for the parties he was giving in camp for 'all sorts of ladies'.

At the Battle of Oudenarde, Anne's father and future father-in-law (watched from a safe distance, incidentally, by James Stuart) took the field together the year before she was born under the command of the Duke of Marlborough... Each acquitted himself so well that they were complimented by the great Duke personally. George Augustus had been in the saddle for a fifteen-mile night march even before he hurled himself into the cavalry charge against a French force outnumbering them by three to one, which earned him the accolade of 'Young Hanover Brave'. He would be spared to regale many a captive audience with the story over the next fifty years, but Friso's time was short. He joined Marlborough again later that year in an aquatic battle outside Lille. The French broke the dykes, drowning the flat plain between the town and the sea, and as Marlborough struggled to get his supplies up from Ostend on narrow pontoons built by the sweating infantry, the French flanking guns sank beneath the water. Friso loved it: 'It was so amusing to see the French take to the water, we were able to shoot them like wild duck,' he wrote to the Hessian Princess – Marie Louise – whom he was to marry six months later;[2] his mother had finally lost patience, sending him the names of two German princesses. He must marry for the sake of the dynasty; the choice was simply between two chairs, she had told him, and he must decide which was the more comfortable.

In the summer of 1711, already the father of a daughter, Friso left his pregnant wife and set off to campaign once more in Flanders. The King of Prussia had not forgotten his outrage over William III's will and he was now blackmailing Marlborough by threatening to withdraw all his troops from the 1711 campaign if the House of Orange did not make concessions; the Duke asked General Grumbknow to persuade his King to be generous, to which the Prussian replied that he would end up in Spandau if he uttered a word. With the year's campaign generally reckoned to be the last one needed to bring France to the conference table, Marlborough had no alternative but to send Friso north to meet the King in The Hague with instructions to make any concessions needed. The journey involved a crossing of the Hollands Diep, the mile-wide estuary of the River Maas: the normal method of travel was by a flat-bottomed barge onto which coaches were manhandled, with the passengers crossing in a separate open boat. As a blustery wind whipped sheets of rain into their faces, Friso announced that he and his two companions would remain inside the coach, and no one dared to argue. They were nearly halfway across when a sudden squall poured waves over the deck and the barge heeled so sharply that the drenched sail pulled it over. The coach fell sideways into the water, and as it momentarily floated one of the men was able to open the door and scramble out: leaning down, he managed to grasp the Prince's hand but could not hold him. Forty years later a nervous French traveller was regaled by the ferryman with the dreadful story. After eight days a fisherman found the body entangled in his nets, and it was embalmed and sent back to Friesland for Marie Louise to view before burial in the family vault. Six weeks later she gave birth to a son, whom she named William, and the title of Prince of Orange revived again.

Left a widow at twenty-three in a strange country, she applied herself diligently and energetically to preserve her son's inheritance. The Frisians, difficult and idiosyncratic as they were, had already warmed to her friendly informality, and they had no hesitation in placing the regency in her hands, to the rage of her strong-willed mother-in-law who had become accustomed to indulging her expensive tastes by running up debts and treating the province as her own property. Marie Louise's immediate problem was the King of Prussia. He showed no mercy, and her youth, inexperience and lack of influence abroad made it impossible for her to do more than prolong negotiations while the valuable Orange properties he claimed lay in limbo with no indemnification. She was also forced to sell sixty of the paintings from William III's bequest to clear Amalia's debts and pay the allowances she demanded for herself and her six unmarried daughters.

At the same time a series of natural disasters hit the province: rinderpest struck the Frisian cattle, which were its main economic support, and there was a sequence of severe winters from 1712–16. But the most serious threat was an infestation of parasites which, by the time it was discovered, was beyond control; brought on ships' hulls from the Far East, these 'sea-worms' transferred themselves to the wooden piles which supported the protecting dykes and began to honeycomb the structure. Without repair, the whole vast system would collapse and reclaimed land return to the sea, but there was no way for the province to raise either the money or the manpower for so enormous a task because the tax obligations to The Hague of provinces loyal to the House of Orange were seldom realistically reviewed. When written petitions were ignored, starvation loomed and lives were being lost to the encroaching sea; whereupon Marie Louise, in an action Friesland never forgot, travelled to the capital and appeared before the States-General to plead in person. She spoke so eloquently that she returned home with not only a remittance of taxation but also a large detachment of soldiers to help with the repair of the dykes.

Friso's early death was of course a devastating blow to the ambitions of the House of Orange. Its supporters were a powerful force and they had exulted in Friso's military success; with peace in sight as the French faltered, they had expected their Prince before long to present himself to the provinces as a worthy stathouder. Now another minority gave the still shaky Republic twenty more years to consolidate its position. Considerable efforts by the Orangists brought the young prince (stathouder of Friesland by birth) the stathoudership of two more provinces – Groningen in 1718 and Gelderland in 1722 – but these were almost as irrelevant as Friesland. In the latter province, even this recognition was subject to restrictions, although there was some comfort in the fact that when Holland, as the most powerful province, tried to thwart its action, Gelderland retorted that a Prince of Orange was 'the only born Resident of this State who can be elected to the High Dignity'.[3]

This was not the sort of clear principle the other provinces wished to perpetuate, for they had eyes on the 'High Dignity' for themselves. For them, a monarchical government was equivalent 'to a death from which there can be no resurrection'.[4] The Republic was totally controlled by the provinces of Holland, and to a lesser extent, Zeeland, both implacably opposed to the House of Orange: for them stathouderless government (which they termed 'True Freedom') was the only possible course. Johan de Witt, the great statesman of the previous century, had expressed it for them: 'It is beyond controversy that the full absolute sovereignty is vested in the states of the respective provinces'... not in the possibly arbitrary rule of a prince.[5]

But for the moment nothing could be done, and Marie Louise devoted herself to her children. She worried about her daughter, Amalia, who was growing up melancholic and introspective, but she soon had a far more serious concern about her son. During the summer before his sixth birthday he had a fall when he excitedly tried to jump down from a moving carriage, and to this mishap was always attributed the deformity which became apparent soon afterwards. This is unlikely: a bad fall would have caused instant paralysis rather than the severely hunched shoulder which inexorably became apparent to those around him; but the natural psychological reaction was to find the cause in a minor and coincidental accident. The increasing curvature of back and chest before the age of sixteen is more indicative of a chronic condition – either a vertebral malformation, which would show no signs of deformity until the effect of gravity and growth; or possibly a tubercular condition, which attacked the spine. His psychological attitude to the handicap was beyond praise. William endured it without bitterness and the constant pain without complaint, while sheer determination and courage gave him as good a seat on a horse as any prince could wish.

Marie Louise retained close links with her family in Germany, and she noted the elevation of the Elector of Hanover in 1714, together with the fact that he had three granddaughters around the same age as her son. She was a childhood acquaintance of Caroline's and she assiduously maintained a correspondence with her until George I's death. She was in a similar predicament to the Hanoverians: the Frisian branch of the House of Orange-Nassau had always married into the secondary princely families of Germany – Anhalt, Brunswick-Wolfenbüttel and her own Hesse – but while the stathoudership of the more important provinces remained vacant a prestigious marriage could influence attitudes. When the news reached her of George's rejection of the Prussian alliance she wrote to him direct, suggesting that any of his daughters would do nicely. He replied, expressing his respect and admiration for her, though promising nothing. However, as other political options dwindled and Anne's twenties took their toll, Marie Louise's cherished plan bore fruit, and the Earl of Chesterfield, the English envoy in The Hague, began serious negotiation. He reported to London that a marriage between William and the Princess Royal would almost certainly result in the prince's immediate election to the stathoudership of the four key provinces of Holland, Zeeland, Overijssel and Utrecht, making him ruler of a united country, and thus the useful ally England needed as Europe seemed about to plunge into armed conflict once more.

Chesterfield was a highly skilled diplomat with considerable experience in Dutch affairs, and yet he completely misjudged the situation. Since William III's death, the Dutch had found republicanism much to their taste in practice as well as principle; the Regent Councils were increasingly made up of the new families made rich by trade rather than the Orangist nobility, and the mercantile class were fearful of change. In the States-General, the interests considered were those of Holland, which virtually meant Amsterdam. There, the discreet shutters of the tall gabled houses concealed enormous wealth – warehouses stacked with valuable merchandise and the paintings, furniture and artefacts which were the tangible signs of business success. Daniel Defoe wrote in 1728, 'The Dutch must be understood… as the Carryers of the World… and the greatest part of their vast commerce consists in being supply'd from all parts of the World that they may supply all the World again.'[6] For these merchants, the House of Orange's warlike reputation offered only the risk of an interruption of trade and loss of their independence and their wealth.

The long minorities had left Orangist supporters weak, inexperienced and paralysed, but as Prince William grew to manhood they began to stir, compensating for the years of inactivity by talking up their support and influencing Chesterfield out of all proportion to their actual importance. The Earl's judgement might perhaps be faulted in other respects also; his views on women were that they 'are only children of a larger growth; they have an entertaining tattle and sometimes wit; but for solid reasoning good sense I never knew in my life one that had it or reasoned and acted consequentially for four and twenty hours together'.[7]

At an early stage, Chesterfield tackled the awkward question of the prince's physical appearance, cautiously reporting that 'his stature is not as good as men might wish but not as bad as I had heard'.[8] William's right shoulder was severely deformed, the hunch was too pronounced for even the court artists to ignore, even though he clung to the long flowing wigs of his youth long after fashions changed. He had yet one more disadvantage as a husband – he had an exceptionally close and emotional relationship with his mother. This was hardly surprising in the circumstances, but it would be a cause for resentment if he married a possessive wife.

Notes

[1] The late-seventeenth century English ambassador at The Hague, Sir George Downing, quoted by E N Williams, *Ancien Regime in Europe*, 1970, p.39
[2] KHA, Johan Willem Friso, 2017, I
[3] From a pamphlet entitled 't'Leven van Willem den IV', 1758, quoted by H Rowen, *The Princes of Orange*, 1988, p.156
[4] Quoted by P Geyl, *The Netherlands in the Seventeenth Century*, 1964, p.192

[5] From the 'Deduction of Johan de Witt', 1654 as quoted by I Leeb, *The Ideological Origins of the Batavian Revolution*, 1973, p.33

[6] D Defoe, *A Plan of English Commerce*, 1728, p.33

[7] Chesterfield, *Common Sense, or, the Englishman's Journal*, 1737

[8] C Tamse [ed.], 'Nassau en Orange', in *De Nederlandse Geschiedenis*, 1979, p.192

Chapter Seven

In London, the prospect of a Dutch alliance was popular, and early in 1733 Parliament received George's announcement of Anne's betrothal with great enthusiasm. William III's conviction that France could only be checked and contained by an alliance between the maritime powers of England and the United Provinces had been a basic principle of European politics, and the English still believed in it wholeheartedly, with the influential merchant classes insisting that the Republic must be a partner in every alliance because abstention might allow it to enrich itself at their expense. But once the two powers were divided by William's death, many interests actually diverged, though English ministers were extraordinarily slow to realise it. The Dutch lost their desire for military glory, while remaining totally obsessive about the fortresses along their southern frontier, and the English began to increase their influence outside continental Europe, although the connection with Hanover ensured a focus there. The 1713 Treaty of Utrecht had brought little to the United Provinces except crippling debts (in large part due to their acceptance of military obligations which were strictly speaking English ones), and the consequent Dutch reluctance to commit themselves to an aggressive foreign policy exasperated the English government. The Dutch view that it was pursuing an essential neutrality seemed to the English a delusional self-indulgence, they were 'sunk in a sweet slumber dreaming of durable peace and the clinking of ducats.'[1] The inner drive, that spark of genius which had flared into the material and spiritual brilliance of the Golden Age, giving the country such power and influence in Europe, had died away. Now the Dutch were normal again, a small country struggling for survival with no inclination for foreign adventure. But London was assured by Chesterfield that a prestigious marriage was all the House of Orange needed to reassert itself at the head of a united country.

For George personally, the announcement gave him a popularity he badly needed. Opposition in Parliament was increasing despite Walpole's skill, and royal absences in Hanover were deeply resented, as a paper nailed to the gate of St James's Palace during one visit showed:

> Lost or strayed out of this house, a man who has left a wife and six children on the parish, whoever will give any tidings of him to the Churchwardens of St James's so as he may be got again shall receive four shillings and sixpence re-

ward. N.B. this reward will not be increased, nobody judging him to be worth a crown.[2]

The King could now be seen as caring for English interests by reviving traditional links and strengthening the Protestant succession. The latter was not merely an idle formula, for until her brothers were married only two lives stood between Anne and the English throne. The anticipated wave of approval swept through a marriage grant to Anne of £80,000. This enormous sum, made possible by the recent sale of colonial Crown lands in the West Indies, was double any previous royal dowry, and threw Frederick into a positive frenzy of resentment.

During the summer of 1733 Anne and William exchanged stilted letters, usually consisting of a single paragraph thanking the other for writing, with an occasional more personal note from William 'how dear you are to me already' and 'how I dream of our meeting'.[3] The King wrote civilly to Marie Louise, complimenting her for all the good reports he had of her son, and the proud mother had copies made which she sent off to all her relatives. In truth, George was increasingly doubtful about the match, having been somewhat shaken by the cool tone of the States-General to his formal notification – it hoped that Anne would be happy in 'the free republic which ours is'.[4] There was no going back now, but he decided to make it clear to William from the outset that he was very much on sufferance.

The Prince arrived in London in November and was accommodated in Somerset House, which had stood empty since Charles II's widow, Catherine of Braganza, had died there. The shabby decorations, damp walls, hastily collected sticks of furniture and grandstand view of the riverboat brothel must have warned the Dutch what to expect. Hervey went to inspect the bride-groom and hurried back to St James's, where the Queen wished to 'know without disguise what sort of hidden animal she was to prepare herself to see'.[5] He assured her that 'the body was as bad as possible with excessive roundings of the shoulder, a short waist and long legs without calves', though his actual countenance was far from disagreeable. He asked if Anne was not anxious to hear about her prince, and was told that she was in her apartment playing her harpsichord 'with some of the opera people' and was as calm and relaxed that morning as her mother had ever seen her.[6]

Anne was showing an entirely characteristic self-discipline, but music had always been her refuge. She was by this time Handel's patron and valued friend, frequently visiting his house in Brook Street to hear new pieces or perform at private concerts. When Handel lost his Italian singers they had taken the best tunes with them, and he had been left with often inferior musicians, no money to heat his theatre and no opera scores. At this point

Anne stepped in, managing to persuade her notoriously tight-fisted father to part with £1,000 a year for a box and, most importantly for the history of music, advising Handel to bring his piece *Esther*, which he had written years before for a private music club performance, to be staged at the Haymarket as a dramatic production.

George had forbidden the Tower guns or any guard of honour to salute his future son-in-law's arrival, and carefully sent a coach with only two instead of the customary four horses to bring him to St James's. However, even Hervey was forced to admire William's diplomatic handling of the discourtesies, and his easy and friendly manner enabled the betrothed couple to carry off the public ordeal of their first meeting with dignity. The wedding was fixed for three days' time and William returned to Somerset House to write to his mother, 'this is the last letter you will receive from me as a boy'.[7] Bonfires and fireworks were ready primed and the newspapers were whipping up a frenzy of excitement over the first royal wedding for fifty years. The Dutch Church in London proudly laid on a service of thanksgiving, but halfway through William collapsed in his pew and had to be rushed back to his lodgings, semi-conscious and delirious. For three weeks his life was despaired of as his servants attempted to nurse him through a severe attack of pneumonia amid the dank pollution and cheerless atmosphere of Somerset House.

George somehow convinced himself that the illness was smallpox, which was raging in London at the time, and forbade the royal doctors to visit him for fear of infection, though he was eventually shamed into allowing a move to the cleaner air of Kensington. Early in the New Year, William travelled to Bath for an indefinite stay, in the hope that the waters would cure his 'extreme lassitude and weakness of stomach', and Anne's patience was further tried by the publication of a little book which seemed to compromise her reputation.

A Court Novel: the Secret History of Mama Oello, Princess Royal of Peru[8] is the story of a princess who by order of her father must marry the prince of a neighbouring but poverty-stricken state, and thus far is no different from the scores of contemporary semi-literary texts which satirised royalty and the government, but London nostrils were set a-quiver by the fact that this princess had a lover. Most of these satirical texts were ephemeral pamphlets relying on their readers to recognise topical allusions and political jibes, but the importance of this one is indicated by the fact that it is a bound book, and the British Library copy has a handwritten title page, later in date than the book itself, identifying every character and place name: Curaca Robilda is Robert Walpole, Curaca Sinchi is Chesterfield, Quito the Dutch Republic and Cacique, lover of the princess, is Lord Carmichael, later Earl of Hyndford. Carmichael at this time in his early thirties and a captain in the 3rd Regiment of Foot, was described later in life by Thomas Carlyle as 'a broad-based shrewdly practical Scottish gentleman with a certain rough tenacity and horse-dealer finesse'.[9]

Perhaps such characteristics did attract Anne into indiscretion, but whether malicious invention or insider information, the book must have aroused much gossip and speculation for the anonymous author was perceptive. Mama Oello weeps that she must marry a Prince of Quito whose land produces nothing but butter and cheese, where the inhabitants 'once famed in the arts and sciences' now indulge only in trade and commerce. She must obey the orders of her father's Wicked Minister, Curaca Robilda, whom all the country hated 'on Account of his persuading her royal Grandfather and Father to impose heavy taxes', and since many noblemen in her country hold wider lands, why must she 'Princess Royal of a mighty empire leave my country and friends to be only a co-Partner in a poor Principality?' Disguised as a gardener, Cacique meets his princess secretly near Hampton Court and presents her with roses and carnations, at which 'the fair Mama Oello lifts up her eyes and feeling her dearest Cacique so near, closes them again in a fainting fit'. Love poems are exchanged until the princess's mother becomes suspicious and watches her so closely that 'when she plays cards to oblige her sisters she hardly knew what she did or what she said'. Here the story breaks off with the note that it will be continued when more material comes to hand. Probably the author felt his point had been made, which indeed it had – the Dutch alliance was offering the Princess Royal a disputed title in a country in decline.

After two months in Bath, William was well enough to return to London. He travelled via Oxford, where he was given an honorary doctorate. He responded to the Public Orator in a witty Latin speech without notes, apologising for the fact that his command of the language was a little rusty; the assembled academics were greatly impressed and a genuine enthusiasm was injected into some of the routine poetic offerings in every tongue from Arabic to Welsh, with which Oxford and Cambridge marked the royal marriage. The standard of composition varied. Mr T Morell of King's relied on cliché:

> Meanwhile with rosy Mantle Love o'erspread
> The generous Blushes of the Royal Maid.
> The Royal Maid consents with decent Pride,
> And crowns her Triumphs with the name of Bride.[10]

The Dutch efforts were equally laboured; the following is better in the original but not much:

> Behold here Anna, Friso's love and crown of women
> Raised high by spirit, figure and by birth,
> In whose eyes men read the things of love on earth.

Back in the capital, William was made a Fellow of the Royal Society and dined with its President, the physician Sir Hans Sloane, showing a knowledgeable interest in his collection of antiquities. Intellectually he would certainly be Anne's equal, if not politically, and their meetings were noticeably animated. 'She made prodigious court to him, addressed everything she said to him and applauded everything he said to anyone else.'[11]

The King remained irritable. At a formal Sunday dinner he suddenly ordered William to join the gentlemen in waiting behind his chair, saying 'What's the Prince of Orange till he has married my daughter?'[12] William kept his own temper and pointed out adroitly that unfortunately his health would not allow him to stand; he was in any case suffering from shock, since part of the dilapidated stonework of Somerset House had just crashed to the ground within inches of him.

The marriage took place at last on 14 March 1734. St James's Chapel had been lavishly decorated at a cost of £117 16s. Crimson velvet and taffeta studded with golden roses veiled the interior forming a background for the priceless tapestries brought from Hampton Court, which then had holes cut in them to fit the candle sconces. A wooden gallery had been built to protect the wedding procession as it passed through from the palace, and the workmen's hammering and bad language had disturbed the Duchess of Marlborough at her home next door. However she termed it 'the King's Orange Box', and repeated her joke ad infinitum to anyone who would listen. Most of Anne's trousseau had been made of English textiles at Caroline's insistence, but the wedding dress was a stiff blue French silk embroidered with silver thread and looped with diamonds. She wore her ermine robes of state, and her six-foot train was supported by eight peers' daughters. The spectacle was rather spoilt by the fact that the bride was escorted to the altar at arm's length by Frederick, who was in a towering rage because she was marrying before him, and she was followed by her four more or less envious sisters who sobbed audibly throughout.

Hervey remarked that 'the scene looked more like the mournful pomp of a sacrifice than the celebration of a marriage and put one in mind rather of an Iphigenia leading to the altar than of a bride'.[13] The choir and an orchestra performed Handel's specially composed anthem 'This is the Day', to a text written by Anne herself paraphrasing Psalm 45 – 'Forget also thine own people and thy father's house'.

The menu for the wedding banquet broadly followed contemporary English custom:

First Course

Large turbot. Mutton 'in blood'. Beef roast. Veal collops. Chicken ragout. Soup. Capons. Boiled potatoes. Ham boiled on napkin. Chicken and cauliflour.

Second Course

Five plates partridges, quails, squabs, larded pheasants, woodcocks. Tartlets and jellies. Marrow puddings. Asparagus. Smelts. Broiled oysters. Dutch beef. Stewed peas. Flyes.[14]

The rather confusing 'Flyes' probably refers to *vlaai* which was (and is) a Dutch speciality, consisting of a large pastry filled with various fruits. William always travelled with his own pastry cooks.

George's patronising attitude had been undermined by the £30,000 worth of jewellery which William bestowed on his bride, and by his appearance in a dazzling suit of gold brocade. But once the carefully cut clothes and flowing wig had been exchanged for nightshirt and tall nightcap for the public bedding ceremony, poor William's deformity was starkly revealed, 'looking from behind as if he had no head, and from before as if he had no neck and no legs'. Caroline was so overcome at the sight of 'this monster lying with my daughter'[15] that she broke down, but again Anne's self-possession and William's calm dignity carried them through the ordeal.

The next day a ball was held at which only the royal family danced, while the guests stood around eyeing each other's clothes, many of which had cost them four or five hundred pounds. The Duchess of Queensberry, a cousin of Queen Anne, had insisted her husband should wear Scottish plaid as a discreet reminder of their Stuart ancestry, while she herself was resplendent in white satin and a brown chenille petticoat over which rambled nasturtiums, honeysuckle and convolvulus in their natural colours. The fashion critic, Mrs Delany, noticed 'a black velvet dress embossed in a pattern of vases and rampant flowers, properer', she thought, 'for a stucco staircase than a lady's apparel.'[16]

For the next six weeks the Prince and Princess of Orange were the centre of attention, as William continued his sightseeing and the aristocracy vied to entertain them. Frederick could not resist inviting them to Drury Lane for a command performance of *The Careless Husband*. The City of London, which had lined Ludgate Hill with two thousand lamps in pyramids on the wedding day, considered it had done enough and, when encouraged to commission a statue, announced that a Loyal Address was quite sufficient, and had the added advantage of not blocking the streets. Its citizens were much more enthusiastic but the press did not fail to point out that the wearing of the orange was also in 'grateful Remembrance of our once Royal Deliverer' William III – whose arrival in London in 1688 ousted the hated James II and sent him into exile. George's temper had not improved much since the wedding, and the circulation of such verses as:

> Remember George when this set led to dance,
> They sent a better King than you to France.

did not help. The final straw came one night at the opera when he was greeted with polite applause but when William moved forward into view 'wild cheers and huzzas were heard'.[17] The newly-weds were sharply informed that a royal escort was ready to conduct them to Gravesend, where William's ships were moored. The farewells at St James's were highly emotional, though Frederick did not attend them, sending a message to his 'beloved' sister that he feared they might both be too affected. George remembered that Anne was his favourite and gave her a superb pair of diamond earrings, and Caroline was distraught: she was losing her only intellectual companion in the family and she was well aware that politically her daughter had a tough time ahead. She wrote the day Anne left,

> Dear Hart,
>
> My sadness is indescribable, I never had any sorrows over you Anne, this is the first a cruel one. Orange is a good man and will ever be a great favourite of mine.[18]

William had managed to win over his formidable mother-in-law.

Notes

[1] J Huizinga, *Dutch Civilisation in the Seventeenth Century*, 1968, p.33
[2] Trench, op. cit., p.184
[3] KHA, Willem IV, 171 I
[4] P Geyl, *Willem IV en Engeland*, 1924, p.26
[5] Hervey, op. cit., p.231
[6] Ibid.
[7] KHA, Willem IV, 171 I
[8] British Museum 1418.d.40
[9] Thomas Carlyle, *Frederick the Great*, 1858
[10] Gratulatio academicae Cantabrigiensis auspicatissimus Gulielmi principis Auriaci et Annae Georgii II nuptias celebrantis, 1733, Cambridge University Library
[11] Hervey, op. cit., p.272
[12] Walters, op. cit., p.86
[13] Hervey, op. cit., p.271
[14] KHA, Willem IV, 171 I
[15] Hervey, op. cit., p.271

[16] J Walters, *Splendour and Scandal*, 1968, p.125
[17] Hervey, op. cit., p.282
[18] Quoted by Arkell, op. cit., p.212

Chapter Eight

As Anne sailed for Rotterdam, her family sought distraction in characteristic ways: George and Caroline anxiously followed the course of the parliamentary elections, Frederick returned to his landscape gardening and his poetry, wounded no doubt by a critic's description of his most recent ballad – 'it has miscarried in nothing but the language, the thought and the poetry' – while Amelia left for Bath. She was a regular visitor, though one of her coarser critics had remarked that the hot spring she needed might be found nearer to home.

At the spa, Richard Nash ruled supreme and even a royal princess had to observe his code of manners. He had single-handedly transformed a little provincial town of dangerous streets, crumbling houses and surly citizens into a beautiful and fashionable spa with fine public buildings and lavish entertainment. Nash was King of Bath; his strictures on dress and etiquette had to be obeyed to the letter. He himself always wore gold-laced clothes and, as an unkind observer put it, 'was taken by many at a distance for a gilt garland'. He stopped John Wesley preaching in the town because it upset people – the Duchess of Buckingham declared, ''Tis monstrous to be told you have a heart as sinful as the common wretches who crawl the earth'[1] – and when Amelia announced her intention of continuing to dance after 11 p.m. Nash firmly told her that this was against his rules. She retreated to a summerhouse on the river bank and held court there in her riding habit and a postilion hat of black velvet; she again scandalised many people by playing cards publicly and 'playing very deep'. She found plenty of time to indulge her passion for gossip, and on this visit she happened to see her father's mistress, the Countess of Suffolk, whom his children had always resented. Watching her closely, Amelia was delighted to discover the lady deep in conversation with Bolingbroke, who had returned to England with a pardon after his involvement in the Fifteen. However he could never quite shake off his past, and Amelia hurried back to London to inform George that Lady Suffolk was consorting with Jacobites.

The King had long been feeling that a mistress approaching fifty reflected badly on his manhood so he was happy to let her go, speeding her on her way with the remark that she had become 'old, dull, deaf and peevish'.[2] According to Hervey, 'Princess Amelia wished Lady Suffolk's disgrace because she wished misfortune to most people, Princess Caroline because she thought it would please her mother.'[3] The Queen's feelings were actually ambivalent, as she feared the inevitable successor might be more of a threat to her;[4] but she and

George were facing the immediate risk of the fall of their chief minister. The word 'their' is exact: although Caroline never instigated policy, Walpole had always relied heavily on her to influence her husband to his own way of thinking. Her political pragmatism chimed with his. In his characteristic words, 'the King has the right sow by the ear'[5] and they understood each other very well. Walpole had ridden out the satirists for fifteen years:

> I believe in Sir Robert Walpole who was accused of corruption, was convicted expelled and imprisoned, he went down into Norfolk, the third day he came up again, he got into the administration and sitteth at the head of the Treasury. From thence he shall pay all those who vote as they are bid.[6]

While he had recently been burned in effigy at Temple Bar, enthusiasm for the Orange marriage had given both Court and government a short-lived popularity, but his parliamentary skills were being stretched to the limit by increasingly stormy sessions which seemed likely to lead to a Tory victory in the 1734 elections. The Septennial Act of 1716, whereby members of parliament, elected for the usual three years, had extended their tenure to seven because of the Jacobite threat, was being attacked as unconstitutional, and the Whigs looked very vulnerable. General elections were annoying interludes for members of the government, but with a record number of contested seats they had to get out into the country and fight. The Earl of Cork grumbled that his 'doors are open to every dirty fellow in the county that is worth forty shillings a year, all my best floors are spoiled... and the Chinese paper in the dining room stinks abominably of punch and tobacco'.

Treasury funds were poured out to ensure a friendly press, whose editions were circulated by government officials. Walpole spent £60,000 of his own money, and the Duke of Newcastle toured the inns of Sussex in an increasingly inebriated state as he canvassed votes. An opposition politician's lofty assertion that he never dined in taverns was to keep him out of office for ten years. The political journalist, Sir Richard Steele, decided to join the world he satirised and won election by 'a merry trick': he offered ten guineas to the first child 'born that day nine months – upon this several that would have been against him and who lived some miles from town posted home to capacitate their wives'. The government won with a greatly reduced majority and the Septennial Act survived until 1911, when five-year parliaments were introduced.

Meanwhile, Anne's introduction to her new country began smoothly – the dreaded North Sea crossing was unusually calm, and at Rotterdam the party transferred to gilded boats which were drawn along the canals by briskly trotting horses, 'the most entertaining way of travelling, you may read and write with the same ease as in your closet'.[7] Lining the banks were immaculate gardens, their statues and topiary skilfully adjusted to a smaller scale than English eyes were used to. She and William were warmly welcomed in Delft and Haarlem but as the procession glided into Amsterdam the atmosphere changed abruptly. To the ruling oligarchy in the republican heart of the country, the Prince of Orange's new wife was irrelevant and must be made aware of it. No guns fired in salute and no decorations were allowed; the couple were received outside the old Lutheran church in the centre of the city by a small deputation whose hostility was barely concealed. Curious crowds had gathered but these were marshalled by watchful guards and no hospitality of any kind was offered.

The party embarked from the harbour for the 22-hour crossing of the Zuyder Zee to Friesland's port of Harlingen. The inland sea was always treacherous, and strong winds this time made many seasick, 'the Princess lay in bed all the time and by that means was pretty well'. She was accompanied by several members of the English royal household, whose happy assumption of foreign inferiority was to be severely undermined. Eight horses 'the finest I ever saw' drew the ceremonial coach into Anne's new capital of Leeuwarden, and the formal drawing room reception the next day revealed 'really very well looking people' in respectable clothes. The town itself was small, huddled round its canals as if to protect itself from the biting winds which swept across a featureless landscape. But William had lavished much care on the decoration of his rambling palace in the main square. Valuable tapestries and pictures from William III's bequest, porcelain and lacquered chests from the East Indies, and walls hung with embossed gold leather formed a rich background to his more personal gifts – a fine harpsichord and a magnificent Moorish bed commissioned from the craftsmen of Limburg. Anne's delight with the latter was fortunate for one of the maids of honour at her wedding, since at her own marriage that autumn Lady Caroline Manners had received George I's State Bed. Bequeathed to his eldest granddaughter, it stands today in Calke Abbey in Derbyshire, with its original hangings of dark blue silk and cream taffeta studded with coiled peacock feathers and embroidered with flowers, mythical beasts and Chinese figures.

As Anne surveyed her new home, Robert Walpole's brother Horatio was in The Hague trying to persuade the States-General to receive her. He was in correspondence with the Queen as well as the government, and Caroline's suggestion that 'the gentlemen of Holland might pay their respects to her not as William's wife but as His Majesty's daughter' became the basis for the finally agreed formula.[8]

Almost immediately, William left to join a contingent of Dutch troops on the Rhine. Augustus of Poland had succumbed to one drinking-bout too many and Louis XV had seized the chance to put his father-in-law on the Polish throne. Ranged against him was Augustus' son, supported by Emperor Charles VI, to whom the House of Orange (though not the United Provinces) owed allegiance. Such split loyalty was echoed in England where George's electorate, though not, of course, his kingdom, had imperial obligations. The War of the Polish Succession was a somewhat desultory affair – neither side considering Poland was worth much effort. Charles's army was commanded by the Prince Eugene, whose joint command with Marlborough in the early years of the century was the stuff of legend. By now a sad figure, virtually paralysed, he was, as he wrote to the Emperor 'dying from the feet up'; he welcomed William warmly for the sake of his father, Friso, and 'although he had dined made me eat with him', but his conversation was only of old wars: 'He forgets what he did a moment before and truly he is no more the same.'[9] William's headquarters offered no beds or even straw, and the horses were fed on vine leaves because the fodder had run out. The two camps were so close that the opposing sentries could (and did) talk to each other until, taking advantage of a thick river mist, the entire imperial army in eight columns of horse and foot moved away, the French 'having the courtesy to let us go', as William wrote to Anne.[10] Every week four or five letters of great tenderness passed between them – the arranged marriage had become a love match, he was 'Pepin' or 'Pip', she 'my adorable Annin'. He assures her that he is distanced 'from the other princes of the Holy Empire who consort with grisettes, for I hope never to be unfaithful to my dear Annin, especially so unworthily'.[11]

His letters were addressed to London, for Anne had seized the opportunity to return during his absence. She happily fitted back into Court life, reporting to William the King's fury at Walpole's determination to keep England neutral. Imperial troops were in action and George longed to be with them: he – young Hanover Brave – was 'rusting in the cabinet while other princes were shining in the field'. Walpole withstood the pressure. 'There have been fifty thousand men slain in Europe this year and not one Englishman,' he declared dramatically if inaccurately.[12] Anne shared the family satisfaction over the disgrace of Lady Suffolk, telling Hervey 'that she cannot be too ill-used, and I wish with all my heart that he would take somebody else, then Mama might be a little relieved of the ennui of seeing him for ever in her room'.[13] The Court waited with interest on the replacement, Walpole promoting Lady Tankerville, 'a very safe fool'. Another possible candidate was Lady Deloraine, governess to Mary and Louisa and married to a member of Cumberland's household. According to a contemporary she had 'a weak head, a pretty face and a lying tongue', George was always happy 'to talk a little bawdy'[14] with her when he visited his younger daughters, but even he may have had some scruples about her official position and, besides, he said, 'she stank of Spanish wine'.[15] Her apartments adjoined that of the princesses, and one evening a planned party had to be cancelled because she had given birth to a stillborn child. George desired to see it and it was duly presented to him on a silver platter, but this was assumed to reflect His Majesty's obstetric rather than paternal interest.

Anne's quarrels with Frederick continued as Handel extended his opera season into July in her honour and Frederick redoubled his efforts at Drury Lane. He was gathering opposition politicians around him, just as his father had done, and his grievances were entirely legitimate. Parliament had settled George's Civil List assuming that the annual £100,000 he had received as Prince of Wales would be given to Frederick. Instead the Prince received an allowance of £24,000 'in small sums without account'.[16]

The treatment of Frederick's younger brother William, Duke of Cumberland, could not have been more different. Care and attention had always been lavished on him, and by the age of ten he had been given his own household and a generous allowance. Both parents doted on him, to the extent that Walpole himself advised the Queen to cool it: 'People already talk enough of the partiality Your Majesty and the King have for the Duke.'[17] Caroline ensured he was tutored in science and the arts by distinguished men, and George was delighted by his son's enthusiasm for all things military. He was taught the principles of ballistics and gunnery, line trenches were dug for his study in the grounds of Hampton Court, and an aged engineer who had planned the walls of Londonderry came to expound on the design of fortresses. He was a precocious and sometimes insolent child: after a severe maternal scolding Caroline was gratified to find him reading his Bible. On being asked what part was interesting him, he replied. 'That part where it is written "Woman what hast thou to do with me?"'[18] He was a fearless rider, taking many crashing falls with equanimity, and he took the greatest of pride in his Englishness, announcing that German was a language for stupid children. It is greatly to Frederick's credit that he showed no resentment of such a sibling and always spoke of him with kindness; the enmity was confined to his three eldest sisters.

Anne was present at the memorable court reception that summer when James Oglethorpe, who had founded the colony of Georgia, named after the King, mainly as a reception centre for debtors, presented a group of Cherokee Indians and their 84-year-old chief to the King. They had carefully painted their faces with red and black triangles and draped themselves in glass beads, but Oglethorpe had problems convincing them that loincloths alone were not the custom at Kensington Palace. He was an extraordinary man who packed many careers into his eighty-seven years – soldier, philanthropist, parliamentarian and ruler of the colony. He served under Prince Eugene against the Turks before returning to Parliament in 1722 as a Tory and flirting with Jacobitism. In 1729 the death of a friend in the Fleet prompted him to head a parliamentary committee into the brutality and corruption of prison officers. As the old *Dictionary of National Biography* puts it, 'in all times colonisation has suggested itself as a remedy for the economic ills of old countries', and in 1734 Oglethorpe received a charter to set up the colony, whose inhabitants included Highland Scots and German refugees as well as English paupers. John and Charles Wesley joined him there to oversee the spiritual life of the new capital of Savannah – causing, it has to be said, much trouble and discord. Oglethorpe refused to allow slavery, and his treatment of the Indians was beyond praise: while in London, one of them died of smallpox and he persuaded a London clergyman to allow burial in his churchyard according to the rites of the man's own race. When they left to return home they especially asked to be presented again to the thirteen-year-old Cumberland, and he was delighted to grant them permission to give his name to the coastal island which is now one of America's most exclusive resorts. Cumberland and Oglethorpe were to meet many years later on the road to Culloden.

While Anne enjoyed herself in London and the armies were at stalemate on the Rhine, her husband was visiting his own sister. At the age of sixteen she had married a prince of Baden-Durlach, and his death just after the birth of their second son had tipped her childhood melancholia into madness. In his letters to his mother William could offer little comfort. Amalia lay in a darkened room sipping endless cups of coffee and scribbling on carefully torn pieces of paper. She seemed to recognise him but asked what religion he was, when he replied that he was a Protestant, she screamed, 'So much the worse for you!' and attacked him. The doctors refused to bleed her until the dog days of August were over, and William spent the rest of the time in the nursery with his two nephews, rocking the baby and comforting the three-year-old Karl, who said, 'I want Mama to look after me but she is not well'.[19] For Marie Louise back in Leeuwarden, where she had faced her own early widowhood with such stoicism and strength, it was like another bereavement: 'I have no other consolation in the world but you,' she wrote to her son.

There was no mention of all this in William's letters to Anne, perhaps because of 'the confirmation of what we hoped for on your departure from Holland'. Her pregnancy served 'but to redouble and augment if that were possible my love and my devotion to you my incomparable Annin';[20] but arguments were already mounting over where the child should be born. Orangists were convinced of the symbolic value of The Hague as the seat of central government, while the republicans were equally concerned to keep the capital uncontaminated. Anne herself desperately wanted to stay in England but William was horrified at such an idea, and Caroline, although sympathetic to her daughter, knew that politically it would never do. She wrote to Horatio Walpole that The Hague would be more advisable than 'a village' – Anne had obviously been grumbling about Leeuwarden – and should not cause problems:

> she will not be in anyone's way and a lying-in cannot be dangerous to a government nor give jealousy especially if she and the Prince of Orange conduct themselves with propriety and discretion and I believe I can answer for both.[21]

In a thoroughly emotional state, Anne set off for Harwich for the crossing to Helvoetsluys near Rotterdam, which physicians and admirals recommended as the better route through possible autumn gales. Tearfully she begged Hervey to let her know 'how those hours passed in which she used to have her share'. At Colchester, on receiving a letter from William which told her he was delayed in Germany, she turned round and rushed back to London, interrupting her mother and sister who were 'drinking chocolate, drowned in tears and choked with sighs'.[22] However they seemed more interested in their wake than the cause of it, and Anne was sent back to Harwich. One day out at sea she insisted she was in convulsions and the ship returned to port. Safe on dry land, she despatched pathetic letters in all directions, together with corroborating evidence from midwives and surgeons that she would miscarry at sea if forced to embark again.

William, having travelled day and night to 'this miserable Helvoetsluys'[23] to meet her, lost his temper and told her to come at once by the shortest sea crossing through Calais. He appealed to George, who had also lost patience, and she was ordered to travel from Harwich to Dover via the Gravesend ferry. As a last-ditch stand, she protested that the condition of the roads made it essential for her to come via London, but her father gave permission only for her closed coach to cross London Bridge without stopping. Finally defeated, the mortified princess was met at Calais by William, who had made another night and day dash along the coast. Her antics had reputedly cost the King £20,000, something which he would never forgive, and she was never to see England again.

Notes

[1] Walters, *Splendour*, p.125

[2] George's attentions might be enough to make anyone peevish since, according to Horace Walpole, no royal mistress ever received less for her pains. She was certainly deaf and three years older than the King, but the astringent critic, Alexander Pope, termed her 'that rara avis – a reasonable woman'. Walters, *Griffin*, p.98

[3] Hervey, op. cit., p.382

[4] Ibid., p.381

[5] Quoted by Trench, op. cit., p.137

[6] Davies, op. cit., p.120

[7] Sundon, op. cit., pp.317–19. All references to the journey and reception in Leeuwarden come from this source – Dorothy Dyves of the Princess's suite was a cousin of Lady Sundon.

[8] W Coxe [ed.], *Memoirs of Horatio Walpole*, 1808, p.190

[9] KHA, Willem IV, 171 I

[10] Ibid.

[11] Ibid.

[12] Quoted by Davies, op. cit., p.128

[13] Hervey, op. cit., p.382

[14] Davies, op. cit., p.139

[15] Quoted by Trench, op. cit., p.202

[16] Ibid., p.97

[17] Hervey, op. cit., p.767

[18] E Charteris, *William Augustus, Duke of Cumberland*, 1913, p.13

[19] KHA, Willem IV, 170 I

[20] Ibid.

[21] Horatio Walpole, op. cit., p.359

[22] Arkell, op. cit., p.222

[23] KHA, Willem IV, 171, I

Chapter Nine

In the spring of 1735 the King left to visit Hanover, leaving Caroline to head a Regency Council from which Frederick was again excluded. He had recently petitioned his father for a regular and increased income and for a suitable marriage: George as ever ignored the first request, and in response to the second offered the supposedly retarded Princess Charlotte Amelia of Denmark. His ministers always hated the electoral visits as they could never be sure what he was up to, and there were endless administrative delays as documents had to be shuttled backwards and forwards. One minister always accompanied him but when this was Lord Harrington, a man who apparently took six hours to do something which should have taken six minutes and ought to have been done six days ago, the frustration at home only increased. This time, settled in Herrenhausen and free from the tiresome shackles of the English parliamentary system, George's high good humour was increased by his successful wooing of a young married woman, Amelia Sophia Walmoden, who came from a family 'with a long and gallant record', i.e. she was closely related to two of George I's mistresses. Dark and pretty and twenty years his junior, she had heard none of his reminiscences before, and he soon accounted himself madly in love with her. Bizarrely, he kept his wife informed of every stage of the relationship, because of 'your indulgence for all my weaknesses... I know you will love Madame Walmoden because she loves me'.[1] As his stay lengthened into the autumn, Court and Queen alike wondered if her influence was at an end. Walpole hardly helped her morale by delivering a harangue to the effect that at her age she could hardly hope to attract the King with her body and must use her brains instead.

Anne too spent a miserable summer. She and William had not returned to Leeuwarden, but as he had wished, awaited the birth of his heir in The Hague. They lived quietly and unostentatiously in the residence of the Frisian stathouders. Dorothy Dyves, of the English suite, noticed a definite improvement in attitudes: 'we meet with great civility from the Ladies, though they did not come to the Princess when she was here last most of them have been now'. A Portuguese Jew named Jacopo Lopez de Liz entertained the couple with lavish private concerts, but Dorothy was doubtful about such company. 'I did not think... to show him any particular civility and chose to stay at home.'[2] William kept Marie Louise informed of Anne's health, remarking that 'she gets heavier and less inclined to move about';[3] but rumours flew on both sides of the North Sea that there was no pregnancy.

Caroline sent over her own physician, Dr Douglas, with instructions that he and Ambassador Walpole should visit the Princess. Walpole reported that Anne answered questions but absolutely refused to be examined: 'if she did not deceive herself or him in what she described she was certainly with child but as HRH would not permit him to be St Thomas' [i.e. put his hand on her side], Douglas would make no diagnosis.[4] Anne had hinted of her pregnancy to William in July, and as spring wore on his letters to his mother become increasingly agitated: 'the accoucheur says next weekend will see her delivered' and 'Saturday and Sunday were the crisis days but she has felt nothing yet'.[5] They clung to the hope that Caroline had had what seemed to be a ten-month pregnancy when Frederick was born, but by 20 April the truth was obvious:

> I can hardly bear to tell you but the accoucheur has told her that there is no child. It is not the fact that she is not pregnant that gives me pain, we are both young and if it is not to be this year then we dare hope for another time and besides it is the will of God… it is the blow to my poor princess that is so terrible. The swelling stays with her though the doctors assure me that there is no danger.[6]

Meanwhile, Anne wrote to a friend in London defending Douglas; he had been justified in his opinion and she would not wish him to be less respected 'for what has lately happened to me'.[7] Her generosity of spirit in the midst of her own shock and depression was not echoed by her father who, in an outburst of viciousness unusual even for him:

> said he could not imagine why any of her friends should be sorry for anything but the foolish figure she made in not being able to tell whether she had a child in her belly or not; for as to her having none he thought it much better so than otherwise or why anyone should think it such a mistake that one crooked beggar should not people earth with more crooked beggars.[8]

Anne hopefully hinted to her mother that she would feel better if she could return home again for a visit, but for Caroline political considerations were more important. She wrote in May to her daughter that she no longer belonged in England, 'You are now William's wife, God has given you skill and judgement, you are no longer a child.'[9]

As Anne recovered her mental and physical equilibrium, another problem loomed large. William's brave show of wealth in London and the extra expenses incurred through his illness there had been subsidised almost entirely by credit. The prestige of the marriage had enabled him to raise far more loans than he could sustain because too much of his wealth lay in goods – his family palaces of Soestdijk and Het Loo and the valuable paintings within them. What he needed was Anne's dowry, and not only were the States-General threatening to tax it, he could not even get Treasury clearance for it to leave England until he had acknowledged her joint ownership of these properties. This he was loath to do – not because of any lack of concern for his wife, for the marriage settlement and his newly made will guaranteed possession to her on his death, but because as Horatio Walpole saw, 'he will find money as long as his lands are free but as soon as they are tied up for a real security nobody will lend him anything and his present creditors will press to be repaid'.[10]

Anne appealed desperately to Caroline. 'I must own I should think it a terrible circumstance to have my future security be a pretence of hurting him in the present.'[11] She also drew Marie Louise into the problem when, possibly without William's knowledge, she wrote to her in the autumn about 'the difficulties in which the prince finds himself', and asked if there was any way in which the dower lands of Hesse could be used to find the money needed – a solution which was typical of her financial astuteness.[12] Marie Louise responded immediately, sending her representative to The Hague to do everything he could.

Anne's loyalty to her husband was total, and may have been severely tried: a large part of the £30,000 which William spent on her jewels went on a diamond necklace of twenty-two enormous stones. It was greatly admired at the wedding, appearing in an English print of 1734, and in the list of goods such as silver and communion plate brought over to Leeuwarden; but then it disappears. No later portrait shows what would have been her most valuable piece of jewellery and, crucially, it does not appear in the inventory of personal possessions at her death (as George's earrings do). It would seem possible that it was broken up and sold quietly, stone by stone, during the months before the dowry came through.

While the arguments about money continued, William tried to divert his wife with visits to the two great Orange properties which were at the heart of the problem – Soestdijk and Het Loo. The latter was William III's 'Versailles', and this was no idle comparison. Designed by a French architect, Het Loo was built in brick with stone pilasters and reliefs and was one of the first buildings to have sash windows. Inside the rooms were painted and gilded by Daniel Marot, a young Huguenot driven into exile, and the gardens, modelled on those of Le Nôtre, were the wonder of their time. Great gardens had always featured in Anne's life, from the dimly remembered Herrenhausen to the formal parterres at Hampton Court and the wooded vistas at Kensington, and although those at Het Loo had suffered some neglect for the past thirty years, they still offered the greatest pleasure.

Nearest the palace were the formal gardens edged in box containing tulips, poppies or sunflowers according to season, through them brick paths led to peacock-tailed fountains and intricate cascades, orange and lemon trees in wooden tubs, a labyrinth, a bowling green and a colonnaded amphitheatre. Further away in the surrounding woods, which merged into the vast hunting estate, stood a summer house with blue cupolas topped with gilded pineapples. Inside the floor was paved with red and white marble, and between wall frescos edged with bronze, large windows opened on all four sides into an aviary of tropical and singing birds.

The cost of maintaining such beauty was of course enormous, but to the couple's relief they received the first of a series of inheritances which ensured that their financial position became stable and was never again a problem. William's grandmother Amalia died in Germany, and there too, distant cousins descended from the twelve siblings of William the Silent died without issue, their lands and goods reverting to him as well as their titles.

The dowry dispute was finally settled when a large part of it was invested in English funds, and the quarterly Treasury accounts give a picture of Anne's spending through the early years of her marriage. Musical expenses include such items as '£2 7s to Mr Halling for his expenses in sending a spinet',[13] and she continued to support Handel by paying £60 annually for the engraved silver ticket supplied to those underwriting his opera seasons at Covent Garden. Alongside small sums such as '£4 for gloves and £63 for a length of the prized Spitalfields flowered silk' are regular payments, varying from £800 to £1,500 'to Princess Caroline to buy Bonds'. Hervey asserts that 'Caroline was as well beloved by her [Anne] as anyone could be'.[14] Perhaps these were generous presents but, more likely, they were intended as some kind of insurance policy through a trusted intermediary in case she had to return permanently to England for any reason. Anne's financial acumen was a feature of her life, and the personal animosity of her father and brother had in no way diminished.

George eventually arrived back in England in October 1735 – in a foul temper exacerbated by fever and piles. He divided his time through the winter between writing letters to his mistress and comparing England unfavourably to his Electorate.

> I wish with all my heart that the devil may take all your bishops, and the devil take the Minister and the devil take your Parliament, and the devil take the whole island provided I can get out and go to Hanover.[15]

He had brought gifts to the Queen: a team of the Hanoverian creams, which he proceeded to monopolise though she was responsible for their keep; and a set of pictures of the balls and masquerades which he had enjoyed while he was away, which she must hang in her dressing room so that he could tell her about them. During his absence, Caroline had discovered in an old bureau the Royal Collection's Holbein drawings and Leonardo sketchbooks which had been lost when the palace of Whitehall was destroyed by fire in 1698; but George did not share her pleasure, since the find contained none of the florid mythological pictures he preferred. She had replaced one of these in the drawing room at Kensington Palace with the Van Dyck of Charles I's family, and he ordered 'those nasty little children' to be taken away and his 'fat Venus' returned.[16]

As Caroline, the princesses, and even Cumberland, suffered under the lash of the King's tongue, Frederick carefully kept a low profile, for a marriage had at last been arranged for him. His father had inspected the sixteen-year-old Princess Augusta of Saxe-Gotha and decided she would serve. On being informed of the arrangement, Frederick 'made answer with great decency, duty and propriety that whoever His Majesty thought a proper match for his son would be agreeable to him'.[17] In view of George's previous offer it is likely the prince had made some precautionary enquiries of his own.

His eagerness and the King's determination to return to Hanover for Madame Walmoden's birthday in May decreed a spring ceremony in spite of Augusta's youth (Frederick was twenty-nine), and she arrived at the end of April. She was tall and gangling, with hair, according to Caroline, of 'a sort of blond sheeps colour'.[18] She was also painfully shy and spoke no English, since her mother had assumed that after twenty years of the Hanoverians everyone in England would speak German. As Hervey remarked, 'the conjecture [was] so well founded that I believe there were not three natives in England that understood one word of it better than in the reign of Queen Anne'.[19] She landed forlornly at Greenwich to find the same lack of welcome that William had experienced. George's excuse was again that until she was Princess of Wales there was no rule of precedence on how she should be received, and she spent two nights there awaiting instructions until Frederick took matters into his own hands and came downriver in his own barge to dine with her, and give her 'the diversion of passing on the water as far as the Tower and back'. He professed himself delighted, and she was anxious to please, prostrating herself before her future parents-in-law, which went down very well; and she was soon to speak English with far less of an accent than they did.

Before the evening ceremony, she and Frederick dined with his sisters, and there was an undignified squabble over the seating arrangements, Amelia, resplendent in crimson brocade and velvet, sulked; Caroline rushed off to tell tales to her father; and the fifteen-year-old Cumberland, who was to give the bride away, proved an unlikely mediator. Handel's wedding anthem was to his fury ruined by bad singing, and the Queen had to translate Augusta's vows for her with Frederick 'bawling' in her other ear. She wrote to Anne:

I told her to look at me and I would make a sign when she ought to kneel. The poor girl clutched my skirt and said 'For Heaven's sake please don't leave me'.

At the moment when they were pronounced man and wife, a fanfare of trumpets and roll of drums gave the signal for a cannon salute. Caroline revealed that the bride's 'under dress' at the bedding ceremony was quite dreadful, and added, rather improbably, that the King 'had behaved like an angel'.[20]

Anne was spending the summer of 1736 at Soestdijk near Utrecht. Formerly a hunting lodge, William III had redesigned it in the French style, and though its severely elegant facade and intricate topiary parterres formed an almost perfect symmetry, one garden wall had been deliberately left unfinished, greatly irritating a distinguished visitor. 'Correctitude,' he remarked, 'dictates that in order to embrace satisfactorily you must have two arms.' Surrounded by forest, it was the prince's favourite palace, where he had spent his childhood summers, and now the couple looked forward again to a child of their own. William broke the news to his mother by sending her an intricate needle case so she could sew garments for her grandchild; this time there was no doubt.

His habit of writing two or three letters a week to Marie Louise had not been in the least affected by his marriage, and every one ends with the careful formula that Anne sends her regards or thanks for the gifts her mother-in-law was always sending – fresh Friesland shrimps, a book of chamber music or fruit from her garden 'because I know the princess loves fruit'.[21] Occasionally William is reduced to the assurance that his wife would write to express her own thanks 'but does not wish to incommode Your Serene Highness by doing so'.[22]

Anne's stubborn refusal ever to write herself reflected the tense relationship between two women with absolutely nothing in common except their possessive devotion to the same man. Marie Louise seems to have had no artistic or intellectual interests whatever, and very little education; she had married Friso when she was barely twenty after a childhood blighted by her mother's early death and her father's almost permanent absence at the head of Hesse's mercenaries in Marlborough's wars. Anne's overweening pride, noted by every observer since she was a child, would not allow her to share her husband with anyone, and, deeply resentful of his relationship with his mother, she obstinately placed herself outside it. Once, with William on the Rhine at Frankfurt, she writes to him from Leeuwarden to ask him to thank his mother for the herbs and salads Marie Louise had sent her from a hundred yards up the street. William was a despairing mediator till the day he died, but it says much for him that he refused to allow his strong-willed wife to deflect him from the recognition of what he owed his mother. Marie Louise was not blameless; she had relinquished her political influence readily enough but may have clung to the emotional one to a tactless extent. Looking forward to being a grandmother, she perhaps hoped that a child would help, but once again there was to be no child.

Anne's labour began after they returned to The Hague at the beginning of December. A male midwife, Dr Sands, had been sent from London and all seemed to be going quickly and well for a time, but according to Sands' report to Caroline, the child's head was too large; after four long days of ineffectual labour Anne's own life was in danger, and William had to make the decision for its skull to be crushed. The baby girl lay swathed in white silk in public state before her burial by the grave of the assassinated William the Silent in the Orange family vault at Delft:

> Hier onder 't Handbeelt van een Nassousse Helden
> Die Balthazar Geraard Moordaanij neder velde
> Rust d'eerste Spruit die Anna Bronswyck droegh…
> Zoo ook d'orange stam God geef dat Zij mag bloeijen.

(Here beneath the statue of Nassau's hero / Who was struck down by the murderous Balthazar Gerard / Rests the first child which Anne of Brunswick bore… So God grant the Orange stem will bloom again.)

The bill for gravediggers and torch-bearers was paid the day after Christmas, and is filed in the archives with the carefully prepared letter to the seven provinces announcing 'the birth of a healthy and well-formed son/daughter to my dearly loved wife'.[23]

Amelia revealed a different side to her character in the teasing, affectionate letter she wrote to her elder sister.

> We all love and adore you, my pretty Annin, my angel, don't overdo things pray to show you are Hercules for it frightens me and I will no more be uneasy for you as long as I live, it's too great a fatigue and doesn't agree with my health or my complexion.[24]

Anne suffered from milk fever, but was able to leave her bed on Christmas Day, William reported to his mother some days later that her appetite was back and she had eaten a small chicken, observing, 'we have much to thank God for'.[25]

Caroline, who had also lost two babies, wrote a letter of comfort:

> Words cannot tell how I have suffered and my joy at receiving you back from God, I have you and that is enough. May He grant you renewed strength and

make you the happy mother of a family, be certain that you will have happier and easier labours than this in the future. May God give you every blessing and you will not lack it, *mein liebes kind*, if you submit yourself entirely to his will.[26]

The sincerity of eighteenth-century piety is always difficult to fathom; those tombstones which bear witness to everyone's perfect adherence to the Christian ideal rouse possibly unworthy suspicions in modern times. In addition, there was the perception of what was fitting, what was expected: Marie Louise, on hearing of Friso's death, had simply exclaimed, 'The Lord does what is right in his eyes.' Deathbeds either were, or were reported as being, times for devout submissions and spiritual pronouncements. In contemporary letters, religious references may be as empty as the lengthy and elaborate courtesy formulae with which they begin and end. The fact that Caroline asked for neither sacrament nor prayers during her final illness had to be concealed; Marie Louise could certainly be said to have embodied many of the Christian virtues, and William's faith was sincere and uncomplicated, but Anne seems to be different She seldom expressed herself in religious terms and her funeral eulogy refers to the fact that 'her piety rose to a very elevated pitch though it carefully declined all ostentation'.[27] The cynical might have their fun with that, but the archives do contain a manuscript in her own hand entitled *Theologia*.[28] This is a commonplace book, kept as she measured her own Lutheranism against the Calvinism of her adopted country. It opens with the quotation: 'So long as men live, they must learn… the knowledge of God is needed above all because without that nothing can be understood,' and this seems to indicate a much more immediate sense of God than is found in the English tradition of the period where He is sought in experience, but is not the starting point. The quotation is given in German and is close to the one from Calvin's *Institutes of Christian Religion* that knowledge of self can lead to despair without the knowledge of God.

Caroline's regency this time had been a difficult one, and had already lasted seven months, as George refused to tear himself away from Madame Walmoden and the son she had presented to him as his. There had, to be sure, been a slight problem in June, when a ladder was found leading to her bedroom window, and a young officer hiding in the garden had been arrested. George was puzzled but eventually decided it was a nasty plot to discredit her. The Queen regularly invited Frederick and Augusta to dinner, but found her lack of education and his sly insolence as tiring as though she had carried them round the garden on her back; though she mostly referred to her daughter-in-law as 'the driveller', she had a pitying affection for her and presented her with 'a most beautiful hat curiously made of feathers in imitation of a fine Brussels lace… the first of the kind ever made in England'.[29]

The King and Anne had always been the most relentlessly hostile to

Frederick, as the most directly threatened by him, and with both of them out of the way family relationships might have been expected to improve. But with the Prince's frustration now much greater and his grievances more legitimate, his private and public behaviour was changing. Since his marriage, he could no longer avoid his family so easily and there was continual tension. Amelia's perversity had meant that she had shown him some friendship – their passion for gossip providing a bond – but her lack of patience with the young Augusta, and Frederick's discovery of the stories she was spreading about him, now placed her firmly in the other camp. His remarks about his siblings were regularly relayed to the Queen: 'I hear he speaks of the Duke with kindness... for Amelia she is to be shut up within four walls and for Caroline she is to be sent to starve.'[30] He and his wife took to arriving late at chapel services, taking their place with the maximum amount of commotion, often dislodging his mother's prayer-book as they squeezed past her.

But such scuffles paled to insignificance as he took advantage of the prevailing political unrest. He no longer indulged in juvenile and undignified escapades but skilfully manipulated tensions in the country: West Country riots against corn exports, strikes by the weavers of Spitalfields, a mysterious bomb explosion in Westminster Hall, and Walpole's failed attempt to curb the excessive consumption of gin (estimated as two pints a week in London for every man, woman and child) spelt danger for a floundering government and an absent King. A notice in the Royal Exchange reported that 'His Hanoverian Majesty designs to visit to visit his British dominions for three months in the spring',[31] and Walpole himself summed up the mood, saying 'if he will have a whore why don't he take an English one and stay at home, there are enough of them to be had cheaper here!'

Frederick stepped into the vacuum, making sure he was seen quaffing gin in a London tavern, though in reality he rarely drank. His common touch was further displayed when fire broke out at the Temple one night, destroying 'a vast number of chambers with manuscripts and writings to a great value'.[32] The Prince rushed from his bed and spent six hours directing and encouraging firemen and soldiers. Fire was of course still the great terror in a city of old houses, labyrinthine streets and erratic water supply, and many of the great houses had recently invested in a new invention of 'a Bomb made Beautiful to hang up or set in any apartment that will extinguish any Fires breaking out though the Inhabitants are asleep'. The main fuel for the city was sea coal, shipped from Newcastle and unloaded at Billingsgate, but its fumes caused appalling pollution; all the vegetables grown in the market gardens surrounding London were tainted, and when a hundred houses burned down one night in the City, many Londoners only knew about it when they read the papers.

When Frederick received the Freedom of the City of London in November 1736, the Lord Mayor was especially unctuous, and the Prince's speech referred to the great importance of trade promising 'to do all possible to promote prestige and commerce'.[33] This was ground-breaking stuff, as were his gestures such as picking up an old woman's oranges when his coach had brushed her in the street, and his playing the 'cello in a village orchestra near his country house. He already commanded public (and much parliamentary) sympathy, for on his marriage George had only increased his allowance to £50,000 a year, i.e. still retaining half the amount allocated to the prince by the Civil List; and his exploitation of his position posed a very real threat to political stability.

It has been pointed out that the Hanoverian tradition of quarrelling between King and heir can actually be seen as a political safety valve, at any rate under the first two Georges while the dynasty was establishing itself. If opposition grouped itself around the heir to the throne, that at least kept it under government scrutiny. The Jacobites 'had not gone away', to use a modern phrase, for a young and more appealing Stuart was growing up on the other side of the Channel, and Walpole never hesitated to use them as bogeymen for his own purposes: 'A set of low Jacobites talked of setting fire to the gallery built for the Princess Royal's wedding by a preparation which they call phosphorus which takes fire from the air.' And at this time they were supposedly behind an idea to supply free gin and take advantage of the resulting chaos – possibly a reference to the saying that all Englishmen were Jacobite when drunk and Hanoverian when sober. Any public figure could be vulnerable if there were whispers of Jacobitism, that 'compound of Highland Rapine, Italian Bigotry and French Tyranny'. In 1732 Lord Burlington had felt it necessary to dispel awkward rumours about his loyalties by commissioning William Aikman to paint the enormous portrait of George II's children which now hangs at Chatsworth.

Urgent representations from Caroline (who had been hissed at the opera) and from Walpole, who feared that the King was doing what 'his predecessors could never do [make] all men of one mind' at last pressured George into leaving Hanover.[34] So late in the year, the roads were bad and it took him an unusually long five days to reach Helvoetsluys where the royal yacht and its escort fleet awaited him, pinned down in the harbour by storm force westerly winds. But it was assumed in England that he had already set sail, and Frederick assiduously brought news to his mother that distress signals had been heard at sea and many men-of-war had been wrecked along the coast. A further report had the yacht tacking in the teeth of the gale only to disappear from view. For ten days there was no news of the King, and Frederick outraged his family by giving a dinner for his new friend the Lord Mayor (for which he had to borrow fifty-four candlesticks and twenty-six dozen sets of cutlery).

Caroline began to discuss with Hervey and her daughters the very real possibility of George's death at sea. Princess Caroline announced that if her brother became king she would run out of the house *au grand galop*, while Hervey assured the Queen that she would be able to rule her son – she only could 'prevent the wreck which so unskilful a pilot left to himself would in all probability, bring upon all that were embarked in the same bottom'[35] – a somewhat unfortunate image in the circumstances. At last, the day after Christmas, the news arrived that the King was safe, and although he disclaimed to his wife any responsibility for forcing the ships to set sail in the storm, numerous letters reached England giving a different story. He had blustered to his Admiral, Sir Charles Wager, that he was not afraid of a bit of bad weather, to which Sir Charles replied that whether His Majesty was or not, he himself was; and when George shouted he would rather be twelve hours in the storm than twenty-four in this godforsaken port, the laconic Admiral remarked that he need not wish for twelve, since four in this weather would see an end to him.

Eventually the royal temper prevailed and they had set out. The yacht shipped four feet of water and three sailors were swept overboard. Only by ordering the hacking away of much of the deck's superstructure and – probably with some satisfaction – jettisoning all the royal furniture was Sir Charles able to save his ship and struggle back to port.[36]

The gales continued for many days, and it was noted that the King's enthusiasm for embarkation was much reduced. He passed some of the time by writing a thirty-page love letter to his wife, which Caroline triumphantly showed to Walpole. Hervey said it might have been written by a man of twenty to his first mistress, and agreed with Walpole that

> they had a most incomprehensible master and (though neither of them were very partial to His Majesty) they also agreed that with a woman that could be won by writing they had rather have any man in the world for a rival than the King... He had the warmest the most natural manner of expressing himself that I ever met with, with the prettiest words and most agreeable turns I ever saw put together.

George spent a thoroughly dreary Christmas in Helvoetsluys, and it is quite extraordinary that he never once travelled the eight miles that separated them to visit his eldest daughter, who was mourning the loss of her child. Part of the reason was undoubtedly political, though even the most ardent republican could scarcely have taken exception in the circumstances.

Notes

[1] Quoted by Trench, op. cit., p.175

[2] Sundon, op. cit., p.337

[3] KHA, Willem IV, 170 I

[4] Hervey, op. cit., p.422

[5] KHA, Willem IV, 170 I

[6] Ibid.

[7] This letter is in the Royal Archive at Windsor Add 28/149. Anne seldom dates her letters and it has been tentatively catalogued as 1734, but I think the quotation above and a later reference to Dorothy Dyes leaving the royal service place it firmly in 1735.

[8] Hervey, op. cit., p.423

[9] KHA, Anna van Hannover, 430

[10] Horatio Walpole, op. cit., p.187

[11] Ibid., p.376

[12] KHA, Anna, 430

[13] KHA, A17 412

[14] Hervey, op. cit., p.276

[15] Hervey, op. cit., p.486

[16] Ibid., p.488

[17] Ibid., p.548

[18] KHA, Anna, 430

[19] Hervey, op. cit., p.548

[20] KHA, Anna, 430

[21] KHA, Willem IV, 170 I

[22] Ibid.

[23] KHA, Willem IV, 22

[24] KHA, Anna, 430

[25] KHA, Willem IV, 170 I

[26] Quoted by Arkell, op. cit., p.262

[27] Benjamin Sowden, 'Funeral Sermon of HRH Anne Princess of Orange', London, 4 March 1759.

[28] KHA, 470

[29] De-la-Noy, op. cit., p.828

[30] Hervey, op. cit., p.828

[31] Quoted by Trench, p.183

[32] Young, op. cit., p.99

[33] *Gentlemen's Magazine*, December 1736

[34] Hervey, op. cit., p.639

[35] Ibid., p.631

[36] Ibid., pp.635–38

Chapter Ten

For George, out of sight would always be out of mind, and for England too the Princess Royal was 'as much forgotten... as if she had been buried three years'.[1] To make things worse, the marriage was now recognised by the government as a disastrous political miscalculation. William was as far from the stathoudership as he had ever been and the foreign policy of the United Provinces was still determinedly neutral. The supporters of the House of Orange seemed powerless to pierce the solid rocks of oligarchic government – those regent-bands who controlled so tightly everything which moved within each province, and for whom the English princess was an irrelevance or a threat. The assembly of each province which sent representatives to the permanent session of the States-General varied in number, but every town of importance had its nominee, and the fact that the province of Holland had eighteen town members and only one for the nobility illustrates an important feature of Dutch life.

In England, ownership of land was the key to power: a man might make his money in trade and then bought a country estate. But in the United Provinces, society – at any rate in the most powerful provinces – was essentially urban. Wealthy men spent their money on beautiful artefacts which they treasured within the high walls of their town-houses, and even farmers would use their spare money to buy pictures rather than more land, which may explain the many small canvases of domestic life. In theory, sovereign power lay with these town councils, though in practice they simply ratified central decisions made by the two most powerful men in the country – the Grand Pensionary of Holland who was effectively, in a stathouderless period, the Chief Minister, and the Greffier (record-keeper) who dealt with every document which came in or out of The Hague. The Pensionary from 1727–37 was Simon van Slingelandt, a political realist 'who did not approve of making mountains out of molehills and a business out of nothing';[2] such pragmatism appealed to Caroline, and from 1734 she was in touch with him through Horatio Walpole in an attempt to smooth Anne's path. They shared a common affliction – gout – and this often dictated Slingelandt's mood: 'What a pity,' sighed Walpole, 'that such a Billingsgate tongue and temper should belong to such an excellent understanding.'[3] While she recommended various tisanes for his pain, Caroline thought she could detect in his public statements an acceptance of the Orange role as a focus for his country's federal structure. She trusted him and assured

Walpole 'my daughter will find in him a friend and she will always receive strict orders to do nothing without his advice'.[4] In fact the States of Holland had extracted a secret promise on Slingelandt's election that he would never propose the restoration of the stathoudership, and as time went on Caroline realised her mistake.

In order to understand the forces William and Anne were facing, it is necessary to understand the Dutch system of government. 'Of all constitutions formed by statesmen or described by historians none was more complicated and embarrassed than that of the Seven Provinces,' wrote the ambassador in a jaded mood.[5] Yet although it seemed tortuous in the extreme to pressured diplomats, it quite simply suited the country's fierce individualism. It had evolved naturally when William the Silent had taken over the function previously held by the Hapsburgs he drove out, but left the provincial structure untouched, and the decentralisation formed a system of checks and balances which had worked well through the seventeenth century. No individual must ever dominate for fear of the base ambition to be found in every man, and so the authority of the Princes of Orange must be weighed against 'the Freedom of the Cities, the Sovraignty of the Provinces, [and] the Agreements or Constitutions of the Union';[6] however the thirty-year-old Republic had now become used to life without the House of Orange, and it would not easily be persuaded to the contrary.

Anne often complained that their marriage seemed to have harmed William rather than helped him, and her mother only disagrees on a personal level; the English misjudgement had simply succeeded in driving a further wedge between William and the States-General. Caroline understood this very well and she was also concerned about Anne's increasing interference in political matters. She warned her daughter to watch her tongue after receiving reports of her interventions in the delicate negotiations over command of the army and the fleet; in her determination to promote William's interests she was advising him to block all promotions until he himself was made General of the Foot.

Walpole was severely tried. 'I shall always be glad to see my old friend Horatio, provided he leaves the ambassador at home whom I must constantly quarrel with.'[7] And at length he had to tell her frankly that she and William should leave The Hague for a time, since indifference to them was rapidly changing into downright antagonism.

They decided to visit William's other northern province of Groningen, and at the end of February 1737 braved the towering waves of the Zuyder Zee. The boat carrying their luggage was separated from them in the storm and they had to receive local dignitaries without a change of clothes. One of these worthies took it upon himself to deliver a long speech of condolence which reviewed every circumstance of Anne's recent confinement. She managed to remain calm throughout but had collapsed in tears afterwards and wept for hours, William told his mother, raging at 'such sottise'. Marie Louise sent an *oeuf de Vanneau* – an Easter egg, perhaps – as an expression of her sympathy.[8]

Anne's correspondence with her mother now concentrated on family rather than political matters. Mary and Louisa, in their early teens, were taking a full part in Court life; the former tall, dark and very shy 'with the softest and mildest temper in the world', the latter much more outgoing and mercurial and the acknowledged beauty of the family. Carefully chaperoned, they had been taken as a special treat to the St Bartholomew Fair to view the exhibits of human freaks and wild animals, and they were allowed to take part in the card games which were the main entertainment at Court, as they were in society as a whole: the teller at a House of Commons vote was once heard to count – nine, ten, jack, queen, king.[9] The royal family usually gave their winnings to charitable causes though Cumberland kept the £2,000 he won in a single night; he certainly lived life to the full, since it was reported in this year that he had gone hunting in a thunderstorm and afterwards swam his horse across the Thames because he was late for a party at the Vauxhall pleasure gardens; it is worth noting that he was suffering from measles at the time.

But the most important piece of news was the birth of a child to Frederick and Augusta. Aware of the pain this must cause Anne, Caroline wrote as amusingly as she could, though in truth the tale needed little embellishment. Frederick had announced the pregnancy in June, and when Caroline had a gynaecological discussion with her daughter-in-law, all her questions were met with a vague 'I don't know'. The Queen had already convinced herself that her son was impotent, though when she questioned Hervey on this delicate subject he assured her that though he gathered that Frederick was 'in these matters ignorant to a degree inconceivable' he was as well equipped as any man in England.[10] But Caroline was still doubtful and began to suspect that there was a plot 'to disinherit my dear William'. On the last day of July the family dined together at Hampton Court, and afterwards the King and Queen sat down to play cards with Amelia and Caroline, while elsewhere in the palace Augusta informed Frederick that her labour had started. His repeated requests that she should give birth at St James's had been refused, but at this moment of crisis the long years of disregard and frustration propelled him into an action which was as lunatic as it was inexcusable.

With the aid of an equerry and his dancing master, he bundled his wife secretly down the back stairs and into a coach with the Mistress of the Robes (who just happened to be his former mistress) in disapproving attendance. With his valet on the top of the coach and two equerries clinging on behind, Frederick ordered a full gallop to London. Augusta's sufferings are perhaps better imagined than described though Hervey did both. The Prince spent his time telling her it would be over 'in a minute' and begging her not to make such a fuss. At St James's, Augusta was manhandled upstairs to a bed made up with table linen borrowed from a neighbouring house, and within the hour she was delivered of 'a little rat of a girl about the bigness of a large toothpick case' – Hervey's description of course.[11]

The outrage of George and Caroline, and indeed of most of the Court, at the Prince of Wales's extraordinary behaviour led to a virtual rerun of the quarrel which had separated Anne, Amelia and Caroline from their parents twenty years before. A letter was drafted by Walpole himself and sent by George to his son:

> This extravagant and undutiful behaviour in so essential a point as the birth of an heir to my Crown is such an evidence of your premeditated defiance of me and such contempt for my authority and of the natural right belonging to your parents... [that] I will not suffer... the division which you have made in my family.[12]

He then repeated, almost word for word, George I's instruction to him after the birth of his second son: 'it is my pleasure that you leave St James's', though he stopped short of his father's vindictiveness in separating mother and child. Frederick was deprived of his guards and his furniture and banished to the White House at Kew. As a parting shot, the Prince announced that he wished his daughter, whom he had named for her mother, to bear the ancient English title of The Lady Augusta rather than Princess. The service to England of 'this little rat of a girl' was to be the mother of Caroline of Brunswick, who was to bring even greater scandal to the monarchy many years later.

The departure of Frederick and Augusta from St James's was far more low-key than that of his parents had been, since this time the King's response was both measured and understandable. Most of Frederick's supporters were as aghast as George at the offence to the Crown and the danger to the heir, and the prince realised he must repair his image. When the assiduous Lord Mayor travelled to Kew (his twenty-coach procession causing a massive traffic jam) with compliments on his daughter's birth, the Prince responded, 'What Children God may bless me with I will infuse into them sentiments agreeable to the laws and liberties of that Country they have the happiness to be born into.' He then handed out copies of his statement and of the apologetic letters of explanation he and Augusta had sent to the King – these were duly printed in *The Gentleman's Magazine*.[13]

His oratorical and lengthy letters to his father begging for forgiveness and protesting his devotion were further published in pamphlet form at threepence a time, but ended with George's curt response, 'The Prince has his Orders and the King does not make any Alterations in them.'[14] The efforts at ingratiation worked with the public at least, since six months later the royal order, 'No person whatever who shall go to pay their court to Their Royal Highnesses shall be admitted to His Majesty's presence,' had to be formally repeated, though by this time both Courts were observing the strict regulations of mourning.

The Queen's health had always seemed good, partly because she knew her husband's impatience with any kind of illness. Gout had long been a problem: she sometimes appeared in a wheelchair pushed by Cumberland, but George hated her to use it, and to accompany him on their long walks she would soak her feet in cold water and suffer the agony afterwards. Such determined stoicism had extended to an internal rupture of either womb or intestine which she had suffered at Louisa's birth thirteen years before; at that time such damage might have been treatable, but her fear of George's reaction led her into a desperate concealment until it became malignant. She ignored all warning signs and concentrated on her plans for a royal library in the stable block at St James's; English diplomats were scouring Europe for the rare and beautiful editions of literary and philosophical works which were to form the foundation for the royal collection later presented to the British Library.

In early November 1738, as she inspected the renovation of the building, she was taken ill with agonising stomach pains and vomiting. Collapsing into bed, she was dosed with Daffy's Elixir, snakeroot, and Sir Walter Raleigh's Cordial, the last two being remedies recommended by an anxious Lord Hervey. She then struggled up to attend a formal reception where she greeted everyone with her usual serenity. At last she was able to escape and Hervey triumphantly produced Ward's Pill – a remedy which he had found invaluable for rheumatism – assuring Caroline that it would drive the pain from her stomach into the limbs, where it would be less dangerous.[15] As her fever rose and the pain increased, more doctors were summoned till there were at least five grouped round the patient – one of them recommended a slug of whisky, and the Queen 'kept it in for about half an hour which was twenty-nine minutes longer than she had kept anything else'. Two bleedings of twelve ounces a time did not improve things, and George began to panic.

He decided to keep her company by sleeping on her bed at night thus ensuring that she dare not turn or move. He alternated between holding her during her paroxysms and fussing about the ruffles on his new shirt, between snapping at her for not eating and assuring her repeatedly that she was 'the best woman that ever was born'. In desperation, Amelia and Caroline appealed to the doctors to advise that she should be spoken to as little as possible; they kept watch at her bedside but neither understood her murmuring that she had an ill which nobody knew of. Princess Caroline was weak herself, having been racked with rheumatism through the summer and was barely able to rise from her chair. Now her distress brought on a series of violent nosebleeds. For this she, too, was treated by bleeding, though the doctor 'was forced to prick her in both arms and at both the blood was so thick he could get but little'.

Eventually the Queen allowed an examination which revealed the rupture, after which a surgeon's effort to lance the swelling by candlelight resulted in his wig bursting into flames. The days dragged on, the wound turned septic and two further operations were performed 'to pare away the mortification', while the doctors, who now numbered seven, continued relentlessly with their purges and bleedings. She endured it all with superhuman courage. Since she could not keep down the usual anaesthetic of brandy she occasionally let out an involuntary moan but 'used immediately after to bid the surgeons not to mind her and make her excuses for interrupting them with her silly complaints'.

Frederick travelled up to London, and the entire family expended an enormous amount of nervous energy in keeping him away from his mother, since they were sure he was merely seeking 'the joy of knowing [the Queen] was dead five minutes before he could know it in Pall Mall'. They also found time for urgent discussions with the Lord Chancellor about her will. After a week she rallied slightly, probably because the doctors had given up their burrowings into the open wound, and she spoke to each of her daughters in turn, telling Caroline to support the retiring Mary and curb Louisa's vivacity, which might lead her into trouble: 'Poor Caroline, it is a fine legacy I leave you – the education of these two young things.' Amelia escaped the task, since her mother had always thoroughly disapproved of the relationship with Grafton, whom she disliked. To Louisa herself she issued a specific medical warning: 'Remember I die by being giddy and obstinate in having kept my disorder a secret.' Fourteen years later this youngest daughter was to die of almost the same cause. Cumberland was weeping as much as his sisters and her words to him focused his life:

You know I have always loved you tenderly and placed my chief hope in you; show your gratitude to me by your behaviour to the King; be a support to your father, and double your attention to him to make up for the disappointment and vexation he must receive from your profligate and worthless brother. It is in you only I hope for keeping up the credit of your family when your father shall be no more. Attempt nothing ever against your brother and endeavour to mortify him in no way but by showing superior merit.

Lastly she turned to her husband and gave him back the ruby ring she had received at their coronation. 'Naked I came to you and naked I go from you. I had everything I ever possessed from you and whatever I had from you I

95

return.' She urged him to marry again, and when he sobbed, 'No, no, I shall have mistresses,' she sighed deeply, 'O, my God, that never stopped you.'

There had been much gossip at Court that throughout her illness she had never asked for a priest, and Walpole, since the King's attitude to religion was well known, broached the matter to Amelia in terms they both understood.

> Pray, madam, let this farce be played. The Archbishop will act it very well. You may bid him be as short as he will. It will do the Queen no hurt, no more than any good; and it will satisfy all the wise and good fools, who will call us all atheists if we don't pretend to be as great fools as they are.[16]

The Archbishop was summoned, and he prayed at Caroline's bedside morning and evening, with George leaving precipitately the minute he was announced. Still she lingered on. 'I wish it was at an end... but my nasty heart will not break yet.' She asked for all the candles in the room to be extinguished so that no one should have to watch her die. The doctors turned to opium and at last, ten days after the onset of her illness, with George, Amelia and Caroline beside her, a rattle in her throat signified the end.

Such is the power of myth that within a few days it was being reported that 'she had poured out her soul several times in a day in the most devout and affecting terms, her Prayers being generally announced in an audible manner', and 'every interval of Ease from her Sufferings were employed in Acts of Devotion'.[17] No wonder Chesterfield remarked, 'I am sorry it did not occur to the Lord President to propose the deification of Her Late Majesty.' As one of Frederick's advisers, he had been a bitter critic of Caroline, mocking her intellectual friends, claiming 'she bewildered herself in metaphysical disputes which neither she nor they understood', and accusing her of cunning and perfidy in her supposed control of government; but most people would have been more inclined to Hervey's simple tribute that 'she was a thorough great, wise, good, and agreeable woman' – probably the only unaffected and generous description that sardonic man ever wrote.

George's grief was deeply felt and caused his family and the court serious concern. At a reception in January 'he stayed but two minutes and had grief fixed on his face', and on opening Parliament he could not begin his speech for several minutes and continually put his hand to his head with his eyes full of tears.[18] He would suddenly succumb to wild fits of weeping, and Amelia ordered all the queens to be removed from his playing cards. He continued Caroline's servants' salaries and all her charitable contributions – such as an annual payment of ten guineas to poor haymakers along the Hammersmith Road – saying, 'I would have no one the poorer for her death than myself,' – and his grief revealed 'a tenderness of which the world thought him utterly incapable.'[19] He allowed very few people – and certainly not Frederick – to attend the lying-in-state, and the Prince was further excluded from the private service held in the death chamber before the funeral.

The pamphleteers showed no mercy: 'O death where is thy sting, To take the Queen and leave the King.' Neither he nor his younger children attended the funeral, and Amelia, supported by Grafton, was the only member of the family present, as Handel's anthem 'The ways of Zion do mourn' sounded for the first of many times in Westminster Abbey, and every church bell in London tolled against the Tower guns.

Notes

[1] Hervey, op. cit., p.289
[2] A Goslinga, *Slingelandt's Efforts towards European Peace*, 1915, p.16
[3] Horatio Walpole, op. cit., p.323
[4] Ibid., p.356
[5] Ibid., p.11
[6] Sir William Temple, *Observations on the United Provinces*, 1703, p.53
[7] Horatio Walpole, op. cit., p.189
[8] KHA, Willem IV 170 II
[9] E Williams, *Life in Georgian England*, 1962, p.44
[10] Walters, *Griffin*, p.140
[11] Hervey, op. cit., p.759
[12] Royal Archives 54026
[13] *Gentleman's Magazine*, September 1737
[14] Trench, op. cit., p.196
[15] The account of Queen Caroline's death is taken from Hervey, pp.877–915
[16] Davies, op. cit., p.166
[17] *Gentleman's Magazine*, November 1737
[18] *Gentleman's Magazine*, January 1738
[19] Hervey, op. cit., p.916

Chapter Eleven

Anne was with her husband in Breda when the news that Caroline was dying reached her. The town was in the south, well away from their own provinces but it had a long record of especial loyalty to the House of Orange, and was thus an obvious target as William strove to establish a position beyond his own narrow base. The couple had been welcomed under a triumphal arch outside the gates in a symbolic ceremony which harked back to the *joyeuse entrée* of the medieval progresses of the rulers of the Netherlands. They had already stayed for five weeks in the splendid moated Renaissance style castle, lavishly entertaining the local officials who had reciprocated with a great feast and fireworks for Anne's birthday on 2 November. Things were going well, as a visiting diplomat wrote, 'Their Highnesses are adored here by people of all conditions... [they] receive all people that come to them with so peculiar a grace that it must needs attach them for ever to their service.'[1] But the despatches from London sent them into seclusion until the end came.

Many letters came from the family, Amelia mourns 'the best of mothers, the greatest queen and most adorable woman';[2] Cumberland 'the best of mothers and the dearest of friends'; while Caroline, more thoughtfully, writes that their mother often spoke of 'my more than dearest Anne' and sends the text of Handel's anthem, 'the finest cruel touching thing that ever was heard'. This had first been sung in a small chapel adjoining the death-chamber where George sat alone to hear it; his wild grief and unpredictable behaviour was alarming the family for one night he had summoned a hackney chair and, accompanied by ten footmen, crossed Horse Guards to the Abbey and spent some time quite alone by the open vault. They were fearful of his possible reaction if Anne returned to London as she wished to do, and frantic messages dissuaded her. Instead she and William travelled to Brussels to meet Horatio Walpole, who gave them an edited account of Caroline's illness and handed over a letter found among the Queen's papers, written to her eldest daughter the previous summer though never sent, speaking of a presentiment of death.

They returned to spend Christmas in Leeuwarden through the bleak landscape and wintry weather which the Electress Sophia had once remarked were 'more conducive to the body than the spirit'[3] – back to the social and cultural isolation of an insignificant court in a claustrophobic provincial town. Anne had been at the heart of one of the most brilliant courts in Europe. She had watched Robert Walpole's political intrigues and discussed opera productions with Handel, foreign ambassadors had paid court to her and cultured men had sought her patronage. No great men came to Friesland, there was little real interest in the arts, and while William busied himself with the minutiae of local politics she must spend long hours with a mother-in-law, whose conversation seldom strayed from concern for her children or her fruit trees. The dining room in Marie Louise's home seated only six people so there could be little distraction, and she also retained firm control over the charitable organisation of the little town; there was literally nothing for Anne to do. In addition, of course, her continued failure to bear a child after four years of marriage must have been deeply felt. Her personal grief at her mother's death was deepened by her realisation that there was now no one of influence left in London who really cared about her. She had relied heavily on Caroline's sympathy and wisdom – her younger sisters could offer no substitute for that – and her exclusion from the family mourning was a severe shock. Yet she never complained. The disciplined self-sufficiency which had always struck English observers supported her; she read widely, studying literary, theological and historical texts in their original languages, and she always appeared cheerful, in public at least.

Of all the arts, music is the most vulnerable to isolation, and Anne concentrated on creating her own musical environment. Within a short time Leeuwarden had a court orchestra of six musicians, one of whom had been trained in London at her own expense. She would conduct the players from her harpsichord and she accompanied her own singing, especially enjoying improvisations and sight-reading. One visiting musician was impressed both by her playing and her erudite understanding of musical theory, declaring her 'a very great master in music'. When staying at Soestdijk a few months after Caroline's death, the couple were visited by her uncle, the King of Prussia, and after she had arranged a concert for him, he stayed up late talking to her, mentioning in his letter of thanks to William his enjoyment of 'the conversation of Madame your wife';[4] as William proudly told Marie Louise, no one had ever seen the bad-tempered and boorish King 'so gracious'.[5] His son was already in correspondence with her, for as he waited for power himself the future Frederick the Great sent his musical compositions for her comments. She was gathering together a considerable musical library, and Amelia and Caroline were continually begged to send her new scores, along with descriptions of the lavish London productions which she missed so much.

Amelia was a more regular correspondent than Caroline. An ingenuous letter soon after the Queen's death alternates wildly between grief and excitement: 'Caro and I now have two thousand apiece for our pocket money and our stable is entirely to us, so that I really believe we shall come out very handsomely.'[6] Cumberland, with the resilience of youth, was deploring the restrictions of court mourning. Seclusion with his sisters led to 'a life of perpetual retirement [which] renders the court to the last degree spiritless'.[7] He often escaped to the chemistry laboratory which he had set up in the cellars of St James's, and a Treasury report of that year requests another situation: 'the Duke finds it very inconvenient and we think it very dangerous'.[8]

After a decent interval the younger members of the family resumed their visits to the theatre, and one night as Cumberland escorted Amelia and Caroline into the royal box they realised, to their horror, that Frederick and Augusta were already there. Augusta affected to admire the ceiling, but the Prince bowed politely, and when his elder sisters studiously ignored him the audience began to hiss, so intimidating Caroline that she fainted. Cumberland rose to the occasion, needing assistance to carry her out (she was by now enormously fat); he also removed the mulish Amelia and returned to the box to give his brother and sister-in-law a formal greeting.[9]

As far as George was concerned, the violence of his feelings towards his elder son seemed muted by his grief. Frederick was being careful to behave with more circumspection, and by the end of 1738 they found themselves for the first time supporting the same policy, though there was still no formal reconciliation. For thirty-five years the West Indies had been the scene of an unofficial quarrel with Spain, as the British traded illegally in the Caribbean and Spanish coastguards appropriated an ever increasing number of British ships. The Parliamentary opposition to Walpole, with whom Frederick had always made common cause, seized on the issue, and oratory took flight about gallant British sailors being subject to evil, swarthy Roman Catholics. The climax came when a certain Captain Jenkins appeared before the Commons flourishing a small object which he announced was his ear, cut off by a Spanish cutlass eight years before. Walpole had kept the peace for so long that a whole generation had grown up who regarded war as glorious, and the ghosts of Drake and Raleigh were conjured up yet again, while George, always spoiling for a fight, was in the van. Walpole held out for many months, arguing that war with Spain would bring in France (both were ruled by Bourbons), and France fostered the pretender to the British throne.

Walpole was also exercised by the problem of who might influence the King after his wife's death. George was expressing admiration for Lady Betty Waldegrave who, he exulted to Princess Caroline, 'has had three children and still looks like a virgin':[10] Caroline, of course, hadn't and didn't. Such evidence of royal recovery led the Dukes of Grafton and Newcastle to suggest that Amelia could now be influential in her mother's place, but Walpole was scornful. 'Does she design to commit incest? Do not tell me that the King intends to make a vow of chastity.'[11] He proposed that after a year or so Madame Walmoden should be invited over from Hanover, and until that time

Lady Deloraine must serve. According to Hervey, he said as much to the shaken princesses: 'people must wear old gloves until they can get new ones.'[12]

Anne, too, seemed to hope that Amelia might now be able to wield some political influence over their father. She believed that external pressure from Britain might force the obdurate provinces to accept William as stathouder, and she sent Amelia a sealed letter to be handed to the King which probably begged for active involvement in Dutch affairs. Utterly devoted to her husband as she was, Anne was a realist and she knew his weaknesses: William was essentially passive, he would assert his rights with absolute conviction but he would take little action in pursuit of them. He accepted such ceremonies as those at Breda as his due but never put in the hard work and politicking which should have accompanied them.

Part of the reason for this was undoubtedly his health – the chest problems aggravated by his deformity caused violent fevers and frequent lassitude, but the deformity itself had its effect. He could often 'make others forget it',[13] but he himself was always aware of the figure he cut, and beyond the physical deformity he was a humble man, knowing he lacked the qualities of leadership possessed in such abundance by every Prince of Orange before him. Unfortunately, he made no effort to remedy his inexperience and inadequacy; for example he claimed the crucial role of Captain-General of the Union yet he never studied military strategy; his understanding of European diplomacy was often flawed, and he had never commanded more than a handful of men in battle. His unfitness for military command was plain for all to see as he misused his limited power over army promotions either by yielding over unwise appointments or by blocking others until he received the personal recognition he claimed.

With the greatest reluctance Amelia gave the King Anne's letter, and there was little joy for her sister in the response. 'My dear Royaux,' she wrote, using Anne's pet-name within the family, 'he read it and bid me tell you he would help you as much as he could but no other things were practicable… you will be sure to know what that means, I write what I was ordered to.'[14] Amelia had very little interest in the world outside her stables and court life, but she was a close friend of Horatio Walpole. In her usual jokey style she once wrote to him: 'I remain your sincere friend upon land but hate you at sea – you take my stomach and rest away and I love both eating and sleeping.' He certainly confided in her and she knew very well that with William's stock so low the King would never get involved. Her letter continues:

> You will certainly be angry with me for talking of things where you will say you askt no advice, but I cant help wishing when you have things to ask of him [the King] you would consult some one body that knows the lie of the land… what makes you never consult Horatio?

The problem was that Anne could not bear to hear what Horatio Walpole told her – that regent rule was stronger than ever and Orange supporters were losing heart: 'the few friends he has are silent and indifferent about him.' The high hopes for the marriage had been confounded, both politically and personally, with the lack of progress and the lack of an heir sapping morale. But in the summer of 1738 Anne was pregnant again, and the couple prepared for the journey back to Friesland from Soestdijk. Marie Louise wrote a worried letter to her son: it was an exceptionally hot summer (in Leiden people fell dead on the streets), so surely it would be wiser to remain in the south? But William assured her they would travel in easy stages, and because the springing of his coach was so soft, the jolting did not bother Anne at all. The pregnancy must have been well advanced, for a public announcement to have been made, but nothing more is heard of it.

Anne's distress must have been intensified by the fact that the brother she so cordially disliked was, by the spring of 1739, the father of three healthy children. Frederick and Augusta were cultivating their domestic image. The Lady Augusta and her two younger brothers would often be included on river trips or walks in the park, and their parents would frequently dine in public, 'the Windows being thrown open to oblige the Curiosity of the People'.[15] His wife was proving all that Frederick could have hoped for; despite her youth, or perhaps because of it, she was conforming to the role both he and the country required – a Princess of Wales who knew her place and kept to it. But as she matured she was to prove more than that in private, for she was included in his discussions with opposition politicians, and his supporters commended 'her right way of thinking' and her understanding of political issues.[16]

The couple travelled widely outside London – to Bristol and Bath in 1738, where Augusta 'talked freely to the Ladies in good English which entirely won their hearts'[17] and to various country houses. In the autumn of 1739 Lady North of Wroxton Abbey was thrown into some confusion by the information that the Prince and Princess proposed to honour her with a four-day visit. Extra cooks had to be hired because, as Lady North wrote to her mother, there must be two dinners and two suppers every day.[18] 'Promiscuous seating', when the sexes sat next to each other would not become the norm in great houses for another ten or twelve years. Ladies entered the room first and sat together, withdrawing at an early stage before the male conversation which so shocked a visiting Frenchman became too explicit; but the prim Augusta apparently requested that the ladies should be served in a separate room. Despite the hostess's concern, the visit was a great success, 'they were most excessively obliging and seemed pleased with everything', even encouraging the North children to be with them as much as possible; (the eldest son was to become their son's Prime Minister). Frederick had arrived with twelve partridges and a very large Banbury cake (a gift to him as he passed through the town eight miles away) and he left a much-appreciated tip of sixty guineas. The couple also often visited Hans Sloane, allowing him to sit in their presence since he was 'ancient and infirm'; Frederick was enchanted by all the artefacts and chatted happily for an hour: 'upon anything being shown to him he was ready in recollecting where he had read of it'.[19]

The Prince's long-lasting courting of the mercantile and commercial community was proving a mutual benefit; the opposition in Parliament had seized on the merchants' grievances to force Walpole into declaring war on Spain, and as Lord Carteret spoke powerfully of commerce as the reason why this nation 'has been able to stand her ground against all the open and secret attacks of the enemies of her religion, liberties and constitution',[20] Frederick's careful strategy was vindicated. Cumberland meanwhile was fretting to put his military expertise to some use, and since the war with Spain was a naval one he decided that the best way to see action was at sea. He joined the flagship HMS *Victory* under the command of the 79-year-old commander-in-chief of the Home Fleet. Strong gales kept the squadron at first in Portsmouth, then limping from bay to bay along the coast, at each one of which local officials happily invited themselves aboard to pay their respects to the King's son. Cumberland's only taste of action was being woken one night by 'a universal scream and outcry' when the *Victory* was rammed in the bow by another warship.[21] He became bored and apparently complained to his sisters; Amelia had a word with Newcastle, and the royal sailor was eventually told he could return to London, no doubt to the relief of his Admiral.

The Navy, although Britain's pride, was in a parlous state. At a Cabinet meeting earlier in the year the Lords of the Admiralty had been summoned to give an assessment, and ministers were appalled to find that 'to fit out only seventeen men-of-war to defend this island', 2,645 men were lacking, and for the twenty-five ships already in commission there was a shortfall of 4,698.[22] The press gangs had been out, but the draft from the Isle of Wight proved especially useless because of their size and youth, and many others were so sickly as to be unfit for service.

Cumberland fitted back into civilian life with relief. He now owned his own hunting lodge in Windsor Forest, where he would wait to receive his father on hunting days, as George drove down from London by night with the Household Cavalry as a protection against highwaymen. He redesigned the hunt kennels, set up his own stud where he planned to breed racehorses, travelled regularly to parties at the Vauxhall pleasure gardens, and still found time to fulfil appointments 'with the daughter of a yeoman' which were kindly arranged for him by the local Member of Parliament.[23]

Notes

[1] Historical MSS Commission II (1925)

[2] All three letters – KHA, Anna, 430

[3] Kroll, *Sophie*, p.91

[4] KHA, Willem IV, 172

[5] Ibid., 170 II

[6] Ibid., Anna, 430

[7] Baron Bielfield, *Letters* IV, 1770. He was an emissary from the Prussian court.

[8] Charteris, op. cit., p.61

[9] R Whitworth, *William Augustus, Duke of Cumberland*, 1992, p.18

[10] Trench, op. cit., p.257

[11] Ibid., p.252

[12] Hervey, op. cit., p.919

[13] Ibid., p.231

[14] KHA, Anna, 430

[15] *Gentleman's Magazine*, June 1736

[16] M Marples, *Poor Fred and the Butcher*, 1970, p.55

[17] *Gentleman's Magazine*, November 1738

[18] De-la-Noy, op. cit., p.174

[19] *Gentleman's Magazine*, July 1748

[20] *Gentleman's Magazine*, February 1740

[21] Add MSS 32694

[22] Hervey, op. cit., p.939. After the Queen's death Hervey had been appointed Lord Privy Seal by Walpole, to the fury of the rest of the Cabinet Council who had suffered for years from his bitter tongue. These naval details come from his minutes of a Cabinet meeting in May 1740.

[23] Whitworth, op. cit. p.19

Chapter Twelve

In October 1739 the preachers of Ameland – a Dutch island loyal to the House of Orange – received their fourth request to pray for a happy outcome to the pregnancy of their Princess. A measure of just how dispirited the Orangists were can be detected in the fact that there was no longer any attempt to claim national status by a confinement in The Hague; Friesland was to be the birthplace of the child who might be no more than Friesland's heir. But in view of previous problems, an especially skilled midwife was summoned from the capital. She at first refused to go and was eventually conducted almost by force: her fears were fully justified when the severest winter of the century isolated her in Leeuwarden for four months, during two of which she had to confront the ultimate challenge of her profession – a bereaved mother. On Christmas Eve the Town Book recorded: 'On the evening of 23 December Mevrouw the Princess of Orange-Nassau was delivered of a young princess in whom the light of life never shone.' On the night after Christmas another tiny coffin was carried by torchlight to the Nassau vault.

Winter lasted into April that year (well to the south, the Thames had remained frozen for weeks, with a fair being held on the ice), and as the midwife hurried back to the bright lights William yet again planned a journey to comfort his wife, this time to his family lands in Germany. Their many carriages taxed the post stations on the way: after the severe winter many of the horses on offer were so poor that William feared they would not be up to their task. Forty servants and mountains of luggage travelled with them, nine cooks overseeing the kitchen equipment and three footmen the linen and silver, while one unfortunate had forgotten to pack the hard mattress which Anne needed. William informed his mother that since she could never sleep on a soft bed she had to use a mattress on the floor of his room. They indulged in local delicacies as they went, buying two dozen hams and dried beef tongues in Frankfurt 'much better and cheaper than those at home'.[1]

The Nassau lordships of Dietz and Dillenburg, Siegen and Hadamar lay between Cologne and Frankfurt, and gave William wealth as well as his imperial obligations. After the Thirty Years War, the Treaty of Westphalia had splintered Germany into between 294 and 348 semi-sovereign states (no one could agree on the number even then). These included duchies, princedoms, counties and bishoprics as well as electorates. They owed varying degrees of allegiance to the Emperor, who in return was the guarantor of their status and rights. William administered these lands well (as indeed he did Friesland). He was at ease with the small scale; the people and problems were familiar; and the wider picture – a concept with which he always had difficulty – was an imperial task.

A further reason for Anne's presence in Germany was for the wedding celebrations in Kassel of her sister, Mary. As the fourth daughter, Mary's dynastic importance was small and the status of her husband unimportant, but there were political reasons for this marriage with Crown Prince Frederick of Hesse. The state was one of the smaller princedoms but it exerted more influence in European affairs than its size warranted: its ruling Landgraves had personal control of the state's finances, and each generation had used this wealth to build up well-trained forces, often led by the princes themselves, who were on offer to the highest bidder (Johan Willem Friso's choice of Marie Louise had been dictated by the fact that her father had been one of his hero Marlborough's most trusted generals). Mercenaries had been an important part of most European armies since the sixteenth century; the Calvinist Swiss now fought for the Emperor or guarded the Pope while Denmark was pricing itself out of the market, so wars and the rumours of wars always sent diplomats with moneybags to Hesse.

As Walpole had prophesied, the sea war with Spain was making a continental land war inevitable, and since the long years of peace and the British conviction after the Civil War that 'there was no danger but in a standing army' had left the Army in an even worse state than the Navy, troops were going to be needed. The money had to come from the only government tax levied – on income from land, at two shillings in the pound – and since extracting that from a Parliament of landed gentry was always difficult, the prospect of raising it at a time when the opposition was at last making an impact was not an attractive one: a dynastic connection with Hesse might offer financial advantages.

The King was at first delighted to discover that he too would save money, since the ceremony would take place in the bridegroom's country. But although always tight-fisted (he once spent a considerable time turning over a pile of logs to find a lost guinea) George was also aware of the importance of ceremonial, and at the last minute he decided it was beneath his dignity to send his daughter abroad unmarried. There had not been a proxy marriage in England for 200 years, and the Acts of Succession and Uniformity actually forbade one, but the King had no patience with such scruples. He informed his Cabinet that Mary was to be married next Thursday and he left it to them to sort out the ways and means. The ecclesiastical lobby gave in fairly easily but the lawyers were much tougher, and after the manner of their kind they produced an incredible hypothesis as an insuperable obstacle: if Mary were not married according to the existing rites of the Church of England her children's right of succession to the British throne would be undermined. Since Mary had three elder sisters and two elder brothers, one of whom already had three children of his own with another expected, George's explosion, 'I will hear no more of your Church nonsense nor your law nonsense. I will have my daughter married here and will have the marriage complete,'[2] seems entirely justified. In the end the precedent of Mary Tudor and Louis XII of France was decided to be a safe one, and Mary was duly married at St James's with Cumberland acting as the bridegroom and partnering his sister at the grand ball afterwards.

Mary was just seventeen, diffident and retiring, so the private ceremony probably suited her well, but she did have to endure the ordeal of the Lord Mayor's Loyal Address: 'Great Britain is thus by Degrees deprived of her Daughters as His Majesty bestows an inestimable Treasure on His Serene Highness the Prince of Hesse,' he announced and, as was his wont, continued in the same vein for some little time: 'The Subjects of Great Britain can never sufficiently adore the Divine Providence for those numerous Pledges of their future security which Your Majesty [is] so happily blest with.'

Frederick, of course, would have responded with similar purple prose, but George was abrupt. 'I return my Thanks. You may always rely on my favour and protection.'[3]

His impatience to get the whole business done with was due to his desire to visit Hanover for the first time since Caroline's death. His ministers had hoped that once Madame Walmoden had joined him in England (where she was created Countess of Yarmouth and behaved with great discretion – it is remarkable how docile Hanoverian mistresses were) he would lose his enthusiasm for his electorate. They made great efforts to dissuade him from going – with a European war looming, the diplomatic negotiations with an absent King would make things difficult – but he got his way and he and his daughter left for Germany within a few days of each other.

The arguments over the ceremony had so delayed Mary's departure that, to her delight, Anne and William were already waiting for her in Kassel when, outside the city gates, she met her new husband for the first time. Not surprisingly, she embraced Anne many times before being whisked to the palace for a change of clothes. Then with a crown on her head, supported by her father-in-law and William, she was married once more by a Calvinist minister. Afterward she and Frederick performed the traditional German torch dance, leading the guests in an increasingly boisterous procession, which ended with the flames being extinguished at the bedroom door. The next night a ball consisted of minuets and English country dances before a carriage procession through the illuminated town.

William described the three weeks of celebration to his mother, who was the bridegroom's aunt, confessing he was very bored 'since you know I hate all ceremonial',[4] and also exhausted since the firework displays lasted until dawn. Even Anne, who thoroughly enjoyed a party, was suffering from earache. But there were sinister undercurrents to all the jollity. Mary's mother-in-law never appeared, and rumours flew that she had died and the Landgrave was keeping the body in his apartment so as not to spoil the occasion; Anne's servants assured her this was true but the family could find out nothing. Even worse was the Crown Prince's treatment of his 'nice little wife'. He was drinking heavily and his bad manners and coldness to her caused much comment. 'I could say more,' wrote William, 'but dare not write it.'[5] Mary clung desperately to her elder sister but told her very little, and the parting was a sad one.

Anne and William travelled to the seventeenth-century castle of Oranienstein on the River Lahn to stay with his father's four unmarried sisters. The place itself was beautiful, but as William rather ominously reported, 'the presence of my aunts make things less pleasant than they might be'.[6] Anne remained here while William visited his own sister Amalia, who was no better – tranquil if nobody crossed her and spending her time scribbling little notes 'which say nothing' and pinning them together – but, knowing George was in Hanover, Anne resolved on a journey of her own.[7] She knew he was always at his most relaxed and approachable when he was out of England: on one journey an innkeeper had charged him one hundred pounds for some coffee and gin. 'Are such things so rare in these parts?' he had enquired. 'No', came the reply, 'but Kings are!' George was highly amused and paid up. She wrote to him directly asking if he would receive them. At first he refused outright, but then said she could come without William, so Anne, swallowing her pride, set off alone. She wrote every day to her 'dearest Pepin', assuring him 'my attention and care will be devoted to advancing [him] whom I love and adore'.[8] She found her father 'rejuvenated rather than aged', and he welcomed her so warmly that her hopes rose. But he packed her ten-day visit with public festivities, at one of which everyone was dressed in white dominos resembling 'spirits from the Elysian fields',[9] and kept the conversation firmly on generalities. 'I have not been able to see the King alone – his manner freezes me and I fear my journey will come to nothing.'[10] Lord Harrington was kindly and sympathetic but had no influence.

At the end of the summer of 1740, therefore, William and Anne journeyed home with the prospect of a national role further away than ever. So happy in her own marriage Anne worried about Amelia, now approaching her thirties, and perhaps suggested after her enjoyable German trip some suitable princes for her sister's consideration. Amelia purported to be horrified at the very idea. Punctuation was dispensed with as she defended her 'easie and comfortable situation' in a wonderful outburst of feminist polemic:

I sometimes believe you think that unmarried women have no places in heaven for you think nobody can have the least happiness without being tied from morning to night to a creature which may tire one's life out and plague one incessantly with their good advice or commands whilst one is full as wise as they and only difference of dress and fashion allowing them all lots of things which women must not do because it's not discreet and that may be they might make a figure in life if they were more to be known or had a more manly education, we poor women have great disadvantages without making them still worse and putting one self into a Jackanapes power. I am glad you are happy... but those things don't happen often...

I want to know how you would have done with a man which had not lov'd you. Make no match for Caro or for me Royaux if you do I shall get you divorced and make Pepin marry someone else.[11]

Caroline, by contrast, had settled reluctantly into depressed spinsterhood. Her only pleasure now was the theatre, where she sat patiently through many Shakespearian productions for the sake of the 'afterpieces' – the short productions of farce or spectacular pantomime which Amelia scorned. But they both loved oratorio and opera, attending productions such as *Rodelinda*, *Rinaldo* and *Ariadne in Creta* many times through the years. They would not have agreed with John Wesley who, after hearing a production of *Judith*, complained that he could not understand modern music. Why did the performers sing the same word ten times over, and different persons sing different words at one and the same time? Good honest hymns were never like that.

Cumberland still accompanied his sisters occasionally when he had nothing more exciting in hand. He was rumoured to prefer his actresses backstage, though he might not have expressed his interest so pompously as Dr Johnson: 'The silk stockings and white bosoms of your actresses excite my amorous propensities.' Silk stockings seem to have been of great public interest. A newspaper published an essay asserting: 'A lady's Leg is a dangerous sight in whatever colour it appears but when it is enclosed in white it makes an irresistible attack on me.'[12] The King had made his son Colonel of the 2nd Regiment of Foot Guards, and he took the appointment very seriously, making himself known to both officers and men and initiating a programme of training and discipline which made the regiment 'an ornament and a safeguard instead of being what they had too often been before, a nuisance and a terror to the places of royal residence they guarded';[13] apparently almost half the footpads apprehended in London were found to be members of the Guards. Acutely aware of his lack of experience, the Duke determined thoroughly to learn his trade – an example his Dutch brother-in-law would have been wise to follow, since unfolding events in Europe seemed to offer him the opportunity he sought, if he was confident enough to seize it.

On the death of Charles VI, William was bound to support the Emperor's only child, Maria Theresa. Charles had hoped to ensure her trouble-free accession to the Hapsburg lands and the election of her husband as Emperor, and to this end he had laboriously woven an intricate tapestry of treaties and agreements which was now threatened by Anne's cousin, Frederick, newly come to the throne of Prussia, and wielding the knife of his inherited army of 60,000 men. This was composed of professionals, drilled and trained relentlessly, and all recruited in the country they fought for – the idea of mercenaries outraged Frederick:

> The institution of the soldier is for the defence of the nation, to rent it out to others to do battle as one might a mastiff [is] a perversion of war and diplomacy. It is said that it is not permitted to sell sacred objects. Well what could be more sacred than the blood of men?[14]

He fastened on the province of Silesia, rich and fertile and paying a quarter of the total taxation yielded by the Hapsburg possessions, and demanded Maria Theresa should cede it to him in accordance with a two-centuries-old treaty. He informed his hapless ambassador in Vienna, 'The question of right is one for ministers, and you had better take it up without delay for the troops already have their marching orders.'[15]

Frederick's action brought the vultures swooping in: two of the Electors, Saxony and Bavaria, declared for Prussia (the latter having an eye on the imperial title himself); Spain ignored its treaty obligation and made no move as Silesia was invaded, and France actually made a formal alliance with Prussia. This was the most important factor for William. It was French aggression which had brought William III the stathoudership when her armies struck deep into the United Provinces and only the House of Orange offered a chance of collective defence; now, with France once more on the offensive, declarations of neutrality seemed a poor protection, and Orangist pamphleteers and preachers began to whip up public feeling. It seemed to be the external catalyst they had longed for, offering fruitful ground for William to seize the initiative, which Anne was desperately urging him to do; but William hesitated and then refused. Just as his republican opponents elevated self-interest into a principle of True Freedom, so he explained his passivity and reluctance to take the lead as a sacred principle – to do nothing that smacked of ambition or impatience. He would wait to be asked rather than seize the moment. So the moment passed. The neutrality lobby in the States-General regained the upper hand as French armies turned south instead of north, the Dutch relapsed again into their 'sweet slumber', and William remained in the shadows.

To his credit, George was the only one of Charles VI's guarantors to keep his word, and Parliament voted the first of many subsidies for Maria Theresa.

However the support came from him as King of England; as Elector of Hanover which was 'so militarily vulnerable that the Prussians regarded it as a breakfast for their generals'[16] he voted for her enemy Charles Albert of Bavaria, as Emperor. Such split loyalties and shifting alliances led to nearly two years of complex manoeuvres – diplomacy or back-stabbing according to your point of view – which taxed brains in the coffee houses and divided parties in Parliament.

Walpole struggled on; the war, against which he had argued so strongly, brought financial problems and neither glory nor excitement for those who craved it, and he was now operating in the Commons with a majority of fourteen. Divisions on mundane matters led to extraordinary scenes as the lobby fodder was carried in through side doors which the opposition tried to block by stuffing the keyholes with sand. An MP wrote to his wife of

> Sir William Gordon, though almost a-dying himself and one of his sons drowned that day sevenight, came to the House out of mourning. He has the longest blackest most emaciated face you ever saw, and he entered the House after night with a dirty flannel hood under an old black wig and with a very long red cloak.[17]

In February 1742 Walpole resigned, and George bade him an emotional farewell: 'the King fell on Sir Robert's neck, wept and kissed him';[18] Caroline must have been on his mind, for the two people he had relied on most were gone.

Notes

[1] KHA, Willem IV, 306
[2] Hervey, op. cit., p.931
[3] *Gentleman's Magazine*, April 1739
[4] KHA, Willem IV, 170 II
[5] Ibid.
[6] Ibid.
[7] KHA, Anna, p.430
[8] Ibid.
[9] Thackeray, op. cit., p.54
[10] KHA, Anna, 430
[11] Ibid.
[12] *Gentleman's Magazine*, August 1737
[13] Quoted by Whitworth, op. cit., p.23
[14] MacDonough, op. cit., p.124
[15] Quoted by R M Rayner, *European History 1648–1789*, 1954, p.227
[16] Davies, op. cit., p.205
[17] Trench, op. cit., p.212
[18] Young, op. cit., p.158

Chapter Thirteen

The King had his emotions well under control when later the same month a public acknowledgment of his son's existence ended the five-year rift. Careful preparations had included Augusta being despatched to the Duchess of Norfolk's ball, covered with £40,000 worth of borrowed diamonds, and firm political pressure applied to George 'who swore he would not speak to the Prince but was prevailed upon'.[1] As Frederick entered the King's levée his father marched up to him, enquired, 'How does the Princess do. I hope she is well.'[2] And, as the prince kissed his hand, withdrew it sharply and turned away. It was hardly warmer than the reconciliation between monarch and heir twenty years before, but as a cynical commentator put it 'it still brought tears of loyalty to many eyes'.[3]

Some time later there was another breakthrough when Frederick and Augusta were present at the opening of the Ranelagh Gardens with Amelia, Caroline, Louisa and Cumberland. The place was planned as a more upmarket alternative to the Vauxhall pleasure gardens developed ten years before. There, supper boxes with paintings by Hogarth lined an area of trees festooned with lights, but these did not reach the far alleyways, where 'indecencies' could occur. But Vauxhall's slightly raffish image was not its only disadvantage: with no bridges over the river the only access was by water which added to the expense of the outing (8d from Whitehall Steps), the watermen were surly (they had not been allowed to raise their charges since the previous century), and stepping gracefully into a rocking boat with high-heeled embroidered satin shoes and spreading skirts could be tricky. It was rumoured that the building of Westminster Bridge, which began in the 1740s, was due to the fact that fashion was dictating ten-foot hoops.

Ranelagh was much more upmarket than Vauxhall; the entrance fee was two shillings and sixpence instead of a shilling, although this did include free tea or coffee and bread and butter. Under a large rotunda, paved with marble and hung with brass chandeliers, people could sit in tiered boxes and listen to concerts played from a canopied bandstand. Situated as it was next to the Chelsea Hospital, fashionable London could take carriages or sedan chairs there rather than boats and it quickly became an acceptable meeting place for the social elite, and for those preliminary encounters to see if prospective partners might suit. Those without access to the aristocratic world but who had money and knew how to behave could find that the pleasure gardens provided an opportunity to break through the class barrier. Women might now have a say in their marriages, but money lay at the heart of any contract; the *Gentleman's Magazine* carefully detailed the fortune of a bride in its announcements, and offered other illuminating details too. About this time the marriage took place of the Earl of Halifax and Miss Dunck, sixteen-year-old daughter of a wool merchant, who was in possession of £100,000. By her father's will she was to be married to 'none but an honest Tradesman, for which reason his Lordship took the Freedom of the Sadlers Company and exercised the Trade'.[4] Lord Halifax was rewarded for his effort, since the couple lived 'in perfect amity' until her death in childbirth twelve years later, but the hopes of a certain Mr Nathaniel Carter seem to have been dashed – he disappeared from his bride's bed on their wedding night and his body with stones in the shoes was later dragged from the Thames.[5]

Differences in age were also of interest. 'Mr R Allen, an eminent Pawnbroker, aged seventy-five to Miss Catherine Powell of about seventeen.' But readers were reassured that she was 'a young Lady of such sedate womanly Carriage as becomes one of three times her Age, nothing of the giddy young Damsel appearing in either her Dress or Behaviour... which enamoured her ancient Lover with the Desire of joining Hymen's knot'.[6] In 1742 the marriage was announced of a Mr Robert Thornton, China Merchant of Doncaster, to a 63-year-old widow. 'It is remarkable,' the paper added, 'that this is his fourth wife, all of them named Mary, and he only twenty-six years of age.'[7]

Once married, of course, the woman's task was to produce children, though Mr Rudeskin, a grocer from King's Lynn, may have felt his wife had taken the Biblical injunction too far when she presented him with quadruplets, though he did baptise them Abraham, Isaac, Sarah and Rebecca.

Augusta was triumphantly carrying out her royal duty (even though her fourth child, Elizabeth, was sickly and deformed, unable at the age of three even to stand); but 'Great Britain's Daughters' were less fortunate. News reached Friesland in July 1742 of the death of Mary's son who had been born on Christmas Day. Anne longed to go and comfort her sister whose marriage, she knew, had all but broken down, but she was in the early stages of pregnancy herself and could not travel. William stayed with her through the autumn and winter, despite the pleas of his supporters that he should come to The Hague and add his voice to the military discussions which were preoccupying the capital.

The Dutch had a treaty obligation with Austria to send men if called upon. When Frederick marched into Silesia in December 1740 Maria Theresa had invoked it, and the States-General had stalled by replying that 'the Republic [could not] grant its Assistance as it doubted if such an Assistance would be effective'.[8] This was an ingenuous but entirely valid defence. The 'Great

Power' of the early years of the century could barely muster either army or fleet. Military spending had been shaved to the bone over the years – and it was easier simply to scrape together a subsidy for the Austrians instead. But they did promise a small force as well, and as an army of British, Hessians and Hanoverians, all supported by the British taxpayer and the villages where they camped, awaited the Dutch in Flanders, the point at issue was who should lead the soldiers who had somehow been found. William was offered a Lieutenant-Generalship, equal in status to several foreign officers yet to be recruited; this was a great advance on any previous proposal but he refused it as being incompatible with his honour.

It is not difficult to see Anne's influence at work. She had always held (rightly) that the appointment as Captain-General of the Republic would be the first step in achieving their objective, but her mother had specifically warned her against interfering in military affairs about which she knew as little as William, and at such a time the Prince's refusal seemed petty and unpatriotic. He should also have been on the spot negotiating in person rather than relying on messengers struggling across the Zuyder Zee, and he should certainly have been listening to experienced advisers rather than his dogmatic wife. So the troops would march south without him, but being the man he was William had no doubts about the choice he had made. At last, on 23 February, a child was born and lived.

She was baptised Wilhelmina Carolina in the Grote Kerk of Leeuwarden; Marie Louise proudly carried her to the font and the Court noticed that the Dowager Princess, who usually cared little about her appearance, had celebrated the occasion with a spectacular new dress. Anne challenged royal tradition by insisting on feeding the baby herself, and after so much heartache, dynastic considerations meant little to the happy parents, though a prominent Orangist grumbled, 'My satisfaction would have been greater if it had been a boy.'[9] Henry Pelham, brother to the Duke of Newcastle, would have agreed. Writing to a friend, he had informed him, 'I was in expectation of an addition to my family, it might have been as I thought of the best sort, but my luck's bad and it prov'd a Girl.'[10]

Anne took the five-month-old Carolina with her when she travelled to Germany in June. William, who was suffering from stomach trouble, stayed behind at Het Loo. As always, they hated being apart: 'It is eight days since I left you and it seems like a hundred.' She visited Mary, who had just given birth to another son: 'the child is small but goes on fairly well, while my sister has gone to church for the first time but is still terribly weak.'[11] She also confirmed that the husband's behaviour had not improved. 'Prince Frederick is as you have seen him, he hasn't gone to sleep under the table yet but there is time for that.'[12]

Anne's ambition seemed to have been lost in motherhood, and she and William paid little attention to the continuing stalemate in The Hague or even the war in the south, where her father, after a gap of nearly forty years, was commanding an army in the field. He and Cumberland had spent the spring in Hanover (the latter for the first time) and their attachment to each other had been strengthened as George showed off his beloved Electorate and taught his son the art of boar hunting. Lord Carteret, now Secretary of State, approved of the Duke, writing to Newcastle that 'his behaviour is in all respects as good as possible, and I who am not easily caught with young men, tho' Princes, begin upon acquaintance to have a very good opinion of him'.[13] Carteret was not 'easily caught' by anybody, treating all with patrician disdain. For many politicians of the time, Parliament was an annoyance, but for him it was a total irrelevance which he loftily ignored: 'Had [he] studied Parliament more and Demosthenes less he would have been a successful minister.'[14] As the finest classical scholar of his age, he would speak in tones 'more calculated for the Senate than for the people', and he was to pay the price.

Cumberland (now promoted to Major-General) and George left Hanover separately, the former travelling to Kassel to visit Mary to cheer her in the last stages of her pregnancy. George, predictably, had no such interest in such inessentials, especially when he was on the way to war. With a baggage train of thirteen Berlin carriages, eighty-nine wagons and no less than 662 horses, he arrived at the village of Dettingen to find the polyglot army hemmed in by the French between a forest and the River Main, with its artillery out of reach. Even worse, the troops were strung along the riverbank for twenty miles, making communication and battle formation almost impossible. As the French crossed the river in two places to attack from both front and rear, their artillery opened up from across the river, and the allied army of 40,000 men was trapped. George galloped excitedly from one battalion to another, exhorting them to hold their ground. Mr Kendal of Lord Albemarle's Troop wrote:

> His Majesty is certainly the bravest man I ever saw. I saw the balls go within a yard of his head and when he was desired to go out of danger he answered, 'Don't talk to me of danger, I'll be even with them.'[15]

Once more the disciplined infantry held their fire until, with the enemy at sixty paces, they opened up and the French fell back; an officer of the Royal Welch Fusiliers reported with some pride:

> What preserv'd us was our keeping close order and advancing near the enemy ere we fired. Several that popp'd at a hundred paces lost more of their men but did less Execution, for the French will stand fire at a distance tho' 'tis plain they cannot look men in the face.[16]

The British muskets used a smaller ball which made reloading quicker and easier, and as 'the smoke blew off a little, instead of being among the living we found the dead in heaps around us'.[17] George seemed to have made the wrong choice from his horses, since at one point it bolted to the rear, but he dismounted, saying that at least he could trust his own legs not to run away; and he then, at sixty years old, had advanced on foot, sword in hand, though the image was slightly marred in English eyes by the fact that he wore the yellow sash of Hanover.

The King was exultant, as he had every right to be, and celebrated the day by creating knights banneret on the battlefield, following the precedent of Charles I at Edgehill. One of them was John Ligonier, a Huguenot soldier of fortune who had become a naturalised Englishman in 1702. Two of his brothers served with him in the British army and they may have been the officers who, it was reputed, would mislead the French in the thick of battle by shouting contradictory orders to them. Sir John had earned his honour since, already sixty-three, he had fought under Marlborough in every major engagement, sustaining twenty shots through his clothing at Malplaquet, and he had served the British Crown ever since in Spain and Ireland. His concern for his men was such that he employed an extra surgeon for them at his own expense, and his respect for the rank and file and his insistence on the duty of his officers towards those under their command meant that he never lost a man through desertion.

Cumberland, at twenty-two, had also acquitted himself well: 'He gave his orders with a great deal of calmness and seemed quite unconcerned; the soldiers were in high delight to have him so near them.'[18] To his fury, a discharge of grapeshot forced him to leave the field with a hole 'the size of a hen's egg' in his leg, but when carried to the surgeons he courteously indicated that a more severely wounded French officer should be attended to first.[19] He flatly refused to return to England, though he was on crutches for many weeks. For the rest of his life, according to his main biographer, Rex Whitworth, walking was painful for him, and the enforced immobility, his small stature and 'imprudent diet' contributed to a massive weight gain.

Dettingen had been more an extrication from disaster than a victory – an illustration of Pelham's maxim that success in any venture is due 'to the want of skill, industry and vigilance in our enemies rather than our own possession or exertion of those qualifications'; but it was marked by Handel with a fine *Te Deum*, and one biblically minded pamphleteer was quite overcome:

> From the blood of the slain, from the fat of the mighty the bow of William turned not back and the sword of George returned not empty. George and William were lovely and pleasant in peace and in war they were not divided.[20]

The return of the heroes in November was described by Horace Walpole, not normally one of George's admirers.

> It was incredible how well his reception was… they almost carried him into the palace on their shoulders and at night the whole town was illuminated and bonfired… he looks much better than he has these five years and is in great spirits.[21]

Frederick, who had been deprived of even a place on the Regency Council in his father's absence, welcomed them home with Amelia and Caroline outside St James's Palace, but George looked straight through him and spoke 'pas un mot', despite the fact that the day before Augusta had given birth to their fifth child. At least the cordiality between the brothers remained strong: Frederick showed no sign of jealousy, named his new son William, and commissioned a painting of his brother on the field of Dettingen.

The delay in their return from Germany was due to the King's travels with Carteret as they conducted diplomatic negotiations to isolate the French. Since this had involved offering substantial subsidies to anyone who expressed the slightest interest in supporting France, and sending the bills back to Parliament, it was little wonder that Walpole was surprised at the loyal reception. The opposition was now led by William Pitt, later Earl of Chatham, 'a well-organised caucus politician' with the face of an eagle and the gift of the sound bite. (He received a considerable legacy from Sarah, Duchess of Marlborough on account 'of his merit in the noble defence he has made for the support of the laws of England';[22] though a more acid commentator remarked that although 'he commands the Passions with Sovereign Authority he is not always a fair or conclusive Reasoner'. He made 'long speeches which might possibly be very fine but were greatly beyond comprehension'.[23]) But his oratorical skills contributed to the downfall of Carteret – not the last man to discover that the heady delights of the international stage were mere self-indulgence without a sound political base at home. He succeeded to the earldom of Granville in 1744 and devoted his efforts to finding a new wife to provide him with an heir, since his only son was somewhat unstable, arriving at a country house breakfast table with a basket of horses' ears which he had hacked off during a tour of his host's stables.

One of Pitt's main lines of attack was that Carteret was 'an English minister without an English heart' who worked for the Electorate rather than England, and George too was carrying through negotiations which could be seen as of greater benefit to Hanover. His youngest daughter, Louisa, was nineteen, and he had long decided on a Danish marriage for her. Denmark had always been an ally of Hanover and was at the time not only involved in a trade war with England, but also reneging on a treaty obligation with her, so this was playing into the opposition's hands. However, the Danes remained popular in London and had provided marriage partners before – Anne for James I, and George for Queen Anne – so the King had obtained his ministers' grudging approval.

Everything seemed set fair when worrying reports from Copenhagen indicated that the Danes were considering a Prussian princess (there were six of them – their father had once been heard to wish that he had drowned some of them at birth, like kittens). Walter Titley, the minister-resident, decided it was time for some creative diplomacy. King Christian VI wished to commission a portrait of his wife and was seeking an artist to do her justice, so Titley requested the urgent dispatch from London of a miniature of Louisa, who was a slim sparkling brunette with, thanks to her mother, that important attribute 'unmarked by smallpox'. He offered it to the King purely as an example of an artist he might wish to patronise, only adding the identity of the sitter as an apparent afterthought. Christian was intrigued and on being assured that the Princess's beauty was 'enlivened by the moving features when she speaks, no picture can express her grace any more than the accent of her voice',[24] he disappeared to show it to his wife and son. Crown Prince Frederick had already, by the age of twenty, an appreciation of the feminine form not always limited to the abstract, and within a very short time the deal was done. He had a sister, also named Louisa, and George proposed that she should be given to Cumberland. The Duke was alarmed: the sixteen-year-old princess was apparently already showing an unseemly interest in the opposite sex, and her physical appearance may have been unfortunate since she was described as a 'bolus' – a clod or a lump of earth. He appealed to Robert Walpole, now Earl of Orford, and received the shrewd advice to accept 'on condition of an immediate and most ample establishment. Believe me, my dear Duke, when I say the matter will not then be pressed'.[25] Nor was it; the government had enough trouble getting Louisa's dowry approved and dared not even raise the subject of Cumberland. After Dettingen, Louisa was sent off to Hanover where her father and brother awaited her, and on 30 October the Duke again acted as bridegroom for a sister before she set off alone for Copenhagen.

Prince Frederick was at first attentive. A courtier wrote of seeing the young couple sitting in their garden feeding each other cherries; but he, like Mary's husband, was a heavy drinker, and there were rumours of sexual violence. When they acceded to the Danish throne in 1746, Louisa took no part in politics, devoting herself to motherhood and for the rest of her tragically short life identifying herself with her adopted country, learning the language, immersing herself in Danish culture and never leaving on even the briefest visit. She apparently said on her departure from England that if she 'was unhappy no one shall ever know it', which perhaps explains the fact that there appears to be no correspondence with her brothers and sisters as Frederick's infidelities increased; though she did retain close contact with Mary who, as her own marriage failed, would spend weeks at a time in Denmark.

Notes

[1] Davies, op. cit., p.195
[2] Walters, *Griffin*, p.183
[3] Quoted by Trench, op. cit., p.214
[4] *Gentleman's Magazine*, July 1741
[5] *Gentleman's Magazine*, July 1749
[6] *Gentleman's Magazine*, September 1753
[7] *Gentleman's Magazine*, November 1742
[8] Rowen, op. cit., p.160
[9] G J Schutte, 'Gouvernante Anna' in *Vrouwen in hets Landbestuur*, 1982, p.150
[10] 1735 letter to the Duke of Devonshire
[11] KHA, Anna, 430
[12] Ibid.
[13] Add MSS 32 700
[14] Horatio Walpole, op. cit., p.101
[15] Trench, op. cit. p.219
[16] *Gentleman's Magazine*, July 1743
[17] Quoted by Trench, op. cit., p.220
[18] B Willson [ed.], *Life and Letters of James Wolfe*, 1909
[19] Whitworth, op. cit., p.32
[20] British Museum MSS 103.k.27
[21] W Lewis, *Letters of Horace Walpole*, 1937, p.391
[22] *Gentleman's Magazine*, November 1742
[23] Trench, op. cit., p.275
[24] J F Chance [ed.], *British Diplomatic Instructions 1689-1789*, Royal Historical Society, 1926
[25] Whitworth, op. cit., p.29

Chapter Fourteen

Cumberland was the only one of George and Caroline's children who managed to remain on generally cordial terms with every one of his siblings. As the continental powers paused for breath he expanded his social life, forging a close relationship with Amelia as they hunted together and moved increasingly in the same circle of friends for private card parties and gaming sessions. Augusta was never at ease with him, but he and Frederick shared many interests: the Prince was laying out plantations of trees and ordering exotic plants in his gardens at Kew, and on visits there Cumberland would accompany him on long walks, no doubt developing his own eye for the major works he was to carry out in Windsor Great Park and Virginia Water. The two brothers presided over one of the earliest cricket matches – Kent v. All England – at which the Duke of Dorset played for the former team, which was captained by his head gardener. Their patronage of artists did diverge: Frederick's portrait of the Duke at Dettingen, and a companion piece of him after Culloden, were commissioned from John Wootten, whose spirited racehorses, hunting scenes and pastoral landscapes made him one of the most sought after painters of his age. Cumberland might have been more likely to patronise the Dutch artist who came to London, rented a garret and painted long landscapes which he then cut up and sold by the yard; his interest was not in paintings as such but in the information they offered, and he ordered maps, military prints and also meticulous depictions of military uniforms from the Swiss David Morier, whom he retained on his permanent staff.

His professional attention was directed to army reforms, both regarding battle drill and discipline. He dispensed with the idea of troops being named for their commanding officers, and brought in dress regulations as a means of improving discipline and raising morale. The first signs of later unpopularity came as he targeted the officers, considering, as Ligonier did, that their lack of professionalism too often betrayed the men; many officers despised those under their command, while standards of training varied widely, as did the battle drill of regiments which must fight together; the moves were unpopular, one colonel, Pelham, even complaining of the Duke's 'outrageously and shockingly military attitude';[1] but gradually professional standards improved.

His experience at Dettingen had taught Cumberland that disciplined flexibility was essential in modern warfare; many of Marlborough's battles had been planned and fought 'in exact formations and with stately deliberation', but those days of polite invitations to the other side to fire first had gone. Commanders must seize their chances and men respond to rapidly changing situations. Despite his enjoyable life in England, he watched with intense frustration as British troops manoeuvred in a haphazard way round the Low Countries under Field Marshal Wade. Known as 'the Grandmother', Wade was over seventy and his main aim seemed to be to avoid the enemy at all costs. Cumberland fretted to be back in the field.

Dutch troops formed part of Wade's army, and his dislike of confrontation suited them well. They had arrived too late for Dettingen, and after a little desultory marching and counter-marching, found it prudent to set off for home before winter set in. Their officers professed themselves exhausted by this 'campaign', and Horatio Walpole, still under instructions to stir the Dutch into a useful fighting force, despaired. 'I really think that an unaccountable infatuation like the sickness of their cattle has possessed and infected the whole country.'[2] Since the great days of William III, things had been kept to the barest maintenance basis, as skills were lost, arsenals were run down and, most importantly, the military ethos was smothered. Many, and not only the Orange supporters, felt shamed by the decline of their once great army, but politicians were too self-absorbed and the military too apathetic to accept the enormous financial and administrative challenge needed to arrest it. Many of the great Princes of Orange might have tried, but not William; he had neither the energy nor the experience even to understand the deplorable state of the forces he aspired to lead.

For the first time for some years, he and Anne spent the winter in the south, first in their favourite Breda and then at Huis ten Bosch in The Hague. The 'House in the Wood' was yet another of William's family possessions. Round a central domed hall decorated with allegorical frescos of the triumphs of the House of Orange, rooms, where even the door-keys were of solid gold, displayed exotic marquetry and the newest Japanese lacquer work. The one characteristic William did share with his brilliant ancestors was a love of beautiful things and an unerring judgement of the right men to provide them; the aged Huguenot Daniel Marot, who had adorned Het Loo, was coaxed out of retirement to add two wings to the house, which provided a chapel for Anne's private use (so large that it is now used as a ballroom) and a white dining room with exquisite rococo plasterwork.

Early in 1745 Marie Louise wrote a slightly offended letter, having heard indirectly that Anne was pregnant again; William assured her that it was early days though it was soon 'the secret of the whole world'.[3] One of the most articulate and dedicated Orangists, William Bentinck, was delighted by their venture out of Friesland:

This... will procure them many friends for they both behave as well and with as much judgement as can be wished and are civil and obliging without distinction. They keep a very good table (always an important factor here!) and keep for supper all the ladies and gentlemen who go there in the evening.[4]

But the public image needed iron discipline. The pregnancy was a difficult one, with frequent bleeding, not helped by a horse bolting with Anne's carriage, and their precious Carolina was ailing as smallpox stalked the capital. In the middle of March, William wrote to his mother that 'her burden has descended a little and she is losing weight'.[5] The celebrated Leiden physician, Hermann Boerhaave, disagreed with a midwife's assumption of a miscarriage, and two more miserable weeks passed until he confirmed the diagnosis.

Cumberland visited them on his way to join the allied army in Brussels. At barely twenty-four he had been named Captain-General, the title last held by Marlborough, and while he comforted his sister and played with his niece he assessed the usefulness to him of the Dutch troops, and was horrified to discover that only half the number promised to him were actually ready. At the beginning of May he faced a French army which outnumbered his by almost two to one at the village of Fontenoy east of Tournai. It was commanded by the German Marshal de Saxe, who was suffering so badly from kidney stones that he was carried on a litter, chewing on a bullet to help him endure the pain. The Dutch contingents were led by the Prince of Waldeck, also a German, an obstinate man obsessed with precedent who 'has no head for the post... and is too wise to learn of others'.[6] He was entrusted with the left wing as the army launched a full frontal attack against withering French artillery. Cumberland was everywhere in the thick of it, appearing 'wherever the fire was hottest and flying wherever he saw our troops fail, to lead 'em himself and encourage 'em by his example'.[7] A travelled British officer compared the ten-hour cannonade to Mount Etna, observing that 'Dettingen was play to it'. The Dutch, to put it politely, were hesitant, though the Duke, leaving himself under strength, despatched two of his own battalions to help them, but they could not prevent a 'withdrawal', a euphemism for the bolting cavalry. This left Cumberland dangerously exposed to the crossfire of two French batteries less than a mile apart, and once more he was only able to get his men out by skilful defence – as the line retreated in good order each battalion halted and turned about to fire a volley. But his casualties were enormous: it took men from three regiments to make up the headquarters guard that night, and he railed in private at 'the inexpressible cowardice of the Dutch, calling them "Goats"'. He managed to write a tactful, if slightly pointed, letter to Anne:

Dear Sister,

I hope that the hurry of business that I have been in for the last week will plead my pardon for not having writ before but the care of the wounded and the changing of the Regiments has taken up all my time. The Right Wing did their duty and have lost between five and six thousand men, and good men they were, how to recruit them is the difficulty now. Count Konigseck [the Austrian Field Marshal] talks of you and the Prince in a way that gives me and all your sincere friends joy (I don't love him the less for that)... My thanks to little Carolina for her remembrance, I remain your tender and affectionate brother William.[8]

Amelia received a flippant but exasperated account describing how, when needed, 'the Chief Goats' had been in retreat, and 'they are not animals to give spirit',[9] while the Dutch commander was incapable of posting an ensign. Konigseck's personal remarks had accompanied a report in which he had told Cumberland that the Dutch were wholly to blame for the allied defeat – only one infantry battalion had made any progress at all under fire, and when it took cover in a convenient ditch and stayed there, the entire advance had stalled.

Back in London, the Duke's personal courage was well documented and Frederick, generous as ever, sent his congratulations. But observers also focused on another aspect of command – his concern for the men. He visited the wounded, especial bravery was rewarded with bounties from his own pocket, and he wrote personally to Louis XV (signing himself, incidentally, 'your affectionate friend') assuring him of his care for prisoners which he trusted would be reciprocated. When he discovered that many regimental surgeons had been captured after the battle while tending the wounded, and that many of the wounds revealed that the French had used shells and bullets filled with shards of metal and glass, his fury knew no bounds, and Saxe received a harshly worded note and a casket containing the offending material. The Regency Council (George was in Hanover) made a formal vote of thanks for 'that spirit of humanity which appears in all His Royal Highness's actions and the justice he has done to those who have deserved so well of him and their country'.[10] Horace Walpole added his voice to the general adulation. 'All are full of the Duke's humanity and bravery, he will be as popular with the lower class of men as he has been for three or four years with low women.'[11]

Walpole's characteristic waspishness seems to imply that Cumberland's liaisons were seldom with his own class. He moved easily in courtly society but his total focus on military affairs left no time for any relationship which might encroach on his independence. As he entered into the most critical year of his life, such focus was important.

Early in July 1745, government agents tracking the movements through Europe of a certain 'young Chevalier', reported that he had set sail from Brittany, presumably for Scotland. The intelligence service was at a high point, as a senior clerk in the French Foreign Office and the chief cipher decoder at the Holy See were both in British pay. A French ship, the *Elisabeth*, was damaged in a desperate encounter with the Channel fleet off the Lizard, and returned to France; but news reached London that Prince Charles Edward Stuart had raised his standard at Glenfinnan in Moidart, and put a price on the head of the Elector of Hanover. But the *Elisabeth* had been carrying two thousand firelocks, six hundred swords and a detachment of French soldiers, so Charles had to rely on youthful charm and on the Scottish and English Jacobites who, he was confident, were just waiting for their leader. The first attribute was easy: a couple of months older than Cumberland, Charles had twice the charisma of his father (though that wasn't difficult) and he was an attractive man of undoubted courage and 'incomparable sweetness of nature' – in public at least. Having landed with seven companions he headed within a month a sizeable force of clansmen as he advanced on Edinburgh.

London was slow to react, partly because the King was in Hanover and ministers were divided as to the nature of the threat, one of them even writing jovially that 'the young Squire is gone a-shooting grouse in the Highlands'.[12] But as Charles spent a month consolidating his position there was time to assess the situation. The complex nature of Jacobitism was perhaps easier to fathom then than now after the accretion of two and a half centuries of furious argument. Nationalists try to come to terms with the fact that the risings of 1715 and 1745 were essentially civil wars, with English and Scots fighting together on both sides; and pragmatists on either side find that every confident assertion of the allegiance of a particular group can be irrefutably contradicted. The whole issue is then overlaid by myth – the romantic Scottish one of the Prince in the misty heather, and the political English one of a secret and all-powerful threat to stability.

In Scotland, as many clans kept their heads down as ever declared for either Stuart prince, and a favourite tactic was to keep a foot in both camps, with the chief professing loyalty to the Act of Union and his sons out raising the standard; or, as happened with the Seaforths and the Mackintoshes, the clan chiefs serving in the royal army and their Ladies out in the hills.

The Jacobite retreat at Sheriffmuir had been forced by an English army commanded by the second Duke of Argyll, head of the Clan Campbell, who had established its dominant position by means of such realpolitik as the Glencoe Massacre and a fairly consistent allegiance to the English crown. Resentment and hatred of the Campbells brought many clansmen to the Stuart cause, as did their desperate poverty – rule from London had brought them little, and at the very least rebellion offered a prospect of betterment. The Earl of Kilmarnock said at his trial that 'for the two Kings and their rights I cared not a farthing which prevailed, but I was starving, and by God if Mahommed had set up his standard in the Highlands I had been a good Mussulman for bread and stuck close to the party for I must eat.'[13] Religious affiliation to the cause was rooted in episcopalianism as much as Catholicism, the former having been increasingly identified with Scottish nationalism since the Presbyterians had triumphed as the established church in Scotland.

In 1715 a pamphleteer had written, 'It well deserves your thought whether it is worth your while to beggar yourselves and your family that the man's name on the throne be James instead of George.' Such apathy, allied with James's personal failings and reluctance to compromise his religious position even so far as toleration for his followers, had doomed that Jacobite effort to failure, and those who remembered the Fifteen seem initially to have been among those most casual about the threat of the Forty-five. George was thoroughly relaxed on his return from Hanover, Pitt was perversely arguing for naval improvements as a hostile army moved through Scotland, and Parliament was preoccupied with the recent outbreak of rinderpest among cattle (in a later debate a speaker repeatedly referred to 'horned beasts' and eventually two prominent Members whose wives were known to be unfaithful, rose and solemnly bowed to each other).[14]

But the young were more alert. Horace Walpole joked rather nervously about what he would do when he was in exile in Hanover, and Cumberland wrote to Newcastle from Flanders requesting a recall: 'It would be horrid to be employed abroad when my home was in danger.'[15] Ten of his battalions were summoned back to England when the news broke of the defeat of Sir John Cope's northern army at Prestonpans just outside Edinburgh. Cope had chosen his ground well, using the protection of a supposedly impassable bog; but local knowledge enabled the Jacobites to cross it and hurl themselves on the royal troops, who were mostly untested in battle. Cope's dragoons rode all over the infantry and his guns were ineffectually manned by the sailors who had brought them down from Aberdeen. Even so, one artillery discharge was enough to break the Highland line, which was about to disintegrate when Cope's men turned and ran. All was over within ten minutes, but the pursuit took longer and consisted of acts of sheer barbarism which England would not forget, as with 'more than Turkish inhumanity' her men were slaughtered:

> The foot seeing themselves naked and defenceless, and the enemy rushing impetuously upon them sword in hand, they threw down their arms and surrendered prisoners. But the merciless enemy would grant them no quarters, 'til they were compelled by their superior officers. The unheard of manner in which the dead were mangled and the wounded disfigured was a great evidence of the truth of this.[16]

Horace Walpole later described the scene when survivors were landed at Tower Wharf 'in a most miserable shocking condition without limbs, eyes or noses'. One Jacobite officer vainly trying to control the Highlanders was Lord Elcho, who commanded the Prince's lifeguards, and he wrote in a private memoir of his disgust when a company of MacGregors, always a law unto themselves, armed themselves with scythes bound to seven-foot sticks and 'had the impression that horses fought as well as men' slicing off their hooves in frenzied attacks after the riders fell.[17]

The battle certainly decided a few fence-sitters, but Charles still crossed the Esk and marched for Carlisle with a pitifully small force, convinced that the many Catholics of the North West would flock to him. However, the main fence-sitter was France. The Jacobites had always accepted the uncomfortable fact that the only way the Stuarts could reclaim their crown was 'at the point of a French bayonet', but they were involved in a frustrating circular argument: the French would only invade Britain to support a successful rebellion, but British Jacobites would only rise after a successful invasion. With Prestonpans, Charles seemed to have broken the circle, but France's unpreparedness when the news reached Paris meant weeks of delay; by the time an invasion fleet was ready at Boulogne it would be too late and the English Jacobites knew it. Nevertheless, despite desperate attempts by Cumbrian local officials, firstly to find money to pay the local militia and secondly to confiscate all ladders which might be useful to the rebels, Carlisle surrendered.

Notes

1 Chatsworth Papers, Pelham to Hartington, September 1748
2 Egerton MSS 1712
3 KHA, Willem IV, 170 III
4 Egerton MSS 1713
5 KHA, Willem IV, 170 III
6 *Briefwisseling*, William Bentinck, CXXXVIII
7 Quoted by Whitworth, op. cit., p.50
8 KHA, Anna, 430
9 Undated letter (ending 'burn this nonsense') in Spencer Papers at Althorp
10 Royal Archive Cumberland Papers 3/36
11 Quoted by Whitworth, op. cit., p.51
12 Sir Robert Trevor to Cumberland, RA Cumberland Papers 4/209
13 B Lenman, *Jacobite Risings in Britain*, 1980, p.256
14 L Picard, *London*, 2000, p.282
15 RA Cumberland Papers 4/30
16 A Henderson, *History of the Rebellion*, 1753, p.87
17 F Maclean, op. cit., p.91

Chapter Fifteen

The news finally caused widespread panic in London: rumours were rife – the militia guarding London had mutinied on Finchley Common and Cumberland had thrown in his lot with Charles, Jacobites stalked the streets to assassinate prominent members of society, and the royal yacht waited in the Thames estuary to take George and his daughters to Hanover. There was reported to be a run on the Bank of England as people tried to withdraw their savings: the Bank blocked its counters with its own agents who were paid out vast sums (in sixpences), left by a side door, handed over the money and entered by another to repeat the procedure. But this brilliant stratagem, which might perhaps be borne in mind for the future, seems, unfortunately, to have been a fantasy: a top Bank official wrote to reassure a worried friend out of town that despite the alarm there was financial stagnation, 'nothing doing in stocks except four per cent annuities which are under par'.[1] Thomas Arne, fresh from the success of his 'Rule Britannia', composed the music for a new anthem which was performed after a performance at Drury Lane, and the audience were encouraged to sing 'God save great George our King'.[2]

George and the recently returned Cumberland refuted rumours with a show of personal courage when they stood side by side for two hours on a terrace outside St James's, first reviewing six regiments of horse and foot, and then remaining in this totally exposed position to acknowledge the cheering crowds. At the Court celebrations for the King's birthday on 30 October – always the most important and lavish ceremonial of the year – the family displayed a united front, Frederick in light blue and silver, Caroline in pink with flower patterns of yellow, green and silver, Amelia, predictably, 'more gay than elegant' and Cumberland in his scarlet uniform 'with quantities of gold';[3] Augusta as usual had just given birth. The Speaker of the House of Commons, Arthur Onslow, was full of admiration; the King 'was void of the least appearance of fear or dejection and just with cheerfulness enough to give spirit to others. I never saw him, I think, show so much of true greatness as he did then'.[4] The cool demeanour concealed inner tensions since, as Amelia wrote to Anne, she and Caroline were 'totally dismayed' by events, while to everyone's outrage, Frederick had arranged a lavish christening party for his new son, ordering a cake in the shape of Carlisle Castle, which he encouraged his guests to pelt with sugarplums.

Anne, too, was controlling her concern over events with 'an inexhaustible fund of spirits and cheerfulness'.[5] She forwarded Amelia's letters to her husband with strict instructions to burn them and she worried for the safety of her sisters and the family's future. William was in Frankfurt to meet Maria Theresa, whose husband's election had made her Empress at last, and along with family news – the 2½-year-old Carolina 'looks for you everywhere with a melancholy air and asks all the time where you are' – Anne pressed him to ask for and obtain marks of recognition.[6] She was forever trying to boost his morale, writing on another public occasion 'your black embroidered coat will be the finest there just as your inner self I know is the most perfect among all the princes and great ones',[7] but William was always ill at ease in any but the most intimate gatherings. His physical handicap was becoming ever more marked, the shoulder more twisted, and as the pressure resulted in frequent bouts of illness it was obvious that even if he had been given a military role he could never endure the rigours of a campaign.

A force of 6,000 Dutch soldiers had been claimed under treaty obligations for the defence of the English crown, but so restricted was their choice, the States-General had to include the Tournai garrison, who had been released by Saxe on parole. Somehow the French discovered this and, unimpressed by the ingenious argument that parole obligations referred to frontiers where troops might not serve, and since England was an island it had no frontiers, they issued a formal warning that any Dutchman captured in England would be shot. Whether Cumberland was sympathetic to their predicament or simply determined to keep them out of his own way, he sent them to north-east England as Charles advanced through the North West, and under 'Grandmother Wade' they were instructed for the moment to protect the sea coal supplies out of Newcastle.

Landowners loyal to the crown in northern England were deeply worried. Lord Glenorchy wrote to his daughter regretting his recent house improvements such as 'taking the iron bars from the windows and sashing them and… weakening the house as to resistance by adding modern wings to it. If it had remained as it was before I might have slept very sound in it for their whole army could not have taken it'.[8]

Everyone now looked to Cumberland. 'The great dependence is on the Duke, the soldiers adore him and with reason, he has a lion's courage,' wrote Horace Walpole.[9] While waiting for the recall from Flanders he had studied government papers on Scottish affairs and briefed himself thoroughly on Highland history and Jacobitism. Because of his calm maturity and his known influence with the King, he was often sought out by ministers, Newcastle having rejected Chesterfield's advice to make up to the Countess of Yarmouth – 'for even the wisest man, like the chameleon, takes up without knowing it more or less the line of what he is often UPON'.[10]

George was supremely self-confident and brooked no advice on military affairs; he saw all the intelligence reports and rejected the more alarmist. 'I believe there must be some mistake in this except the rebels shall have permanently divided their forces which is not probable.'[11] He flatly refused the panicky suggestions of arming loyal Scots, and he quickly grasped the significance of reports from Lancashire and Cumbria that the invaders were marching into empty towns: English Jacobites had been happy enough to drink to 'the King over the Water' in the privacy of their own dining rooms, but as he arrived at the head of an often ravening rabble they looked to their silver.

Cumberland billeted his main army over a wide area of Staffordshire as Charles marched south. He knew that Manchester was the one town where the Prince would find recruits – as indeed he did, though only two or three hundred formed the ill-fated Manchester Regiment: they came mainly from the ranks of the unemployed and were issued with plaids and white cockades. A Miss Elizabeth Byrom put on her new twelve-shilling blue and white dress and set off to see the Prince who, to her delight, was wearing a blue and silver waistcoat: 'He sat on a cavorting horse – a noble sight.'[12] She then attended church where prayers were offered for 'The King and the Prince of Wales' with no names mentioned. When the local constables were ordered to proclaim King James III at the market cross, one of them pleaded that he had left his glasses at home and the other that he suffered from a severe speech impediment. The royal army was poised to block any advance on Chester, if the rebels swung into Wales they would be trapped, and Cumberland devoutly hoped the Jacobite spy system was unaware of the unreliability of Wade's army, which was meandering vaguely on the far side of the Pennines; Arne's anthem been optimistic:

> God grant that Marshal Wade
> May with his mighty aid, victory bring,
> May he sedition hush,
> And like a torrent rush,
> Rebellious Scots to crush,
> God Save our King.

But in reality Wade, hampered by the terrain, the weather and the Dutch in equal measure, never came within thirty miles of the rebels, and it is certainly arguable that he never planned to – he had spent years in Scotland after the Fifteen improving the defensive infrastructure of forts and roads to consolidate Hanoverian control, and he had bitter experience of the Highland claymore and the strength of the Highland myth: 'Their notions of virtue and vice are very different from the more civilised part of mankind.'[13]

Cumberland's continental experience led him to expect a set-piece battle on ground of his own choosing where he was confident his disciplined troops could be deployed to the greatest advantage; just outside the town of Stone he found the space he needed for the unimpeded cavalry charge and infantry squares of continental warfare, and he settled down to wait according to his aide-de-camp 'all in spirits and jollity'.[14] The experienced Ligonier, who was with him, considered that the tide had turned and advised his London friends to buy bonds; at the same time, mindful of the northern weather, he ordered blankets for the infantry who, unlike the cavalry had no greatcoats to keep them warm. But unexpectedly Charles turned east and entered Derby – in the words of Robert Chambers:

> The last (and the least) of all the armies Scotland ever sent against the Southron had thus reached the Trent, traversed five counties and insulted the very centre of England.

But as Horace Walpole wrote, 'though they have marched into the heart of the kingdom there has not been the least symptom of a rising not even in the great towns.[15]

The Gentleman's Magazine later published an account of the arrival in Derby on 4 December. The vanguard under Lord Elcho rode in first, well-horsed and well-dressed in scarlet and blue with gold lacings, followed by 150 clan chiefs, also on horseback, in their Highland dress bearing double-handed broadswords and huge bull-hide shields embossed with silver. It is worth recording that the Lowlanders, and even the French, in Charles's army were ordered to wear Highland dress in a deliberate attempt to trade on the potent myth, which had developed since before the Union, of the Highlander as true patriot – a cultivated man holding himself aloof from 'the lure of England's gold'. Derby was impressed, rang its bells and lit bonfires 'to prevent any resentment from them that might ensue on our showing a dislike of their coming among us'.[16] But then to the brave sound of the pipes the foot came in, 'a parcel of shabby, lousy fellows, mixed up with old men and boys, dressed in dirty plaids and many without shoes', while, according to the town clerk, 'they jabbered like hottentots'.[17] All through the next day the public crier toured the town inviting 'all persons who had any duties to pay [i.e. uncollected excise] or any public money in their hands' to take it to the Prince, who would submit it to 'King James III'. It was already being announced in the *Gazette de France* that James Stuart would be crowned in Westminster Abbey on Christmas Day as William the Conqueror had been.

Charles was exultant. By his jink to Derby he believed the road to London lay open for him, but as he entertained his commanders to dinner that evening they issued an ultimatum. Many had argued fiercely against the invasion of England (in fact he had won that decision in Edinburgh by only two votes), and they now pointed to the pitiful lack of English support. It was the final showdown between the Prince and his commander, Lord George Murray, whose disagreements and mutual dislike had marked the whole campaign: the Prince 'whose optimism blinded him to the realities of any situation and "Lord George" whose appreciation of those realities bordered upon insubordinate pessimism'. Lord George was a fine soldier but, 'he desires always to dictate everything by himself and knowing none his equal he did not wish to receive advice.' Charles was emotional, intuitive and immature, aware of his lack of military experience but relying on the power of his cause and his own charm to conceal the fact. He was also vulnerable to the many whispers in the Jacobite camp that Murray was looking for 'an opportunity of deliver him up to the Government'.[18]

Ironically, their very success was at last stirring Jacobites in the woodwork, but it was too late. Cumberland had moved his men by forced march down to Coventry, and one of Newcastle's most able secret agents, Dudley Bradstreet, managed to convince the Prince's council that Wade's army was on their flank. Not one voice was raised for anything except retreat, Charles 'fell into a passion and gave most of the Gentlemen who had Spoke very Abusive Language'; when he could not prevail he relapsed into a sullen demoralised apathy.[19]

All through the night preparations were made for the long march back to Scotland, though the secret was kept from all but the most senior officers. Whatever the decision, there was a desperate need for fresh horses, and a letter to the son of Sir Nathaniel Curzon from his old tutor, Dr Mather, writing from Kedleston Hall, gives an account of the methods used in the search for them. The Curzons were the leading Tory family in Derbyshire and might therefore be expected to have some Jacobite sympathies, though in the county's subscription list 'to defend our excellent constitution in Church and State against the threat of rebellion', their contribution had been second only to that staunch Whig the Duke of Devonshire. Kedleston lay just north of Derby, right by the Ashbourne road, and Sir Nathaniel's servants had watched the rebels march by; Lord George Murray himself had wheeled his horse to invite some of them to enlist, though one that did was later sent back 'as too great a rogue to keep with them'.[20]

According to Dr Mather the household was roused between eleven and twelve by a thunderous knocking at the door and a demand to open up for King James's men. Seven Highlanders, each carrying two brace of pistols and a broadsword and two with slung muskets, stationed themselves round the hall, but their officer was extremely courteous – he had been told he might get from them nine or ten horses, though half that number or even less would be sufficient, and he had no desire to incommode the family, though he would also be greatly obliged if any good pistols could be spared. But his men were jumpy, and when Mather's current pupil, Sir Nathaniel's sixteen-year-old younger son, was seen peering into the hall from a skylight one of them threatened to shoot him. The pistol was knocked to the ground by the officer who continued to chat amiably to the tutor, telling him they expected to be in action soon with Cumberland's men outside Leicester (in other words, on the way south).

Before dawn the next day the drums beat to arms and the troops prepared to leave, as they thought, for the next stage of their advance on London. A few hardy townspeople had risen to see them go and they were the first to realise to their utter astonishment that the orders indicated the northern road – the retreat had begun. The soldiers themselves only gradually understood, as the winter sky lightened, that they were retracing their steps and 'there were howlings, groans and lamentations throughout the whole army'.[21] The Kedleston servants rushed out again to watch – Sir Nathaniel had taken the precaution of removing all his best horses to the furthest corner of his estate, and the previous night's raiding party had yielded only an aged coach horse and a highly nervous brown mare, who was observed galloping uncontrollably through the throng.

Thanks partly to what has been termed 'the spectacular incompetence' of Wade and the exhaustion of Cumberland's men, the invading army withdrew through hostile territory and appalling weather to reach the Esk once more, virtually unscathed and with all their artillery intact. Cumberland was in hot pursuit with two regiments of dragoons, and at Preston he joined General Oglethorpe, who had volunteered for government service the Rangers he had just recruited in London to take back to Georgia; as the Duke rested his troops, Oglethorpe pursued the rebels up to Shap Fell where an inconclusive skirmish ended when heavy snow blanketed the ground. Oglethorpe withdrew and spent the night at a local vicarage, but unfortunately for him he overslept and as he rode into Shap village was mortified to discover his furious commander-in-chief already there. The enemy had managed to cross the high moors the previous day, despite the weather, and the General was court-martialled for dereliction of duty.

On his twenty-fifth birthday, Charles shook off his depression and took personal command of the recrossing of the swollen Esk, he and the rest of the horse wading in 'to break the stream that it should not be so rapid for the foot [who] marched in six in a brest in as good order as if they were marching in a field... without any losse but two women that belonged only to the publick, that were drownded' – presumably camp followers.[22] Cumberland decided not to follow them into Scotland for the moment. He stayed a couple of nights near Penrith with a Quaker, Thomas Savage, who described his guest as 'a man of parts, very friendly with no pride in him',[23] and planned his siege to retake Carlisle Castle, which had been left with a Jacobite garrison of 400 men, since Charles still convinced himself that he was simply staging a tactical withdrawal before attacking again in the spring.

After a three-day battering from ten heavy guns shipped to Whitehaven from Liverpool, Cumberland formally received the surrender of Carlisle. Many judicial delays later, trials of 127 of the captured rebels resulted in the acquittal of thirty-six, conviction of the remainder, many of whom pleaded guilty, and execution of thirty-three – a proportion which should be remembered. The Duke returned to London, confident in a job well done, leaving a cavalry general of sixty-five, Henry Hawley, in charge of the army which would pursue the rebels.[24] He arrived at seven o'clock one morning in early January and it was noted, went straight to a service in the Chapel Royal. He was fêted everywhere, Newcastle himself writing 'all the world is in love with him and he deserves it'.[25] He was voted to receive the Freedom of the City of London, but before the ceremony could take place a communiqué came from Hawley, who had advanced on the Jacobite army near Falkirk: 'My heart is broke, I can't say we are quite beat today, but our left is beat and their left is beat.'[26]

Thanks to his enjoyment of a lavish meal, good wine and much flattery from the Jacobite Lady Kilmarnock the night before, Hawley had not been at his best, had underrated the enemy, walked into a trap and misdirected the ensuing battle. He blamed his men, summarily shooting several dragoons for cowardice, and his ruthless reaction was to be repeated in the coming months on friend and foe alike, despite the recorded efforts of 'Butcher Cumberland' to restrain him. The news from Falkirk revealed the continuing danger. 'I tremble for fear that this vile space [Scotland] may still be the ruin of this island and our family,' Cumberland is reported to have said as he left St James's by torchlight at one in the morning,[27] sped on his way with a hundred sentiments similar to those of Horace Walpole: 'we paid too great a favour to Scotland in 1715, the Duke must make an end to it.'

Notes

[1] HMC Lothian MSS
[2] Walters, op. cit., p.190
[3] Whitworth, op. cit., p.60
[4] W Speck, *The Butcher*, 1981, p.76
[5] *Briefwisseling*, Bentinck, CLXV
[6] KHA, Anna, 430
[7] Ibid.

[8] Lord Glenorchy probably felt he was at risk from both sides. He was a staunch Hanoverian having served as ambassador in Scandinavia, but he had had to report to Sir John Cope before Prestonpans that he could raise no men from his own lands for the Government army.

[9] Charteris, op. cit., p.246

[10] Davies, op. cit., p.247

[11] Quoted by Trench, op. cit., p.233

[12] Manchester City Council Education Department, *Jacobites in Manchester*

[13] Whitworth, op. cit., p.59

[14] Ibid., p.63

[15] Letter to Horace Mann, 9 December 1745

[16] *Gentleman's Magazine*, December 1745

[17] Ibid.

[18] MacLean, op. cit., p.69, 116, 240

[19] R Marshall, *Bonnie Prince Charlie*, 1988, pp.117–24

[20] 'A Letter found in Lord Scarsdale's Papers' published in the *Derby Telegraph*, 23 April 1869

[21] David Daiches, *Bonnie Prince Charlie*, 1973, p.169

[22] MacLean, op. cit., p.138

[23] *Transactions*, Cumberland and Westmoreland Archaeological Society, 'Clifton Moor', X, pp.186–225

[24] Rumour had it that Hawley was a bastard son of George I, conceived on his visit to England in 1680.

[25] Add MSS 32, 700

[26] RA Cumberland Papers 9/99

[27] Waldegrave, op. cit., p.39

J Faber's print from the portrait of Princess Anne by H Hysing which was painted from life and presented by Her Royal Highness to the late Countess of Sussex. From the author's private collection.

The Drowning of Prince John William Friso in the Hollands Diep in 1711. Engraving by R Vinkeles, after H Kobell Jr, 1766. From the Prentenkabinet der RU Leiden.

Marie Louise of Hesse and her children Princess Amalia and the later William IV.
Portrait by A van Boonen, early 1720s. On Loan to the Ambassador's residence at The Hague (as of 1995).

Georgio II^{do} Mag: Brit: Franc: & Hiber: Regi

Nuptias Ceremoniales inter Annam Mag: Brit: Principissam Regalem et Gulielmum Principem Aurantenensem habitas in Capella Regia S.^{ti} Jacobi apud Londinum Martis 14ta An: 1733.
Devotissimus et obligatissimus servus Gul: Kent.
Humillime offert, dicat, dedicatque

Wedding Ceremony of Princess Anne and Prince William of Orange in the Royal Chapel, St James's Palace, 1733.
Engraving by J Rigaud after William Kent. © The Trustees of the British Museum.

Double Portrait of William V and his sister Carolina.
Engraving by P Tanjé after G Sanders, 1751. From the Prentenkabinet der RU Leiden.

Willem IV (1711-51). Portrait by Jacques André Joseph Aved, begun 1751, finished after the Prince's death. From the Rijksmusum-Stchting, Amsterdam.

Prince William Augustus, Duke of Cumberland (1721-1765), Youngest Son of King George II. Portrait by Sir Joshua Reynolds (1723-1792). © The Devonshire Collection, Chatsworth.

Representation Perspective de la Salle et Lit de Parade en etat Exposé le Corps de Son Altesse Royale
Perspective-Afbeelding van de Parade Zaal en Bedt waar op het Lyck van H.K.H. geleegen heeft.

Anna's Lying in State at The Hague, 1759. Engraving by S Fokke after P de Stewart, 1759. From the Prentenkabinet der RU Leiden.

Chapter Sixteen

The Duke rode hard and was in York in two days, Edinburgh in five. His arrival, and the fact that after Falkirk many of Charles's army left to return to their homes and farms, prompted the Jacobite command to recommend withdrawal into the Highlands. The Prince disclaimed in writing all responsibility for the decision which was, as he saw, a strategic mistake. He had argued since Derby that the retreat should be conducted as a tactical withdrawal, and now that a victory had raised morale again, to retreat still further into the isolation of the high mountains seemed perverse. It discouraged the French from offering any more than token support, and most serious of all, it meant jettisoning their cannon and heavy artillery which were duly retrieved from rivers and barns and handed to Cumberland as he advanced up the coast road towards Aberdeen. Although he issued orders that his soldiers should only seize arms and ammunition, with supplies uncertain and the weather bitter 'some of the Men did venture to transgress when they saw a good Opportunity', and he certainly, to put it mildly, 'marked his sense of the disaffection of this part of the country by subjecting it to military law'.[1]

The Dutch had returned home and the Duke was now backed by 5,000 troops led by his brother-in-law, Frederick of Hesse; the marriages of both Mary and Louisa having been planned with an eye to military advantage. However, the Danes flatly refused to send any troops to Scotland, and the maverick Frederick rather warmed to the rebels, announcing that since he was 'not enough interested in the quarrel between the House of Stuart and the House of Hanover to sacrifice his soldiers' lives in combatting men driven to despair',[2] he would not move north of Pitlochry.

In Aberdeen, Cumberland settled down to six weeks of hard work. He had studied the Jacobite tactics at Prestonpans and Falkirk, and he evolved a defence to the yelling Highland charges with claymore and Lochaber axe which had prevailed there. The men were relentlessly drilled in a manoeuvre whereby they thrust their bayonets to right front rather than straight ahead so as to pierce the enemy shield wall. He was also looking ahead to ultimate political solutions, 'Mild measures won't do,' he wrote to Newcastle, 'don't imagine that threatening military execution and many other things are pleasing to me but nothing will go down without in this part of the world.'[3]

By the beginning of April, two factors signalled the beginning of the end – a French ship carrying 12,000 gold guineas for the Jacobite cause was intercepted, and spring at last reached the North. The former meant that Charles, though without many of his best men who had returned to their homes after crossing the border, simply had to stand and fight within the next week or two because his money had run out, the men already being paid in meal; the latter that the road from Aberdeen to the last Jacobite stronghold of Inverness was passable.

Cumberland marched north-west to Nairn, fifteen miles short of Inverness, and a public relations exercise told how he carried the musket of one of his sergeants who was obliged to bring his baby because of the illness of his wife. He stayed on the way with James Findlater, a prominent government supporter whose home had been sacked by a party of Jacobites. Hardly any glass remained in the windows, furniture was carried off, mirrors and china broken and 'parchments torn and trampled and mixed together with dust and feathers and jam and marmalade and honey and wet and all sorts of nastiness mixed together'.[4] It was another small piece in the jigsaw of the Duke's attitude to the task ahead.

Their choice of Culloden Moor as the battlefield was another Jacobite mistake – a stretch of open ground where 'regular troops had full use of their cannon so as to annoy the Highlanders prodigiously before they could make an attack'. The choice was made by the Prince in consultation with his close friend, John O'Sullivan, an ex-seminarian turned soldier of fortune, and Lord George, arriving later, could not reverse the decision: 'I did not like the ground, it was certainly not proper for Highlanders.'[5] Even worse was an utterly hare-brained scheme for a night march to Nairn. Now it was Cumberland's twenty-fifth birthday, and Charles somehow persuaded himself that after drinking their commander's health, the royal army would be too drunk to resist a surprise attack. After five or six miles over unfamiliar ground, progress was so slow that it was realised they would be launching an attack in daylight, so the literally starving men were halted, turned round and marched back to Culloden. Due to the general chaos, the main body returned by a different route and nobody thought to inform the rear division, who had become separated in the confusion and who doggedly marched on to the enemy camp – only to discover they were alone. As one of Lord Elcho's life guards put it, 'O for Madness, what can one think or what can one say here!'[6]

Straggling back through the dawn to Culloden, officers and men alike were so exhausted that they slept where they dropped, but the royal army was close behind them. Having slept well and enjoyed their tot of brandy and an extra piece of cheese for each man, they were on their way before five o'clock, giving the Duke a rousing reception as he rode through their ranks on his grey charger, the Lizard, though an embarrassing moment occurred when he noticed some of his loyal Highlanders were carrying bundles of sticks, and ordered new weapons for them; it had to be explained that these were bagpipes.

The Jacobites fought with desperate courage, earning a rightful place in myth, but they never stood a chance. Cumberland's powerful artillery raked their lines as they stood fast waiting for the order to charge which did not reach them because of chaotic communications. Donald Cameron of Lochiel, in tears of rage and despair, stood among his dying men, brandishing broadsword and pistol, until both his legs were broken by grapeshot. His gentle courtesy, honourable conduct and unswerving loyalty had been a dynamic of the whole campaign, although he had desperately tried to persuade Charles even at Glenfinnan that the enterprise was doomed.

The Prince, in his own words 'was led off the field by those around him',[7] and by all accounts was in a state of paralysed shock. Lord Elcho writes of 'his deplorable state', and a story of possibly doubtful authenticity has him begging Charles to lead a charge and die sword in hand, and, when this was refused, calling his leader 'a damned cowardly Italian'.[8] The prince issued a *sauve qui peut* order, refused any further contact with either the battered survivors of the battle or with the still loyal (and not inconsiderable) force which mustered at Ruthven, begging him 'most earnestly to come thither quickly to put himself at their head'.[9]

The dream was over, and Charles was to live the remaining forty-three years of his life in drink-sodden exile; but as a fugitive through the glens and the islands he lived up to the name he has been given. He recovered the courage, stamina and gaiety which had first drawn men to him and which he had lost at Derby, and through five months of desperate hardship and hair's breadth escapes, with a price on his head and the entire northern army baying at his heels, he established forever the legend of the Bonnie Prince whom the impoverished clansmen refused to betray.

Scottish legend also gathered round Cumberland, as the defeated told of the finishing off by bayonet and club of the wounded lying on the field and of the murder of women and children. Undoubtedly there were acts of sadistic and unjustified revenge in the aftermath of battle, and also pillage and rape by the detachments sent out to scour the mountains, but never the systematic brutality which was alleged. Cumberland ordered a thousand lashes for any such defiance of his authority, but he could not oversee everything carried out in his name. Charles's French contingents (and the Irish serving with them) were assured of fair treatment under international law, but the rest were, in the Duke's eyes, guilty of treason: he ordered that any who surrendered could go in peace but those who did not would be liable to summary execution. He was thus dealing with them by military law which was notoriously severe and which he never hesitated to use on his own men. Lawyers in London and

Edinburgh fretted, and rightly so since in time of peace civil law should prevail, but, as his most recent biographer put it, Cumberland considered he had given the rebels their chance: 'If they chose to continue to resist they would have to take the consequences… many of them did [and] the myth-makers found their ammunition.'[10]

It is important to realise that Culloden was not seen then as it can be now – as the death of the Stuart cause: Charles had escaped, while many of his best regiments had not even been engaged on the moor and were massing else-where. The royal army was far from base, deep in relentlessly hostile territory, and dared not risk losing control. A defence of Cumberland is a dangerous exercise, but it is valid to try one. He was convinced throughout the Forty-five and afterwards of the immediate danger posed to his family: this was for him a personal struggle with his father's throne at stake. The fierce undisciplined savagery of the rebel army was quite outside his experience on the continent of professionalism in battle and generally honourable treatment of prisoners, and he was genuinely at a loss when he surveyed 'the villainy and infidelity of the Highlands'. The driving force of his life was loyalty – to his father, to his men and to his country – and he would serve the first, champion the second and defend the third at whatever cost. But the crucial factor in his actions was the attitude of London. The instructions and recommendations he received were quite specific – this from Newcastle: 'the rebellion must be got the better of in such a manner that we may not have another';[11] from the urbane diplomat Chesterfield: 'starve the whole country indiscriminately, put a price on the heads of the chiefs and let the Duke put all to the fire and sword';[12] while many were warning against sowing the seeds of future disloyalty by too easily pardoning the present, 'we must not have another [rebellion] next year.'[13]

In July, Cumberland returned to London to overwhelming public acclaim. Fireworks, church bells and gun salutes shook the streets, while the roaring crowds threatened to 'devour him with fondness'.[14] Handel wrote 'See the conquering Hero comes' and popular ballads lionised him:

> Then Scotland did rejoice
> O that the Youth had come
> The Glory of the Nation
> King George's youngest Son.

The manager of the Savile Row Theatre reported 'not inconsiderable damage' when mention of the Duke's name in a patriotic piece caused 'numbers of Gentlemen to exert their canes in a Torrent of Satisfaction'. Ecclesiastical spin doctors produced an account of his praying on Culloden field: 'Lord what am I that I should be spared when so many brave men lie dead?'[15] Though even they must have jibbed at the shop window in the Strand which displayed his portrait under the title 'Ecce Homo'. Only the Chelsea veterans were disappointed because they had been looking forward to displaying the conquered standards, which Cumberland had sent to Edinburgh to be burned, since he said 'they were the business of the hangman';[16] there had been no honour in the taking of them. The King shared their feelings, because he had wanted to parade them through the streets, but reluctantly accepted his son's apology and gave him the post of Ranger and Keeper of Windsor Great Park, which would provide a role and a solace in the hard times ahead.

With the Duke back in London, Scotland was at the mercy of the brutal and ruthless Hawley, now nicknamed 'lord chief justice' on account of his 'passion for sudden and frequent executions' – an appointment which initially gave Walpole satisfaction, since he was afraid Cumberland was too soft and would 'wield the sword of mercy'. James Wolfe, who was later to meet a glorious death on the Plains of Abraham when taking Quebec and was aide-de-camp to Hawley, declared 'the troops dread his severity, hate the man and hold his military knowledge in contempt'. It was probably Hawley, and not Cumberland as Jacobite tradition has it, who ordered Wolfe to kill a wounded man on the field of Culloden. Wolfe refused, offering his commission instead.[17] The overall commander was the Earl of Albemarle, who wrote tellingly, 'It is absolutely impossible for the person who commands here to do his duty like an honest man.'[18]

So Scotland suffered, and as autumn came euphoria faded and guilt crept in to the public mood, fuelled by both legitimate grievance and downright lies. Cumberland was held solely responsible for everything done in the Highlands in England's name, and 'the glorious youth beloved of Britain' became 'the Butcher' – a reviled scapegoat for the policy ordered by a government facing dangerous rebellion; he never defended himself, and the evil reputation remained for the rest of his life and long beyond. The sober Lord Waldegrave, whose reflections on the personalities of George II's reign are measured and restrained, wrote that 'all his good qualities are overlooked, all his faults were exaggerated, false facts were advanced against him and false conclusions drawn from them'.[19] One of the accusations was connected with the order paper in which Charles had instructed his men to give no quarter – i.e. to kill prisoners: the Jacobites swore that the Butcher had forged it. But the order was actually known about long before Cumberland can have felt any need to justify his actions, and the French troops who had held themselves aloof at the last battle claimed that they had done so because, as professional soldiers, they refused to accept such an order. The Duke's 'generosity and compassion of prisoners' which had long been remarked upon was forgotten and rebel atrocities ignored; for example, a Jacobite raiding party had descended on the house of the Presbyterian minister at Nairn, set it ablaze and against the flaming background submitted him to five hundred lashes. This was obviously an isolated incident by men breaking out of their leaders' control, but exactly the same argument applies to the Duke. Out of reach of his strict discipline 'men transgressed', as happens in every war.

Cumberland acted with stoical dignity through both adulation and discredit, though to his distress even his father was affected by the public mood; discussing the matter with a courtier he deplored the fact that the nation was so changeable and felt that 'though he had not gone there to please them, William had been rough with them'.[20] The Duke was a brooding presence at many of the rebel trials in which eighty-four men were condemned to death out of over 3,000 tried. Manchester has, in fact, a much greater reason to hate the Hanoverian Crown than the Scots, for twenty-four men from their pathetic little regiment were put to death as against forty from all other Jacobite units put together (and thirty-eight deserters from the royal army). Peers were condemned to the axe rather than hanging – Kilmarnock, who pleaded starvation not treason; and Balmerino, whose surrender did not save him, but who impressed Walpole as 'the most natural brave old gentleman that I have ever seen'; his young wife visited him in the Tower 'whereupon he stripped her and took her to bed'.[21] But he also devoted himself to trying to cheer Kilmarnock by showing him exactly how to angle himself on the scaffold so as to ensure that the first blow hit his neck rather than his skull or his shoulders. Balmerino's endearing friendliness had led him to meet an acquaintance in Preston and chat to him about the numbers and names of all Lancastrian Jacobites; since the man was one of Newcastle's spies, the information was invaluable. On the scaffold, he invited Kilmarnock to go first, watched as the executioner was 'given something to prevent him fainting', and 'conversed cheerfully the while with his friends, refreshing himself twice with bread and a glass of wine.'[22]

A year later, when he was eventually captured, the 77-year-old Lord Lovat was also executed after reminding his judges that he had once carried the infant Cumberland through the gardens of Hampton Court to meet his grandfather, George I. Balmerino and Lovat 'died game', an important factor in the days of public executions. The highwayman Dick Turpin had conducted his hanging in style. Since he could not control his shaking foot he performed a little tap dance and then 'looking round him with an unconcerned Air threw himself off' before the cart on which he stood was driven away, and died within five minutes. A certain amount of fear and struggle was amusing, but a footman convicted for murdering his mistress was such a quivering wreck that the crowd lost interest and moved on to Hyde Park to watch the shooting of deserters instead. Lovat died better than he had lived. After a career of intrigue and shifting allegiance he thanked his judges in Westminster Hall for their kindness: 'God bless you all, I bid you an eternal farewell... We shall not all meet again in the same place, I am sure of that'.[23] Vast crowds had collected as he mounted the scaffold and he expressed surprise: 'Why should there be so much bustle about taking off an old grey head that cannot get up three steps without two men to support it?'[24] On his way to trial a woman had shouted, 'You'll get your head chopped off, you ugly Scottish dog!' To which he had responded, 'I believe I shall, you ugly English bitch!' But now, with more dignity, he settled himself comfortably on a chair which was provided and delivered several appropriate Latin quotations from Horace before removing his enormous periwig and coiling his tall upright frame onto the block.

A carpenter had built a high stand for those demanding a good view and enterprisingly set up a bar underneath it, but the whole edifice collapsed, killing several and maiming more. In a letter describing the scene to Anne, Amelia admitted to some sympathy with Lovat, whom they had known well in their childhood, and she had no patience with the spectators.

> They have suffered finely for their nonsensical curiosity... Adieu, my dear Royaux, I am going to Handel's new oratorio tonight [*Judas Maccabeus*, composed in honour of Cumberland] where I am sure I shall be pleased.

Frederick's sympathies were also roused, and he interceded successfully for a fourth peer, the Earl of Cromarty, and even visited Flora Macdonald, who had engineered Charles's escape, when she was imprisoned in the Tower. His father and sisters attributed this to perversity, saying 'he is the hatred and despair of everyone,'[25] but there is no reason to doubt his compassion; and though Augusta, too, was thoroughly annoyed by his interest in Flora, he was later instrumental in obtaining a pardon for her, and sharply told his wife that he hoped she would have shown the same courage and loyalty.[26]

Notes

[1] Daiches, op. cit., p.201
[2] Ibid., p.203
[3] Add MSS 32 700
[4] Whitworth, op. cit., p.82
[5] S Reid, *1745 A Military History*, 1996, p.129
[6] Ibid., p.138
[7] Whitworth, op. cit., p.86
[8] Reid, op. cit., p.174
[9] Ibid.
[10] Whitworth, op. cit., p.89
[11] Charteris, op. cit., p.274
[12] *Private Correspondence of Chesterfield and Newcastle*, 1933, p.130
[13] Charteris, op. cit., p.274
[14] Whitworth, op. cit., p.98

[15] *Gentleman's Magazine*, May 1746

[16] Whitworth, op. cit., p.91

[17] B Willson, op. cit., p.280

[18] Albermarle Papers, East Suffolk County Records Office

[19] Waldegrave, op. cit., p.155

[20] Lewis, *Letters of Horace Walpole*, 1926, p.222

[21] Ibid. and for account of execution

[22] *Gentleman's Magazine*, August 1746

[23] *Gentleman's Magazine*, April 1747

[24] KHA, Anna, 430

[25] Ibid.

[26] In 1788 she was granted a pension by George III

Chapter Seventeen

The Princess Royal's main preoccupations were now elsewhere. French misjudgements following the failure of the Forty-five were profoundly affecting Dutch attitudes to her husband, and she was pregnant once more. William's chief adviser, William Bentinck, visited them at Soestdijk in August and wrote to his mother, who had been Anne's governess:

> she is prodigiously big. Her burden begins to be troublesome. I have seen her once or twice shifting every minute the position she sat or stood in so that one could see she was very uneasy, tho' she keeps up always her courage and spirits.[1]

The companionship offered by Bentinck and his then wife had been very important to Anne in her early times in The Hague when she was ostracised by so many of the regent families; the very notion of Friesland horrified the sophisticated Bentincks and an early letter from Anne ends 'tell your husband that I have not fallen into the Dykes, and in spite of his baleful warnings I am managing very well'.[2] But friendship did not survive the couple's divorce. Both Anne and William came to dislike him, mocking him as 'our fat friend', whose unctuous manner and never failing self-esteem irritated them, although his energy and loyalty in the service of their cause was at last beginning to bear fruit.

Anne's stoicism was not shared by Mary who, on a visit to London that autumn, complained bitterly about the strain of attending a formal reception: 'You laugh at me dear Sister, but I am so sylly that there is no bearing of me.'[3] She had been forbidden by her husband to bring her sons, aged three and eighteen months, but she stayed several weeks visiting Bath with Caroline and attending performances of *Richard III* and *Hamlet* with Amelia. She was always a favourite in England, and this was to be to her advantage when misfortunes overtook her.

On 16 November another daughter was born to the Prince and Princess of Orange, and congratulations poured in from all the rulers of Europe, aware that William would soon enter their charmed circle. She was baptised Anna Maria two weeks later, and even George and Frederick wrote affectionate letters – the latter, unusually, in German, the language of their childhood: he told Anne that he had hung a portrait of Carolina in his bedroom, and her little cousin (the future George III) was very interested in it. But just after

Christmas there was yet another blow. William wrote an incoherent letter to his mother mourning 'this special and dear baby, we hope she will find peace and that one day we shall all be reunited'.[4] Anne had broken down completely, weeping day and night. 'Her milk is still plentiful which makes things worse.'

For the rest of the winter she remained in Leeuwarden, sunk in deep depression and devoting herself to Carolina. The townspeople would see her walking the narrow streets muffled in furs against the bitter wind, with the child in leading strings or a little cart drawn by a pony.

In The Hague everyone could sense the changing national and international mood; through the 'whispering capital of Europe', all diplomatic correspondence came by flying seal which meant they could be read by representatives there before onward despatch, and the British had especial knowledge since, with several key postmasters in their pay, most of the secret reports about French attempts alternately to bully and coax the Dutch into an alliance ended up on Newcastle's desk. Domestic discontent was rising, as the ruling regents made many enemies. They could be seen as being a thin veneer – immensely strong and needing a hammer blow to split it, but once an outside agent provided that blow, it would be swiftly splintered by the swelling pressure from below.

Influential families long excluded from power were being skilfully courted by the Orangists, and the merchants of Amsterdam were incensed by French threats of an embargo on their merchant shipping; neutrality no longer seemed to be offering protection. Regent corruption had become increasingly blatant and tax collectors, raising revenue larger than England's from half England's population, took a generous share. The popular uprising needed active leadership, and Bentinck worked tirelessly to increase suspicion and hostility towards the regents and to orchestrate that 'voice of the people', without which William utterly refused to move.[5] An English envoy, the Earl of Sandwich, assured Bentinck of discreet financial support for provincial opposition, while Cumberland, still trying to assess Dutch military strength, stayed for a month over Christmas, conferring with both Sandwich and the Prince until William rushed back to Leeuwarden to comfort his wife when their daughter died.

They were together there at the beginning of April when a French army of 2,000 invaded the Dutch Republic in what it seemed to view as a friendly warning to cease diplomatic negotiations with England and Austria: the Dutch should throw in their lot with an ally who could produce such a show of strength across their borders. It was the long awaited external catalyst and at last focused Dutch minds; the States-General recognised it as the turning point, and one of the deputies rounded on the French ambassador, saying 'You're ruining us, you're making a stathouder.'[6] The western maritime province of Zeeland was the most immediately threatened by the French and crumbled first – rumours of atrocities and the sight of a squadron of warships offshore caused panic, which was directed by Orange supporters as the English money poured into eager hands.

From Zeeland the popular risings swept north and east like beacon fires. When they reached the capital, the States-General were in emergency session, threatened by hostile crowds who were ready to lynch any deputy who tried to escape. As a cry went up for the blood of traitors, the Pensionary Jacob Gilles nervously recalled the fate of his predecessor De Witt, torn to pieces by the mob in 1672, and turned to the Orangists for help. He was smuggled out of the building, crouching on the floor of a coach decorated with orange streamers under the feet of Bentinck, who beamed and acknowledged the cheering mob. Within a month William had been elected to the posts of Admiral and Captain-General and was stathouder of every one of the United Provinces. The revolution was complete when an Orange banner was hoisted on the town hall of Amsterdam, for so long the symbol of republican power, and it was to that city that William and Anne travelled first.

They travelled by land (since the parsimonious Frisians had reclaimed the yacht bestowed on the couple as a wedding present), but their procession was joyfully acclaimed by every town and village along the way, as children dressed in orange scattered spring flowers under the carriage wheels. A member of the large Jewish community of Amsterdam watched with pride as the rabbis of different national synagogues were presented to the 'slightly hunchbacked but affable and well-spoken prince'.[7] City dignitaries paid homage, while carillons pealed and trumpets blared. Porcelain merchants with warehouses along the canals had been advised to wrap their most fragile stock because of the expected noise, and far into the night the rejoicing crowds milled round the narrow streets as William, Anne and the four-year-old Carolina embarked on a glass-topped boat and toured the city. Many fell into the water, though, according to a newspapers, 'most of them' climbed out again. High on a wall in illuminated letters was written:

> De fiere Leeuw ontwaakt en brult
> De Franschman is met schrik vervuld,
> En zal zich bevend rugwaarts ijlen,
> Nu Friso pronkt met zeven pijlen.[8]

(The proud lion wakes and as he roars / the Frenchman, full of terror, cowers / Trembling now, he backward hurries / For Friso's armed with seven arrows.)

The number was significant, none of William's predecessors had held all seven provinces, and his power within each one extended beyond theirs. But to whom much is given, much is expected, and in no way at all could William be compared with past holders of his proud title. For the moment however the English were exultant – the Batavian lion referred to in the verse was now ready to stalk the field as in the days of William III, Newcastle wrote of 'all the good consequences, a perfect Union between the two Nations and a Firmness and Stability in Measures'. It was an illusion to which he would cling longer than anyone else.

Amelia, of course, rejoiced for the sister she had tried so hard in chatty letters to comfort through her bereavement: their sister, Caroline, was much better... 'though pray don't mention it to her as she will only allow of her not being worse'.[9] London's spring heatwave was terrible: 'rain would be very acceptable for one is quite blind with dust'; and 'Billy's account of his army puts us in great spirits – we shall soon be as strong as the French in Flanders'.[10]

'Billy' seems to have shared her optimism, since he chose to confront Saxe in June near the key town of Maastricht.[11] Backed by a strong Austrian contingent, he had been assured by William that the Dutch would now be a power to be reckoned with. *The Gentleman's Magazine* reported that before the battle 'the British lay on their arms all night in the open field, but as it was very wet and cold the Austrians and Dutch thought it more agreeable to pitch tents';[12] foreigners seldom got a good press in London.

From dawn, both sides exchanged an exceptionally heavy artillery barrage and the French infantry had to be 'stiffened' by sending the cavalry behind them with drawn swords. Three Dutch squadrons of horse on the left wing were then ordered to wheel right 'to make a front against the enemy', but they either misheard the order or panicked, depending whose story you believe, and turned right instead, cutting straight across a line of advancing cavalry.[13] The ensuing melee fell back on two regiments of foot, who were trampled into the ground. Cumberland, whose ADC standing beside him had just been decapitated by a cannon ball, rode immediately into the thick of things, trying to restore order, but the French had seized their chance and were already there – it was reported that the Duke had coolly severed the hand of a French dragoon whose sword was poised to strike him. He was then threatened by a French battalion of Scots and Irish who flung themselves 'like devils' on the victor of Culloden, and he was only saved by a cavalry charge hastily mustered by Ligonier. The number of casualties – 15,000 – was staggering. The French suffered most but as an English officer wrote, 'we lost more of [our] people that Day than Ever was known at any Battle before'.[14] Ligonier was captured and brought before Louis XV, himself who had watched from the sidelines. The King was deeply upset by such loss of life, and sent his compatriot back to Cumberland on parole to start the search for an honourable peace.

Recriminations flew. *The Gentleman's Magazine* had no doubt about it. 'Why did we not win a victory when we did so well? Because of the monstrous tide of Dutch cowardice.' Then they reported the casualty of 'one Dutchman who was a little bruised in his flight'.[15] The Dutch defence was robust: the oral commands issued against the thunderous cannon were unclear, and because of Cumberland's failing eyesight he had mistaken French troops for his own men. The Duke himself wrote to London, 'I am sorry to say that I am convinced every Day of the melancholy Consideration that we must actually reckon on the Dutch troops as Nothing.'[16] But Newcastle still believed in the magic of the Dutch revolution, for the secret reports from his postal spies told him of massive army augmentation. The trouble was, these referred to orders issued – few of them ever carried out in the bureaucratic chaos that passed for Dutch administration.

In the autumn of 1747, Cumberland visited his sister and brother-in-law in The Hague to discuss strategy, since Saxe was still in the field using the familiar manoeuvre of grabbing everything he could to use as a bargaining counter in the peace negotiations and threatening the barrier fortresses which historically defended the United Provinces against French aggression. The once relatively warm family relationship deteriorated sharply. Anne was at her most combative, deeply jealous of her brother's military reputation and embarrassed by Dutch shortcomings, Cumberland hardly bothered to conceal his utter exasperation, while William resorted to his usual approach to any problem – arguing laboriously, logically and at inordinate length. Sandwich wrote resignedly that 'the Prince can always find arguments for his conduct even when it is wrong',[17] and Newcastle's brother noted, 'our two young heroes [Orange and Cumberland] agree but little, our own open, frank, resolute and perhaps hasty, the other pedantic, ratiocinating and tenacious'.[18]

Anne's determination to protect her husband's interests seems to have banished all common sense, for William is unlikely to have produced the ultimatum he did without her prompting: he told Cumberland that since no alien should command Dutch troops on Dutch soil he, who had never led more than sixty men in battle, should replace the Duke as commander-in-chief of the allied army. Cumberland was so flabbergasted at such audacity (and so concerned to avoid delay) that he proposed a similar division of responsibility as that between Marlborough and Prince Eugene. George, who had served under their unique command, speedily vetoed the idea, and William gave in, assuring his brother-in-law, 'I know what subordination is.'[19]

At this point Cumberland fell ill with a severe kidney infection and was cared for in the official palace of the stathouders. It had stood empty since William III's death in 1702, deliberately left to rot by the States General who met in the same complex, and even after six months' work the damp and decay were so bad 'it is a wonder everyone does not catch their death there'.[20] Anne was supervising the restorations, and working to a deadline since she was pregnant once more. The year before, in her Danish isolation, Louisa had been the third of 'Great Britain's Daughters' to lose her first child (at the age of three); Anne had lost five, but at the beginning of March 1748 a son was born to secure the Orange succession in the male line. William wrote exultantly to Marie Louise, 'He takes the breast though he's still a little clumsy about it, but he grows in strength and weight while we watch.'[21] Anne was unusual among royal princesses for insisting on feeding her babies herself.

There was of course great rejoicing, fireworks flared every night for a week in all Dutch cities, George gave the messenger who brought him the news one hundred guineas, and even the sullen States-General voted a christening gift of 3,000 guilders a year. But within a short time rumours surfaced which persisted well into the twentieth century that the baby was not William's child. The defeated republicans revenged themselves in the only way they could – by whispers and slander. Undeniably, the birth of a healthy son to a 37-year-old woman with Anne's unhappy gynaecological history seemed too good to be true; but the argument was that William was impotent because of his disability and that Anne had indulged 'in domestic misbehaviour'.[22] This at once made nonsense of the rumours: it is *her* capacity rather than William's which could be questioned. Disregarding the false pregnancy, she conceived at least six times before her son's birth: the anti-Orange faction must either believe that she was consistently unfaithful or that she decided to celebrate their political triumph with an act of adultery. Neither scenario easily survives a reading of their lifelong private correspondence. But it would be one more burden for Anne in the years ahead.

The still convalescent Cumberland shared in the celebrations, family tensions eased temporarily when he was invited to be godfather, and he kindly spent much time with his five-year-old niece, Carolina, who had developed measles and was kept away from her mother and brother. But his enforced stay in The Hague had convinced him that peace must be made quickly: his reports on the Dutch political and military situation finally convinced Newcastle that 'we seem to have been all in a dream. It appears that they have no army at all or any which they can or will employ'.[23] Without them there was no hope of defeating Saxe's army of 100,000 men. Perceptions in London, summed up by the comment of a minister that Britain was tying itself to a corpse and calling it an ally,[24] lent impetus to the peace talks on Aix-la-Chapelle. William arrived there to find himself sidelined and treated with contempt, Newcastle referring publicly to the sacred cow of Dutch foreign policy – the string of fortresses along its southern frontier – as 'your damned Barrier', prompted by Cumberland's assessment in a letter to the English envoy at The Hague:

Will anyone say that any business can be continued with the assistance of so weak and infatuated a Government, I am clear it cannot.[25]

Anne in her letters mocked 'the fat generalissimo' [her brother] and alternated an account of the baby's teething problems with urgent advice on how to assert himself, but in vain – the terms of the Treaty, eventually signed in October 1748, marked the end of a delusion.

The Republic had managed to keep its weaknesses decently veiled for thirty years, but as William was forced to accept humiliating peace terms, its bankruptcy in every sense was starkly revealed. The Orange revolution had been based on a promised return to the greatness of the country's past, and William was discredited: he had been in power just eighteen months – long enough to be a viable scapegoat for all foreign and domestic ills.

Notes

[1] Bentinck, op. cit., CLXV
[2] W van Huffel, *Willem Bentinck van Rhoon*, 1923, p.86
[3] KHA, Anna, 430
[4] KHA, Willem IV, 170 III
[5] Rowen, op, cit., pp.161–2
[6] P Geyl, *Willem IV en Engeland*, 1924, p.213
[7] Baker-Smith, op. cit., p.103
[8] Ibid.
[9] KHA, Anna, 430
[10] Ibid.
[11] This was the Battle of Val or, as Cumberland referred to it, the affair of Laffeld, although it was actually a greater numerical confrontation than Waterloo.
[12] *Gentleman's Magazine*, June 1747
[13] Baker-Smith, op. cit., p.118
[14] *Diary of Royal Artillery Officer Wood*, RA Institute, Woolwich
[15] *Gentleman's Magazine*, June 1747
[16] J Wilkes, *A Whig in Power*, 1964, p.122
[17] Memoirs of Horatio Walpole, p.335
[18] Ibid., p.330
[19] Charteris, op. cit., p.340
[20] Bentinck, op. cit., CCLX
[21] KHA, Willem IV, 170 III
[22] Rowen, op. cit., p.213
[23] D B Horn, *Great Britain and Europe in the Eighteenth Century*, 1967, p.100
[24] The Duke of Bedford quoted in D B Horn, *The British Diplomatic Service*, 1961, p.19
[25] Record Office – Military Auxiliary Expeditions, Cumberland to Sandwich, April 1748

Chapter Eighteen

Back in London, the celebrations for the peace of Aix-la-Chapelle took six months to organise, a huge firework display being planned for Green Park. Handel's 'Music for the Royal Fireworks' was delayed when George insisted it should be scored for brass instead of the violins the composer wanted, and everything else went wrong. George, Amelia and Cumberland watched from the library window at St James's as catherine wheels refused to turn, rockets shot forwards instead of upwards setting fire to a spectator, two people were killed falling out of trees, and the delays were so long that the audience began to drift away – though they hurried back for the best part when the specially designed backdrop went up in flames. This was a 100 ft pavilion in the form of a Doric temple 'adorned with frets, gilding, lustres, artificial flowers'[1] and a bas-relief of the King, but since it was built of wood it burned well.

The mortified display designer challenged His Majesty's Comptroller of Ordnance and Fireworks to a duel and was arrested on grounds of public safety. Duels were illegal, though they still occurred. Members of Parliament being especially fond of issuing challenges on the floor of the House; Lord Shelburne once sustained a wound to the groin and as he lay on the ground, reassured his anxious supporters, 'I think Lady Shelburne will be none the worse for it.' The Master of the Horse, the Duke of Richmond, bought up the remaining fireworks cheaply, and staged a highly successful spectacular of his own a few weeks later.

The end of the war with France and the virtual end of the Jacobite threat made the season of 1749–50 the grandest since Caroline's death. At a masquerade George was so well disguised in 'an old-fashioned English dress' that somebody mistook him for a servant and handed him their cup of tea to be replenished. Cumberland was dressed in a similar way, though his by now immense corpulence made him unmistakable. Amelia refused to leave the card table all evening, and Augusta was so shocked by the appearance of one lady 'in an almost primitive state of undress' that she firmly wrapped a veil round her.[2] The festivities were observed by a certain Madame du Bocage, now feeling herself able to travel to London from Paris. She attended a concert where Handel played his own concertos during the interval, barely able to make himself heard above the chatter and clinking of glasses; and she met the (supposedly incognito) Prince of Wales at a lunch party, where he impressed her with his knowledge of French literature. Her favourite meal was breakfast when delicious toast and biscuits were served 'on the richest plate; the glittering cups containing exquisite tea'[3] and chocolate lavishly laced with cream. The latter delicacy was also a favourite of Dr Johnson's, who, when his doctor advised him to give up alcohol, would add butter as well as cream.

Madame du Bocage also observed the excitement when an earthquake shook the capital in the spring of 1750. Horace Walpole was awoken when 'I felt the bolster lift up my head and thought someone was getting from under my bed, but soon found it was a strong [shock] that lasted near half a minute with a violent vibration and great roaring'.[4] At the same time locusts had been seen in St James's Park, and opportunist clerics announced that London had been hit by the plagues of Egypt. To avoid aftershocks and divine retribution, 10,000 people fled to the country – Madame du Bocage was thoroughly scornful: 'Such would never have occasioned so much terror in Paris.'

She left England herself shortly afterwards, travelling to Holland where she contrasted the ill-paved and dirty London streets with 'the brick surfaces here, which are cleaner in all weathers than the best scoured pewter'. She was presented to the Prince and Princess of Orange, and watched with admiration as they conversed with their guests *in five languages*. After a gap of a hundred years there was now a formal Court in the capital, and foreign visitors were always warmly welcomed. Many Dutch also responded to the generous hospitality offered, but the republican opposition was stiffening dangerously and William and Anne were well aware of it.

Despite the long years of waiting, William had been unprepared for power. Since he had seldom indulged in politicking and glad-handing outside his own power base, this was limited to his three hereditary provinces of Friesland, Groningen and Gelderland. These were the poorest and most obscure of the seven, seldom impinging on the awareness, let alone the consideration, of the others. William and Anne committed the classic, if laudable, mistake of rewarding those who had remained loyal through the years of exile, and when they more or less transplanted their entire inner circle of officials and advisers to The Hague, they excluded any national figures from it. This 'Frisian cabal' was totally unversed in the art of political management required in the south, and, realising this, William confirmed in office virtually all the ruling regents who had opposed him for so long. A dangerous division thus opened up between the unaltered personal and national power bases. For the time being the republicans wore their orange cockades, licked their wounds and waited.

William had accepted the constitutional status quo but this would be threatened by the enormous groundswell of domestic discontent which had brought him to power. The collapse of the old regime had seemed, as William described it in a letter to Frederick the Great, 'astonishing and sudden',[5] but the very fact that the anti-Orange ruling elite collapsed so totally revealed the strength of opposition to it. That opposition now expected the stathouder to give it what it wanted. The House of Orange had always been supported by the landed nobility, by orthodox Calvinists and by those who believed that unity under princely rule would somehow restore the country's political fortunes and bring back its golden age, but now there were three new elements.

The first was a group of disaffected merchants who joined with members of certain regent families barred from the narrow oligarchy: wealthy and articulate, they were frustrated by the lack of recognition of their talents and the impossibility of acquiring any influence. Longing to break into the charmed circle themselves, they probably resented the endemic corruption less than the second group – those below them on the social scale, who both observed it and convinced themselves that in the good old days it did not exist. Long the butt of the pamphleteers, regent corruption had become increasingly blatant, with a small number of families holding in its gift every appointment to local and provincial office which they often sold to the highest bidder. Profits from the postal service went into private pockets, and while the tax farmers were generally assumed to remit little more than half of what they collected, their venality was actually, by the standards of the day, not particularly bad; office was bought and sold through most of Europe, if perhaps more privately. In the essentially pragmatic Dutch Republic, it had been accepted as such a fact of life that the bribes themselves were taxed and thus made profitable. The middle-class agitators had too much at stake to take to the streets themselves but the third element of opposition to the oligarchy was the *grauw* – the rabble. It was they who had been so skilfully orchestrated by Bentinck and the others to surge round the town halls, threaten violence and intimidate the regents. Their feelings were formulated in the vaguest terms: the stathouder was their friend and protector and his rule would transform their lives and right all wrongs. The powerful aspirations of all these groups had now to be taken into account, they had been used as the Orange storm-troopers and they expected a good deal of the man they had swept to power.

But the revolutionary changes they looked for could not have been further from William's mind. He viewed his achievement as the end rather than the beginning, and believed that it had righted the only wrong. There was certainly no thought in his mind of becoming 'Prince of the mob'. His awareness of physical deformity and sense of the ridiculous would in themselves have barred him from the role of demagogue, but he was, of course, entirely alienated from the popular movement by both temperament and background. He and Anne (who had little time for the minor nobility, let alone the bourgeoisie) shared the conventional contemporary view of the social hierarchy; the *grauw* complained that the Prince had done nothing for them:

'there none we see to make us free but we ourselves, the common folk';[6] but William never even thought of it nor, to be fair, had he ever promised it either. They had been misled by the euphoric rhetoric of those who had directed the revolution for him. Personal lethargy played its part, and he was always acutely aware of what he could not do, but he had neither the intelligence nor experience to understand what he could. The regents' loss of nerve had offered him an extraordinary opportunity. He had a tremendous fund of goodwill and a political clean slate; as the weeks passed he was invested with more power than any of his predecessors, for in addition to their rights and privileges which were re-enacted, his patronage in civil and military appointments was now extended well beyond theirs. He was created chief director of the East and West India Companies (previously controlled by shareholders), and the stathoudership of every province was automatically made hereditary for the Frisian line, with the important extension to include female succession, which has been relevant through the last century.

Trouble came quickly as celebrations for the birth of the heir were hijacked by riots directed against the tax collectors. Violence spread, and years of pent-up rage at their system of spying and extortion led to their houses being ransacked and families threatened. The regents were reluctant to order the militias into action on their own initiative for fear of refusal, and everyone waited for William to take the lead. He hesitated, consulted, agonised and finally fell ill with fever and delirium, whereupon Anne took over, sending troops into most of the towns with orders to use what force was necessary. It was her first taste of supreme authority. The Prince's inertia and lack of initiative during this crisis and the previous months did not pass unnoticed. It was not William's fault that he was never able to take the wider view (though it has to be said that he would not have known what to do with it if he had been) for he was always stretched to the limit by purely local problems and situations. He worked so slowly and carefully, for example, over his choice of local magistrates or the service appointments that other vital decisions were delayed and looming dangers ignored.

William Bentinck was, as ever, fully alert and took it upon himself to present the Prince with a series of memoranda, in which he explained the problems and issues to be faced. Gradually however he switched tack and began to submit them through Anne. One of them lies in the royal archives in The Hague with Anne's comments scribbled in the margin; it shows Bentinck's unctuous, long-winded and didactic style which too often detracted from his astute analysis; but most of all it shows Anne at her most obstinate and overbearing as she twisted the points back into personal attacks on Bentinck himself. When he mentioned the offence caused by William's tolerance of a corrupt official, she retorts that only old women worried about such things, she blames Bentinck's own laziness for the delays of which he complained, and when he writes of 'laying bare his heart and his conscience' to her she comments, 'continuation of sermon'.[7] Finally, in a cruel and unfair attack she accuses him of self-centredness; he was simply bitter, she insists, because he expected some reward for his service.

He bore no grudge but soldiered on, his notes revealing many difficult interviews through the summer of 1748 in which she constantly kept him waiting, disputed every point and on one occasion walked out while he was speaking and did not return. There was of course more to Anne's behaviour than simply her personal irritation with his manner and her resentment of him as prophet of doom; she knew things were going badly wrong, and although she mistrusted Bentinck's activism she knew that her husband's passivity and indecision were allowing control to slip away. However, fiercely protective as she was, she viewed any suggestions for improvement as an attempt to undermine him, and she could never control her exasperation. 'I left her presence,' Bentinck recorded once, 'quite bewildered by her extraordinary agitation and having said only a quarter of what I planned.'[8] He had very little imagination or understanding of the strains she was under as she watched her beloved husband struggle and fail; on one occasion when Bentinck visited them privately, William sat slumped in a chair as if he slept, although his eyes were open and he never stirred as Carolina romped about the room; the baby cried and Anne desperately tried to keep the conversation going.

As they all knew, Amsterdam was the key, for if William allowed its challenges to his authority to succeed his prestige in the country would be irretrievably lost. The city's implacable opposition to the House of Orange had been a fact of life for a hundred years and the balance of power there was reverting inexorably to its former character, but there was now a further complexity as radical groups, calling themselves Orangist, pressed on the streets for a form of democracy. There is definite proof that Anne herself had a connection with these groups since their leaders, a Rotterdam pastry cook and an Amsterdam porcelain merchant, were received secretly by her at Huis ten Bosch; but they had taken on a dangerous and violent life of their own and the regents were forced much against their will to look for help. Very early one morning, Bentinck brought a regent delegation to William's bedside: only his presence in Amsterdam could prevent a massacre.

He left The Hague on 1 September – his birthday – and wrote to Anne that night to apologise for some kind of quarrel. 'My dear Annin, I am sorry for my stupidity when I left, I don't know what possessed me and I feel very ashamed.' Whatever the personal problem, he must have been affected by trepidation at the task ahead, for he was facing the most intractable of situations with the eyes of the whole country on him. He started off well when in a theatrical gesture he dismissed his personal guards at the city gate, saying he had no need of them while under the protection of the good burghers of Amsterdam. That night he dined with the regents at the town hall; it was a tense occasion, the meal consisted of badly cooked chickens and pigeons, few people spoke and the *burgemeester* ate nothing and looked 'pale as death', having been warned by the most radical opposition group that they planned to chop him to bits.[9]

For three days William was petitioned and harangued by the various factions as they quarrelled and postured around him. He had no time even to write his daily letter to his wife, though one of the household assured her somewhat optimistically that 'despite all his worrying occupations His Royal Highness maintains his customary gaiety'.[10] Anne begged to join him, complaining 'it is so horrible without you'; but his advisers were concerned to keep her away from so delicate a situation. Wringing his hands and often in tears, William yielded as always to pressure and dismissed seventeen out of the thirty-six regents as he tried to find 'a happy medium': only a man of such dogged goodwill could have imagined such a thing were possible. Some of the radicals actually burst into his bedroom at three in the morning to lecture him about his reliance upon unworthy men. It is tempting to imagine their fate at the hands of some of William's forbears, but this Prince of Orange told them, 'My life is in God's hands and I will await what happens,'[11] advising them to do the same.

He left the city quiet, which was something of an achievement in itself, but his new appointments were, as they could not fail to be, carbon copies of those which had gone before, for they were the only people with sufficient experience. He would receive little loyalty from them, as they continued to defend their personal and class interests, and the popular opposition would not wait on God for long.

William's attempts at reform and conciliation were doomed to failure partly because he was always ready to believe that resistance to them came from men of principle and integrity, although in reality that resistance was rooted in republican feeling and the determination to retain personal privilege. Amsterdam merchants were the majority shareholders of the East India Company, whose prevailing attitude seemed to be that there were no Ten Commandments south of the Equator, and when the Prince, as the new Director, began to investigate the claims of venality and cruelty, he was stopped in his tracks by their threats that business could not be carried on any other way. He produced a scheme for economic reform involving a poll tax and the ending of exclusive family rights to office nomination; but the opposition to a switch to direct taxation meant that the poll tax met its usual fate, and the regents simply defied his decree and continued as before. Every time William gave in, a little more of his authority drained away.

The peace of Aix-la-Chapelle brought new problems as urban discontent was fuelled by the disbandment of thousands of soldiers without payment of arrears. These were the troops hastily commissioned by the Republic through the 1740s when the French invasion threatened and England called in the treaty obligations; administration had been so chaotic that the numbers of troops were not known – 'not that their members exceed all Arithmetick, but because they really don't know where they are, who they are or whether they have any at all,' as a despairing observer put it. Often recruited from the dispossessed and the unemployed, badly led, under-trained and always poorly equipped, these men had brought shame on the country through every campaign, and their presence on the streets could be explosive. The Dutch army had once been admired throughout Europe, and its decline was, as Bentinck lamented, 'the effect of a Peace of twenty-eight years, such a want of Spirit... that it's like a body without a soul'.[12] The end of the wars against Louis XIV had left the country exhausted, and ever since the government had kept things on the barest maintenance level, as the military ethos was smothered and capital investment in either army or navy denied by the lobby for the other. The longer the Republic could avert trouble by diplomatic means, the more difficult and expensive a policy reversal had become.

Fifty years on from its Golden Age, the United Provinces were not far short of bankruptcy. The level of taxation accepted by the Dutch had always astonished observers. In the previous century the English representative to The Hague had commented on 'the readyness this people doe consent to extraordinary taxes when their ordinary ones are so great',[13] and by 1696, after years of war, the tiny country was somehow raising a revenue larger than England's. The 1713 Peace of Utrecht had brought little relief, only the crippling debts imposed by a badly negotiated treaty, and although taxation had steadily risen again to wartime levels, 'Money is now more scarce [there] than ever' with the soldiers' pay as the lowest priority.[14]

In England, too, the army had to be demobilised, although for political rather than financial reasons. Cumberland's view of the Aix peace was that it marked no more than an interlude, representing European exhaustion rather than European unity; but he had to recognise that a standing army would not be tolerated in the country, and 40,000 men were disbanded. Cumberland's concern for the welfare of those he termed his 'Flanderkins' brought him into conflict with the government, which refused any re-establishment measures. He therefore organised a privately funded scheme, to which he contributed generously himself, to send some of them to the American colonies for a new life. He also found employment for many of them nearer home. As Ranger of Windsor Great Park, he planned to excavate the largest artificial lake in Europe

– Virginia Water. The project continued for years as waterfalls and grottoes were constructed, vistas created and hundreds of trees planted; the settlement in Nova Scotia was ordered to 'send him the seeds of all the trees we have not here, particularly evergreens'.[15]

Amelia, now happily established in her own house in Cavendish Square which she had decorated with her usual flamboyance, took a great interest in her brother's work. When George made her Ranger of Richmond Park, she too set about draining and landscaping, and years later when she managed to afford her own country house at Gunnersbury, she built a shell-lined grotto decorated with coloured glass and statues, containing a cold plunge-pool for the water parties she enjoyed. Her card parties were well-known for the high stakes she insisted upon, the reek of the snuff she took as she played, and the high quality of the food offered. Horace Walpole, a frequent visitor, often found the length of the meals tedious and he describes her as 'the oddest or at least one of the oddest that ever was known'. Grafton was still her constant companion and they hunted regularly; Amelia's stable was her pride and she accepted enthusiastically the gift of a fine bay gelding after carefully explaining to its owner that she was unable to afford its purchase price of sixty guineas.

The family gathered together amicably enough on formal occasions, but George never missed an opportunity to frustrate his heir. He wrote to Cambridge University, which had wanted Frederick to be its Chancellor:

'tho His Majesty does by no means intend to interfere in their election, yet he is persuaded from the regard and affection which he has always show'd for the University, and from their duty to him, that they will not chuse any one of his family without his approbation.[16]

Such an attitude was in marked contrast to Frederick's devotion to all his children: he agonises over the frail health of Elizabeth and Louisa, commends the twelve-year-old Augusta's letters, so particularly 'full of good sentiments', teases Edward with, 'I did not care to shew myself at the Drawing Room... my face is a little like Edward's usual face, which in these times is not a good Drawing Room face';[17] and he is forever encouraging and advising his heir:

God has given you so high a Mark to govern one day so many Nations and if you do not please them, they won't please you in return. Read this carefully and keep it as it comes from a Father who (what is not usual) is your best friend.[18]

He drew up an instruction list for the young George 'according to the ideas of my grandfather and best friend George I', harking back to his lonely youth when the King's visits to Hanover were his only family connection. A strange postscript reads: 'I shall have no regret never to have worn the crown if you do but fill it worthily.'[19] Whether this was rhetoric or premonition, the Prince of Wales was dead within months at the age of forty-three.

He had attended the House of Lords (still the only contribution to government allowed him) and returned to his London home of Carlton House

> very hot, where he unrobed, put on a light unaired frock and waistcoat, went to Kew, walked in a bitter day, came home tired, and lay down for three hours upon a couch in a very cold room that opens into the garden. Lord Egmont told him how dangerous it was, but the Prince did not mind him.[20]

Pleurisy was diagnosed, but after being bled he seemed better, and his dancing master was playing the violin one evening to amuse him when he suddenly cried out and died, as the frantic Augusta snatched up a candle and rushed to his side. She fulfilled his trust in her by burning all his political papers and plans for government before announcing the death. The King received the news bravely, breaking off a card game to remark, 'But they told me he was better.'[21]

Frederick thus – undeservedly – became a mere footnote of history, as his contemporaries mostly consigned him to oblivion, and the genealogical elision has led later historians constantly to confuse his family with other generations. A London preacher produced an extraordinary 'tribute': 'His Royal Highness had no great parts but he had great virtues, indeed they degenerated into vices; he was very generous but I know his generosity has ruined a great many people, and then his condescension was such that he kept very bad company.'[22] Only Tobias Smollett summed up the worth of this Prince of Wales, declaring that his death afflicted

> all who wished well of their country [since he was] possessed of every amiable quality which could engage the affection of the people – a tender and obliging husband, a fond parent, a kind master, liberal, generous, candid and humane… well disposed to assert the rights of mankind in general and warmly attached to the interest of Great Britain.

Notes

[1] *Gentleman's Magazine*, April 1749

[2] This was Elizabeth Chudleigh, a beautiful adventuress who, by dubious means, became a maid of honour to the Princess. Horace Walpole, *Letters*, p.153

[3] Madame A-M du Bocage, *Letters Concerning England and Holland*, 1770

[4] Quoted by L Picard, *Dr Johnson's London*, 2000, p.269

[5] *Archives de Maison Oranje Nassau*, IV I VIII, henceforth AMON. These are manuscripts from the Koninlijk Huisarchief dealing mostly with political matters. Such published material is distinct from the often rather vague source references under the KHA headings.

6 'Invallende gedagtenbij het overdenken der tegenwoordige tijds omstandigheden', a pamphlet published in Groningen in 1748

7 AMON IV I CVII

8 Ibid., IV I CXLI

9 Ibid., IV I CXII–CXXXIII

10 KHA, Anna, 430

11 Rowen, op. cit. p.178

12 Bentinck, op. cit., I XVI

13 Sir George Downing, English Ambassador to The Hague in 1659. Baker-Smith, op. cit., p.152

14 *Gentleman's Magazine*, May 1753

15 Dorset County Record Office D86/X4

16 Harris, *Life of Hardwicke*, 1847, p.529

17 There was something strange about 'Edward's face'. He is described as 'a very plain boy with loose eyes' and, rather enigmatically, as 'a sayer of things'. Marples, op. cit., p.178

18 Walters, *Griffin*, p.208

19 De-la-Noy, op. cit., p.214

20 Walters, *Griffin*, p.214

21 Davies, op. cit., p.285

22 Marples, op. cit., p.117

Chapter Nineteen

Since her relationship with Frederick had mellowed with time and absence, Anne received the news with the sense of shock and disbelief that the death of a sibling always evokes, but she had far more desperate worries – her husband, too, was dying. The previous year had been a happier one: during the fiercely hot summer of 1750 William had been able to escape to Het Loo, and despite frequent attacks of colic had been able to hunt for the first time for three years; though the fact that he only caught one hare reflects the poor condition of the hunting runs on which his predecessors had lavished so much care. Anne also had a rare treat that autumn, when it is probable that Handel visited her at Het Loo. She was having an organ built for the chapel there and must have seized the opportunity of the best advice available, since Handel gave a public concert in the Great Church of Deventer a few miles away in the presence of the Prince and Princess of Orange. Details of the music played are not given; presumably it was a more decorous occasion than a concert in their honour in The Hague, when the newspapers advertised that the special attraction of the evening after the music would be a competition to climb a greasy pole.

But the Prince was failing visibly through the spring of 1751. The curvature of his spine had so increased over the years that the bone structure was pressing on lungs and heart. The fevers, stomach problems and searing headaches from which he had suffered all his life were now practically continuous. On a journey to Middelburg in May he wrote to Anne that the pain was so bad that he had developed a facial twitch; typically, he joked that this made him look like a monkey and – also typically – he spent three weeks there wrestling with the problem of a single official appointment. His letters to his wife were as tender as ever, 'Hug the children for me, I shall have difficulty finding something pretty for them here, for you I would like to give something better but it will be myself and above all my heart.'[1]

Bentinck travelled to London in June, using his friendship with Newcastle to study the regency arrangements for the future George III, who was only twelve years old. The question had caused a prolonged struggle in Parliament. Cumberland might have seemed the obvious choice, but his reputation had not yet recovered even five years after Culloden, and there were doubts the country would accept him. One of his friends strode out of the chamber in fury when William Pitt suggested that Cumberland's loyalty to Augusta and his nephew would be lacking. So much public argument about what would happen after his death probably riled the King too, and he complained bitterly that his son's authority and experience were being passed over: 'The English are so changeable, I don't know why they dislike him. It is brought about by the Scotch, the Jacobites and the English that do not love discipline.'[2]

This last category was a reference to Cumberland's unpopularity within the army itself. He was adored by the rank and file but his army reforms antagonised many officers, as he targeted the purchase system whereby advancement relied on money rather than merit, and he carried out the revolutionary step of extending the tough army punishment code to include the officer class. As he wrote to a friend, 'till you make an example of the officers you will never make a Regiment.'[3] They had been accustomed to come and go as they pleased but now 'absent without leave' penalties were to apply to them, and their protection from civil prosecution was limited to actions 'in execution of their [military] office'.[4] The feeling against the Duke in the country was, or was perceived to be, so strong that the Princess Dowager Augusta would become Regent, although in conjunction with a council headed by Cumberland. In the event, of course, the King was to live for another nine years until his grandson was well past his majority; but regency in The Hague was certain, since the heir was only three, and Bentinck's visit was timely.

In view of his son's youth, and the state of his own health, William had already appointed a de facto military commander for what remained of the Dutch army, realising that such a figure would ensure continuity and much needed support for the House of Orange. William had surveyed the European military scene and had settled on General James Keith, a former Jacobite who had fought at Sheriffmuir in 1715 and had since served (as so many Scots did) in various European armies. He had once led a Russian force against the Turks, and when the Sultan's envoy came to discuss terms, Keith had been shaken to hear a broad Scots accent from beneath the turban and through the beard – the man turned out to have been the bell-ringer in the General's home village in Kincardineshire.[5] But Keith was snapped up by Frederick the Great, and the second choice was Duke Louis of Brunswick-Wolfenbüttel, who had been a field marshal in the Austrian army since 1740. His disadvantage was that he was recommended by Cumberland, which almost damned him outright in Anne's eyes, but his family connections were much more to her taste than Keith's. She set great store by birth, and Brunswick was Maria Theresa's nephew and Frederick the Great's brother-in-law. More importantly, he was a man of tact, sympathy and understanding.

Brunswick had already been in his place for six months, noting with some dismay the administrative chaos, but William absolutely refused to delegate any of his rapidly dwindling civil or political authority. When one of his oldest friends ventured the complaint of ambassadors that everything was in confusion, William simply shrugged hopelessly and replied, 'I know.'[6] A member of the States-General, Gijsbert van Hardenbroek, wrote in his diary of the 'dreadful triviality' of the stathouder, he had no financial sense and was simply unfit for the great responsibilities he held – such criticism from the heart of government had grave implications for the future of his family.

As his doctors desperately advised him to rest and ordered a cure at the spa of Aix-la-Chapelle, the Prince decided on one last effort at major reform. He appeared before the States-General at the end of August to present a proposal to make Amsterdam a free port. Nothing, he said, caused him so much anxiety as to hear the daily complaints of the decay of Dutch trade. Other countries were fast developing their own systems and no longer required a go-between; no longer, in Defoe's words, were the Dutch 'the Factors and Brokers of Europe'.[7] In Amsterdam, formerly the entrepôt of the world, the great warehouses along the canals where goods had been received and stored were falling into disrepair. William's proposal was a radical one – abolition of the duty charged on import and re-export of goods – and was designed to reverse the trend which was transforming the country from 'an active controlling force in world trade to a passive storehouse'.[8] The merchants would warm to a plan to help them, but like all his efforts it would attract massive opposition too: excise duty had long been the bedrock of the national economy, and lack of protection for local manufactures, such as textiles or pottery, would arouse the powerful industrial lobby within the States-General. As he prepared for his departure to Aix, William had few illusions about the likely fate of his 'darling project', as the English newspapers ironically termed it; but the fact that it was being studied meant that Anne, instead of accompanying him, had to stay behind to coordinate the discussions.

He set out on his journey south on his fiftieth birthday, and endured three days in a jolting coach from five in the morning to nine at night; the only bright spot was the hospitality offered by a nobleman who provided a finely furnished bedroom and a supper of 'most excellent grayling and trout'.[9] The spa doctors examined him, and he wrote to Anne that the consultation was worthy of Molière: 'You would have laughed, but I am very bored by all their preaching and prescriptions, I must even have the water in my wine, at least the taste is less bad than the smell.' He obediently drank ten glasses a day and took the baths for which the town was famous:

> It was at the beginning so cold that I shook all over but then they added a little warm water about blood-heat and I stayed there for a good half-hour. Then I was rubbed down... I would not have believed a single bath could make me so exhausted.

> Your Pip, faithful unto death.[10]

Anne was obviously enjoying being in charge, and her letters were more brisk and businesslike than usual. Reactions to William's trade reform were being collected from the commercial houses and she assured him, 'they are singing your praises in the Bourse at Amsterdam'.[11] This was of course as unlikely a scenario as William's insistence that he was getting better.

Then one day they told him, 'there is no letter here from the Princess Royal'... 'I could not believe it, still in my night clothes I went through all the letters and packages and had the mortification of finding they were right.'[12] Anne was trying to conceal the fact that Carolina had fallen ill with a very high fever, but once William knew, he collapsed himself; the child quickly recovered but her father did not; for the first time he admits to deep depression and lists his symptoms with none of the usual leavening of humour – severe head pain, swelling legs, failing eyesight, blue lips and *'entre nous'* diarrhoea, which only eased when he could sip a little hot chocolate. But he could still take comfort in his wife:

> Farewell dear heart, Pearl among women, my joy whom I love more every day. As God is my witness you are my life's good fortune. Know that I am your most faithful, most tender and best of friends, Pepin.[13]

Anne responds with good news of Carolina, who has been presented with magnificent flowers by the Austrian Ambassador. She mentions 'a dreadful storm... but I have been singing in her room. I find as always a great void in your absence'. She longs for his letters, but adds in a catty aside, 'those of Madam your mother are not very brilliant.'[14]

After four weeks the doctors somehow managed to convince themselves that the Prince was greatly improved. He ordered a coat to be embroidered in Aix in the French style, sent a present to Anne of the town's special trout pâté, and told her he was coming home. The weather was still appalling. Anne had had to cancel several official receptions at Huis ten Bosch because falling trees made the woodland roads too dangerous, and she urged William to stay on. But he had had enough and must have known his time was short. As a last defiant gesture he summoned Brunswick to meet him at Maastricht and spent six hours in the saddle through the height of a storm as they inspected the town's fortifications. Brunswick never forgot it; at the time he was only aware of his own discomfort and the courage of the man riding beside him, but afterwards he recognised it as William's way of emphasising to his military successor the strategic significance of the town as 'key to the Republic'.[15] Maastricht was the most easterly of the fortress towns known as the Barrier which had protected the Dutch from French aggression since the time of William III. They were the cornerstone of Dutch foreign policy, and William's last task was to convince the Austrian Brunswick of their importance and, incidentally, to show him the disrepair into which they had fallen, in the hope that his influence with Maria Theresa could conjure up the subsidies which alone made them viable.

He arrived back at Huis ten Bosch and collapsed into bed. After a week's rest he wrote to his mother, promising to visit her in Leeuwarden in the spring, declaring 'my cold is much better and I am sleeping well so I have much to thank God for';[16] but this last letter must have warned Marie Louise that his true condition belied the brave words. Always previously firm and legible, his handwriting was now a pathetic scrawl. A further strain was standing for several hours while a French artist made preliminary sketches for an oil painting commissioned by the States-General. It had to be completed from memory – on Sunday 18 October he insisted on attending church, but as he entered Anne's chapel, he complained of the heat, became drowsy and suffered a massive stroke. The doctors bled him twice and the fever increased. He lay unconscious for three days and then broke into a sweat and a delirium which was hailed as a hopeful sign. His pulse strengthened, he became tranquil and recognised his wife, although he could not speak, and died at two o'clock in the morning of 22 October with Anne kneeling beside him.

In William IV the hereditary principle had failed: that quality of leadership which was 'the task and test of the stathoudership'[17] and was possessed in full measure by every Prince of Orange before him had been lost. He was irresolute by nature and passive by inclination, ever shrinking from the challenge of economic reorientation and institutional reform. 'Goodwill to all men' is a praiseworthy code to live by, but not one which carries much weight in politics. He was totally irrelevant on the European stage, but even Dutch historians have been hard on him; one of them writes disapprovingly that 'his timorous mind was suspicious of popular movements';[18] few eighteenth-century rulers would have been anything but appalled at the very idea of using a popular movement to their advantage.

The other argument, put forward with hindsight, is that he should have swept away the provincialism which by now choked the Dutch system and imposed centralised government. But a 200-year-old constitution cannot be swept away so easily, especially when defended by historic attitudes and strong structures; the achievement of a centralised Dutch state would take another sixty-five years (with the exile of William's son as part of the process). To say that he could have created it in 1750 is to say he should have thought as a nineteenth-century man, William was, as a more perceptive Dutch historian has put it, 'a child of his time and milieu'[19] – a very ordinary man whose ineffectuality was a reflection of his country's decline into the second-rate.

The year 1751 was to bring yet another death. Louisa had been Queen of

Denmark since 1746, and she and her husband had been popular as he had presided over an important programme of agrarian reform and modernisation of farming methods. She meanwhile devoted herself to her children, insisting on teaching them herself, and always in the Danish language. After the death of their elder son, two daughters had brought consternation, since women could not succeed; in 1749, to great rejoicing, another son was born but he was already, at two years old, showing worrying signs of the insanity which would ultimately bar him from the throne. Frederick, for all his faults or perhaps because of them, was utterly devastated when Louisa died at the age of twenty-seven after an operation for intestinal rupture went badly wrong. The English ambassador, trying to deliver George's letter of condolence three weeks later, found the King unable to speak for his tears.

George's grief for his youngest daughter, at least, was genuine. According to Horace Walpole he spoke in characteristic style of this

> fatal year for my family. I lost my eldest son, but I am glad of it. Then the Prince of Orange died and left everything in confusion. Now the Queen of Denmark has gone. I know I did not love my children when they were young; I hated to have them running into my room but now I love them as well as most fathers.[20]

He had observed the proprieties on his son's death, visiting Augusta (who was pregnant with her ninth child) and weeping as he told his grandchildren to be 'obedient to their mother and deserve the fortune to which they were born'. He had especial words for his new heir and 'bid him to be brave and honest and mind his mother who was the best of women'.[21] Frederick's posthumous daughter – Caroline Matilda – born in July, also became Queen of Denmark, where her blatant affair with the court physician led to divorce and banishment like Sophia Dorothea eighty years before.

Cumberland had accepted the regency arrangements with relatively good grace: 'I am neither in luck nor in fashion just now, the time may come; if not I make myself happy as I am.'[22] He presented his sister-in-law with the first French-style carpet from a Paddington workshop that he had helped to establish. His pursuit of happiness extended to breeding and training race-horses, and he now put his administrative skills to good use as he tackled corruption in the racing world. He and Amelia gambled heavily on horses, but the more ordinary racegoers needed protection, and the Duke was influential in the setting up of the Jockey Club to regulate and supervise the sport. His purple colours remain the royal ones to this day, and he authorised such punishments as a £200 fine and forfeiture of the horse for running below the declared weights.

Notes

[1] KHA, Willem IV, 171

[2] Quoted by Whitworth, op. cit., p.149

[3] Ibid., p.137

[4] 'Articles of War', a draft paper submitted to Parliament in 1749

[5] Baker-Smith, op. cit., p.124

[6] F Krämer [ed.], *Gedenkschriften van Gijsbert Jan van Hardenbroek*, 1901, p.47

[7] D Defoe, op. cit., p.291

[8] J Israel, *Dutch Primacy in World Trade*, 1989, p.397

[9] KHA, Willem IV, 171

[10] Ibid.

[11] KHA, Anna, 430

[12] KHA, Willem IV, 171

[13] Ibid.

[14] KHA, Anna, 430

[15] Baker-Smith, op. cit., p.133

[16] KHA, Willem IV, 170 III

[17] H Rowen, op. cit., p.231

[18] A Barnouw, *The Pageant of Netherlands History*, 1952, p.284

[19] G J Schutte, op. cit., p.200

[20] H Walpole, *Memoirs*, pp.227–8

[21] J Bullion in *Queenship in Britain*, p.226

[22] Royal Archive Cumberland Papers 57/200

Chapter Twenty

For most dowagers there is time to mourn as power moves to the next generation, but Anne's feelings of desolation and her responsibilities as the mother of two young children who adored their father had to take second place to the instant demands of government. She went directly from the deathbed to sign the letters of notification, and measures to ensure calm and facilitate acceptance of the regency arrangements were well in hand before the startled town woke to the news. The supporters of the House of Orange had been skilful in their preparations for this moment; before dawn William's body had been taken in secret along the woodland roads to The Hague, where the embalming took place and a public lying-in-state announced. William's enemies failed to seize their chance and, shrewdly manipulated by members of the Household, the States-General were hustled into proclaiming Anne as '*Gouvernante en Vooghdesse*' – Governor and Guardian.

The Dutch word *vooghdesse* means more than just the English 'guardian', since it implies personal care: this role Anne would obviously fill, but of far greater significance was the word *gouvernante* – the female form of *gouverneur* – a word only ever applied to the Stathouder himself. This was its first use. William III's mother, Mary (though also Princess Royal of England, daughter of Charles I) was guardian only, and although she had fought for the regency her sullen and ambivalent attitude to the Dutch counted against her. Anne's whole-hearted identification with her adopted country was recognised and thus gave her, theoretically, a powerful and unique position for an English princess: she could be seen as a ruler in her own right rather than simply representing her son. This might have been exploited by an experienced politician, but Anne's political competence – though far greater than her husband's – was to be unequal to the task.

For the moment, however, public sympathy and vigorous action by Bentinck and others ensured acceptance of the novel situation: the States-General accepting the stathoudership was now an integral part of government, and even if it was in the hands of a child, it could no longer be left vacant as in 1650 and 1702. Van Hardenbroek cruelly noted in his diary, 'there was no consternation in the world',[1] but there were some outside his hard world and beyond the family who did grieve. William's warmth and patent sincerity had touched people over the years, and, anyway, there is nothing like a royal funeral to make people forget the realities of a royal life, for in the United Provinces, unlike England at that time, the ceremony was one of great pomp and circumstance. It was the first funeral of a Prince of Orange to be paid for out of voted public funds and the scene attracted enormous crowds, the owners of houses overlooking the route being able to charge 800 guilders for the hire of a room.

William's body lay in state for over three months in the *lyk zaal* – the corpse room – in the Binnenhof, the government complex at The Hague. Although his post-mortem, details of which were published as was the custom in the newspapers, had revealed that his twisted backbone had so narrowed the gap between collarbone and breastbone that the jugular vein was all but severed, the print of the Prince's lying in state still conceals the disability. It shows the small figure clothed in a simple robe of silver silk on the black velvet bier, guarded by grim sculptures of crowned and grinning skulls, and at the foot of the bier was displayed a helm with orange plumes and his Garter star.

At the beginning of February a solemn procession conveyed the gilded leaden coffin to the Nieuwe Kerk at Delft for burial beside the tiny coffin of the firstborn daughter. One hundred Swiss Guards, with reversed halberds, marched with members of the Household in knee-length black coats and flat hats from which long black streamers fell to the ground. All the military trappings were there for this most peaceable of men: the helm, sword and coat of mail were carried by army officers and a riderless warhorse caused problems as it cavorted and plunged behind the hearse. It was bitterly cold, and the only sound above the shuffling feet came from the steady rhythm of two drums.

Back at the Binnenhof, Anne heard the gun salute which marked the moment of burial. She wrote to Marie Louise as 'the mother of that most worthy of men and tenderest of husbands', wishing she could join 'my dear prince';[2] it took William's death to draw the two women closer together, as memories became stronger than rivalries, and for the rest of Anne's life they exchanged letters every month or so, while Anne saw to it that the children wrote also, endorsing a letter from the five-year-old William that it was written 'without help from anyone'.[3]

But with the children's other surviving grandparent there could be no such improvement, as the always barometric relationship between Anne and her father assumed direct political significance, and English spirits rose at the prospect of a more malleable ally. George's first letter after William's death seemed to offer a new beginning:

> Never doubt my dear daughter the very sincere share I have in your great affliction. But great though it is I hope that the situation of your family, the public good and your own interest will enable you to overcome it... and be careful for your health which interests me very particularly. Holderness who will bring you this letter will give you all the assurances of my love and the efforts I shall make for you.

Love me always, my dear Anne, and be sure you will always find in me a father who will cherish you tenderly.[4]

But after years of being rebuffed and ignored Anne, would not be so easily won; and she received the Earl of Holderness very coldly although they had previously been on friendly terms since he shared her passion for opera. His report on the meeting spurred the King into further action a week later: 'I can assure you that I regard your interests as my own and I am always ready to help you and show you the tenderness I have always had for you and your family.'[5] In the midst of her grief, Anne must have been wryly amused at that. Even if she had been close to her father she was far too intelligent to allow him the slightest influence. She had suffered many taunts of *'Engelsche vrouw'* over the years, and to seem to acquiesce now to English demands or even English advice would be a terrible mistake. After nearly twenty years in the country she had both experience and confidence, and as the first sharp shock of bereavement faded she faced her new life with energy and some degree of optimism.

However, with Europe in a state of comparative calm, domestic problems were her main concern. In the last six months of his life William had made an effort of centralisation by setting up an informal cabinet without executive power which was known as the Conference, consisting of the Stathouder and various officials. Anne now took her husband's place, joining Brunswick, Bentinck, Pieter Steyn the Pensionary, and Johannes Hop the Treasurer. The latter was perhaps not the ideal committee man: emotional and hot-tempered, he quarrelled with most of his colleagues and, to make things worse, he was highly indiscreet. Since one of his cousins was a deputy of Amsterdam and another had been Dutch ambassador to England since 1723, this latter charac-teristic was especially serious – even the Dutch equivalent of the *Dictionary of National Biography* says that Ambassador Hop did nothing of importance during his thirty years' service, but his cousin's information gave him plenty to gossip about in London.

The Conference could be seen as a genuinely representative body, but no attempt was made, now or later, to incorporate it into the constitutional machinery of government, and without executive power all its decisions had to be placed before the States General and the provincial assemblies, with appropriate Conference members lobbying for its acceptance, Steyn in the States of Holland, Bentinck in the College of Nobles, Hop if the matter was financial and Brunswick if it was military. The system worked only if every member was in full agreement. Anyone by not pulling his weight could cause endless delay, and personal relationships were thus vitally important. These had been William's strength but were his widow's weakness, for she too often allowed personal feelings and grudges to blind her to political realities.

The key triumvirate of Steyn, Bentinck and Anne were always at odds with each other. She could not overcome her irritation and resentment of Bentinck, and since he continued to send helpful memoranda to her pointing out her faults this was unlikely to change; but something might have been salvaged if she had been able to work with Steyn. However, she was to prove arrogant and impatient in her dealings with him also. He was an honest moderate, though always watching his back, too careful of his own position to make common cause with Orange. Also, he had his own resentments, since Anne had ruthlessly used him while William lived, as a scapegoat for all their problems. Another difficulty was language, since Steyn spoke no French and Anne's Dutch was still, surprisingly, far from fluent. To make things worse, Anne would not always work within the Conference anyway. She relied heavily on the old Frisian cabal who had come south in 1747 – men who were profoundly mistrusted in the country, and often rightly so.

Jan de Back had been William's secretary in Leeuwarden, a pompous and self-opinionated man who had made himself unpopular even there. He loathed Steyn and, above all, Bentinck (the two had actually come to blows over William's corpse when de Back exceeded his authority), while he tried to dictate military strategy to Brunswick without the latter's expertise. He was later to be revealed as a traitor 'working against [her] and weakening the authority of Stathoudership of which he is a minister'.[6] A bundle of letters between him and the French Ambassador were shown to Anne, and to avoid public scandal, she gradually and skilfully detached him from the loop; for two years she managed to keep him unaware, until she abruptly dismissed him.

Douwe Sirtema van Grovestins had been master of the household since Anne's marriage and had, himself, married one of her ladies-in-waiting; but his blatant corruption had become a by-word, though his name has a sinister sound in Holland to this day for very different reasons. It is always difficult to date a rumour, but certainly by William's death anti-Orange circles, which had always hinted at the young Prince's illegitimacy, were naming Grovestins as the true father. In 1782 at a time of Orange crisis a pamphlet specifically asserted William V's illegitimacy, and well into the twentieth century opponents of the monarchy were repeating the story, asserting Anne's infidelities during her marriage, and quoting contemporary comment on the physical likeness of the supposed father and son. Further proof of the liaison was seen in the fact that Grovestins would spend long hours alone with the Princess, and that during a casual dinner conversation in 1756 when he was asked what was his first thought in the morning, he replied 'my wife and children' and looked hard at Anne.

Such 'proof' is unlikely to rock the House of Orange today, but the issue is still a sensitive one. An accusation of illegitimacy is the approved weapon for anti-monarchists, and such a rumour had even briefly surfaced after William's own birth, although Marie Louise's popularity swiftly silenced it.[7] Popularity, or the lack of it, is the key; unusually persistent though it is, the story seems little more than a vicious extension of the canards Anne had always endured, flourishing because of antagonism to a foreign widow and surfacing later because of disappointment in her son. As far as physical characteristics are concerned, William V may or may not have resembled Grovestins, but portraits reveal him looking quite depressingly like William IV.

Anne's obstinate defence of Grovestins in face of his proven corruption – her attitude seems to have been one of resigned amusement – is far more characteristic of her fierce loyalty to those who had shared the Leeuwarden exile than of any emotional attachment, but it was the most telling example of that lack of political sense which was to undermine all her efforts. She inherited little from her husband: his mistaken policies and ineffectual methods had already forfeited most of the popularity which had swept him to power, and it is clear that to a large degree she had to reap what he had sown. But this question of the advisers she chose was a crucial one; even twenty years was not long enough for a foreigner to master those intricacies of patronage which were the source of power. Familiarity with the way things were done in Friesland was no help and could even be a handicap in understanding the political scene elsewhere. The double or triple list of nominations to office – burgemeesters, magistrates, etc. – which the States passed to the stathouder, contained many traps. Anne could not be expected to break their codes, but she should have turned to people who could; her inability to accept advice outside the small circle of people she liked and trusted, and her flawed judgement in choosing those few, resulted in a steady erosion of the power she had been given.

As early as February 1752 the city of Amsterdam defied her and she lost control over the choice of burgemeester there. Stung by this, she tried to seize the initiative by actually withdrawing the commissions of three magistrates in Utrecht: Anne always got a bad press in England, but The Gentleman's Magazine was probably right when it smugly pointed out that these three 'are looked on as patriots and are men of much reputation', so that the matter has 'given a handle for much murmurings and is represented as contrary to the rights and privileges of the States of the province'.[8]

The town of Haarlem provided another example of her tactless conduct of affairs, despite the fact that it should have been treated with the greatest care, since it had the highest rate of unemployment, and therefore unrest, in the country. The details of the problem are irrelevant now: one of Bentinck's memoirs takes four pages to examine them and concludes despairingly, 'it is all very complicated'. Suffice it to say that Anne first offended the town by ignoring their petition to her for help, then rounded on Steyn, who came from the town and accused him of fomenting opposition; and finally alienated everyone by plunging personally into local lobbying and politicking which devaluated the independence of her office. Patronage in her adopted country, unlike England, was not a princely prerogative by right, it had to be exercised with discretion and an understanding of its limits; the concept of stathouder as simply 'Keeper of the Ring' was alien to her, as was the vital importance of personal restraint: 'In every town and province,' wrote Bentinck, 'her arrogance is remarked upon, and day by day her personal credit and the love of the people is lost.'[9] She knew it herself, but seemed unable to control the emotional tension which led her at this time to whirl into sensitive situations without due thought; her characteristic self-discipline deserted her, and court and advisers alike suffered her outbursts of furious temper.

Notes

[1] Kramer, op. cit., p.75
[2] KHA, Anna, 430
[3] Ibid.
[4] Ibid.
[5] Ibid.
[6] AMON, IV III DXXXIX
[7] Baker-Smith, op. cit., p.141
[8] *Gentleman's Magazine*, June 1753
[9] Baker-Smith, op. cit., p.142

Chapter Twenty-one

George missed nothing of all this. On his way back from Hanover in the autumn of 1752, he was once more trapped by storms in Helvoetsluys and though – yet again – he refused to visit his daughter, he summoned Brunswick to give him a personal report. William's choice of Brunswick had been a good one – his dedication and undeniable ability was winning over his critics, and Anne herself increasingly turned to him for advice, since he handled her with charm and tact. His admiration for her was conveyed to her father; she was better informed than William had ever been and she did 'far more work in a day than the prince did in fourteen'. Brunswick's notes on the meeting show that both men were extraordinarily frank. George agrees that Anne has a talent for business but says 'I know my daughter, she is arrogant, imperious, false and foolish.' Things should be better now without her husband – 'he was always a fool, a man without character' – but she is deemed capable of spoiling everything. Brunswick reports her quarrels with Bentinck, which George smugly deplores: 'It is not fitting, she is the daughter of a King.' He has picked up on gossip too 'Who is this fellow Grovestins, is my daughter in love with him?' Brunswick prevaricates, clearly startled by such bluntness; though he asks for English support, he has to be content with the lofty promise, 'All my friends can count on me.'[1]

The King's Hanoverian interests were being considered in the desperate attempts to influence negotiations for Frederick of Denmark's second marriage as he turned again to Prussia. Ambassador Titley was instructed to warn Frederick that his choice of Frederick the Great's sister as stepmother to Louisa's four children was unwise: 'She is disagreeable in her person, ill-natured, proud, and with all these qualities a coquette.'[2] The bare six months between Louisa's death and talk of remarriage can be explained by the fact that the mental state of her only surviving son, Christian, made the country's future uncertain; the personal warning may have been heeded, since a princess of Brunswick became Queen of Denmark, providing the requisite heir and attending the King's deathbed as he repeatedly spoke of his first wife.

Louisa's two younger daughters were to marry their cousins of Hesse – Mary's sons – but this family also was now facing a crisis with political implications. Mary's marriage appears to have been doomed from the start; her gentle passivity and emotional insecurity found no support from her capricious and indifferent husband, and she had spent long periods abroad either in

Denmark with her sister or in England where 'the beauty and charm of Her Serene Highness of Hesse' was always much remarked upon in the newspapers.[3] Crown Prince Frederick's sudden announcement that he had converted to Roman Catholicism some years before now horrified her and shocked Protestant opinion in Europe.

Rumours that the Prince's Catholic lover had exacted conversion as the price for her favours quickly expanded to an assertion that he kept a harem of Catholics in Frankfurt, although his lifelong interest in religion and elaborate liturgy might argue a genuine conviction. Certainly he must have been well aware of the scandal it would cause and the political price he would have to pay. His father was enraged, and although unable to disinherit him since the necessary ratification for such an act could not be obtained from the Catholic Emperor, he was placed under house arrest and finally despatched to Berlin and a commission in the Prussian Army. Mary was refused a divorce, for fear that Frederick would marry again and produce Catholic heirs and a disputed succession for Hesse; but a formal separation protected her sons from the terrible threat of Rome. George invited her back to England, but in an unusual display of resolution she announced that it was 'her Duty to remain in the situation in which it had pleased God to place her [and] she would make her own terms for the sake of her sons'. She withdrew to Hanau, an estate on the River Main, where she rebuilt the castle, and her health was later reported to have greatly improved 'since her release from her tyrant'.[4]

Anne had been in frequent contact with Marie Louise, as Frederick's aunt, and their letters become notably more affectionate as they agonised over the crisis. Anne's letter of December 1754 refers to 'the arrangements made for the young princes and for the Protestant religion', and prays for 'the deliverance of my poor sister from the dangers with which that unworthy Prince Frederick has sought to ensnare her'.[5] She personally ensured the States-General's recognition of her brother-in-law's exclusion from the succession and the declaration of his elder son as heir. Her formative years had been spent in the shadow of the Jacobite threat, aware of the almost sacred importance of the Protestant succession, and she was as anti-Catholic as any Calvinist could wish. On his last stay in Aix, William had told her of a church fire near his lodgings when vestments were destroyed and silver plate melted while, according to him, the people made no effort to save anything but simply lit a great candle and prayed to it. Anne had shared his scorn, saying, 'This is called devotion in a place where blindness and superstition rule.'[6]

It was a relatively easy matter to make recommendations about religious controversy abroad, but those at home were fraught with complication. In many of the towns of the United Provinces, religious affairs were inextricably linked with political manoeuvring, for the Dutch Reformed Church was linked to state authority in many ways: its ministers were paid from public funds, it was universally held that ecclesiastical organisation was essential for the well-being of society and the Church had an influential voice in the wielding of civil authority.

The system worked smoothly, and Sir William Temple's opinion in 1688 had been that 'Religion may possibly do more Good in other places but it does less Hurt here'.[7] It was never 'established' in the English sense. Dutch provincialism would never tolerate a national synod, but the provincial synods included regents who then passed the laws the Church requested on such matters as Sabbath-keeping and days of repentance. The eighteenth-century House of Orange had inherited the goodwill of the Church from the seventeenth-century stathouders, and the orthodox ministers were always Orangist; but as the new 'enlightenment', which stressed the importance of individual human reason in religion as in other areas of life, lapped ever higher round the exposed island of Calvinism, the traditionally orthodox lost ground. Tracts encouraging freedom and tolerance were produced and factions began to open up.

In the town of Zwolle in the province of Overijssel, a bold and inspiring preacher called Anthonie van der Os began openly to question the absolute authority of the Church and its doctrines of justification. His appointment had been pushed through in the face of church opposition by the regents, many of whom welcomed such views; when the opposition appealed to William, who had the technical power to depose a minister, the Prince had extricated himself by stating that he considered the matter a strictly ecclesiastical one, since it was a question of orthodoxy. However, he was placed in a quandary when the civil authority announced that a deposition was against the law and the Church appealed directly to the stathouder to uphold his affirmation that the affair was ecclesiastical.

At this point William died and the problem passed to Anne. Her own spiritual inclinations as far as they are known seem nearer to those of van der Os, but he was directly challenging the one public institution which whole-heartedly supported the House of Orange. On the other hand, Overijssel's support for the stathouder became crucial as that of the other provinces fell away: some towns in the province were for Orange, but Zwolle was not one of them, calling itself a free town ruled only by God. By taking sides Anne risked antagonising either her natural ally or the civil authority which she must win over.

She moved cautiously, first making new appointments to office in Zwolle which included men favourable to Orange, and among those she displaced were some of van der Os's supporters, thus delighting the Church, which had been further outraged by a recent sermon in which he announced that God's revelation to the present generation had superseded many old doctrines. She continued to mark time as she observed the preacher becoming ever more audacious and alarming many of his political supporters; playing on these fears, she suggested to the regents that it might be better to let the willing Church deal with so turbulent a priest. At the synod to discuss the case, van der Os predictably refused to compromise, asserting his personal liberty to interpret the scriptures and deliberately challenging all authority. He was duly deposed and Anne was instrumental in ensuring that his successor was a man of similar views but more diplomacy. This case was one of the few occasions where Anne acted with both patience and skill, emerging with her own authority intact and close links with both sides; the fact that she studied the problem carefully and listened to local advice may reflect her interest in its spiritual dimension. Recognising its complexity and accepting its significance, she related the local issue to national problems instead of riding roughshod over it.

Dutch historians detect a pattern in the loss of Orange authority through the 1750s. Power and control of patronage were lost in a rapid slide from well before William's death to about the middle of 1753, and thereafter there was a plateau until Anne's own death in 1759. Many reasons are offered for this, and a compelling one is that Anne's mishandling of situations was gradually improved by Brunswick's advice and the consequent weakening of the Frisian cabal. There is a change also in Anne herself: she became less arrogant, more sensitive to the restrictions on her position and to the realities of the Dutch situation. She seemed to accept the fact that a natural balance was asserting itself in Dutch political life, that the events of 1747 had produced an unnatural scenario which had to be corrected, and that consolidation of the power which that climactic year had given to the stathoudership could never be sustained. As the national kaleidoscope of power settled to a new pattern, so also did the Dutch place in European affairs, and it would ironically be her task as an English princess to ride out a diplomatic revolution – one that would be of advantage to her adopted country, but would cause resentment and bitterness in England.

Notes

[1] 'Memorie van den hertog over zijn bezoek aan den Koning van Engeland', quoted by D Nijhoff, *Hertog van Brunswijk*, 1889, p.216
[2] J F Chance, op. cit.
[3] *Gentleman's Magazine*, October 1746
[4] Baker-Smith, op. cit., p.146
[5] KHA, Anna, 430
[6] Ibid.
[7] Sir William Temple, *Observations on the United Provinces*, 1703, p.107

Chapter Twenty-two

The Treaty of Aix-la-Chapelle had settled very little; or, more accurately, its clauses had left far too much resentment for it to be permanent. Its recognition of Frederick's annexation of Silesia could never be accepted by Maria Theresa – economically it had provided a large part of her tax revenues, ethnically it had balanced the nationalities of the tower of Babel which was her Empire, and geographically its loss gave Prussia easy access up the River Oder into the Hapsburg heartland. For such an impulsive and devout woman the incursion into Catholic lands by a Protestant country led by an ungodly King could not possibly be God's will, and it was for her to help Him right the wrong. To do so she was willing to try anything and she was responsive when one of her Council of State, Anton von Kaunitz, suggested a radical change of alliance. Kaunitz has been likened to Disraeli: devoted to his Empress, politically astute and pragmatic but also a flamboyant eccentric; terrified of fresh air and refusing to eat anything but boiled chicken, his private life was colourful, and when the virtuous Maria Theresa once ventured a remark about its immorality, he told her they were met to discuss her affairs, not his. Kaunitz argued that Austria's traditional allies were useless: George II would never risk Hanover by attacking Prussia, while the Dutch had simply ceased to matter. Without her obligations to the latter, Austria could use the Austrian Netherlands as a bargaining counter to gain support from France. From this initial idea the intricate stately quadrille of a diplomatic revolution unfolded, and by 1756 a Bourbon-Hapsburg pact had forced an uneasy alliance between England and Prussia – religious affinities reasserted themselves.

Through the early 1750s, Austrian loss of interest in the Netherlands and thus in the Barrier fortresses forced the Dutch to question their own foreign policy. Brunswick's private diary reveals his thinking: the garrisons were never viable without subsidy, which neither England nor Austria ever willingly gave, and the 12,000 men who had to be committed to their defence would surely be better employed augmenting the Dutch Army within the Republic's actual frontiers. Perhaps mindful of his tour of Maastricht with the stricken William in 1751, he made an exception for Namur, to the south-west of Maastricht, to protect the route into the country which was most vulnerable to French attack; but all other fortresses should be abandoned, and their artillery and ammunition concentrated on Namur.[1] Since England was still pressing for a Dutch presence in the southern Netherlands, Anne asked secretly for English help in this fortification. However, with George in Hanover, Cumberland was acting as regent, and he made it very clear that any such assistance to an army he despised and a sister whose judgement he distrusted would deeply offend him. Her approach became public knowledge and she was blamed for her lack of influence in London, even as others were attacking her for being an English puppet. Her nationality made her an easy target, and Bentinck's passionate support for the English connection did not help. He was by far the most vocal Orangist, and, thanks to what Newcastle's brother referred to as 'his proneness to hobbyhorses', his personal conviction that Dutch and English interests were compatible was equated in the public mind with Orange ideas.

Most evidence actually points to Anne's understanding of the Dutch position; she, and William before her, had strongly disagreed with Bentinck's judgement. Brunswick wrote to Maria Theresa in 1755, when the Austrians were still probing Dutch attitudes as the international crisis deepened, that Anne 'had asserted in her usually passionate way, "I will not abandon the allies but I will have no war"'.[2] Such a contradictory statement exactly sums up what the Republic had been trying to achieve since the collapse of the Grand Alliance in 1710. While the myth lived on, the true interests of those allies had long been diverging, and yet the Republic had always fulfilled its commitments, sending troops (however useless) to England in 1745 and, though it could ill afford it, giving financial help to Austria in lieu of men in 1740. On the other hand, avoidance of war had to be the paramount aim; only neutrality could ensure the acceptance of the 'free ships, free goods' principle on which commercial prosperity depended. Non-alignment secured the world-wide trading position of a small country with no desire for the military glory or aggressive foreign policy of the previous century.

The issues between France, Spain and England of maritime supremacy and colonial rivalry had not even been considered at Aix – most of George II's ministers still thought in purely European terms (and he himself in Hanoverian ones) – and the treaty had simply reinforced the 1742 status quo, with various New World possessions being exchanged for Indian ones. Only Cumberland was focusing his attention on the colonies, not only as a new home for the demobilised troops he called his 'Flanderkins' but also as a strategic influence on the next continental war; while Pitt, who had called ten years before for colonial rather than continental campaigns, was beginning to see that his argument, probably put forward then for the sake of opposition to the government, had validity after all.

Through the early 1750s Anglo-French clashes in North America became increasingly serious: the fifteen widely scattered English colonies there each had a governor appointed by the Crown and a local executive assembly; there was as yet no resentment of the fact that their legislation came from London, but the settlers were by their very nature aggressive, expansionist and unpredictable, and as they spread westward they collided with the French military presence based on Canada to the north and Louisiana to the south. This presence was disciplined and controlled by an autocratic government working to a coherent imperial policy which involved seizing the headwaters of the Ohio and the Mississippi and thus containing the English in their coastal settlements. With no agreed frontier, isolated skirmishes became all-out battles, and the troop reinforcements forced on a reluctant government by the Duke increased tensions without bringing any resolution, partly because of the colonies' flat refusal to surrender their independence and work together. The French made much use of the native Indians, whose predilection for woodland ambushes and English scalps spread alarm and despondency among the veterans of continental warfare, and the four-month delay between a request for instruction and its delivery doomed any military effort.

Still the English government concentrated on Europe, and as France and Austria drew closer together George II had no option but to make a defensive alliance with his hated nephew, Frederick of Prussia, which, he trusted, would at least keep Hanover secure while measures could be taken to defend the English coast. Rumours of flat-bottomed boats in French Channel ports had the customary effect of spreading panic, and 6,000 Dutch troops were requested under the old treaty obligations. The request was not at first made public, and Anne duly lobbied for it to be fulfilled; she was playing a devious diplomatic game, for she had actually discussed the matter and cleared it with the French ambassador in The Hague. The invasion plan had little substance, since French military capacity was already overextended, but they were happy to encourage English fears, and knew that the continuation of the Dutch alliance would involve England in extra continental obligations when she, too, was already stretched to the limit to protect Hanover – not to mention the colonial rivalry in two hemispheres.

On the strength of the French assurance, Anne gave a secret promise (which she had no power to do and of which even the English Ambassador, Joseph Yorke, was in ignorance) that if George was 'really in need', men would be ready when transport ships arrived.[3] But within a month everything fell apart. There was uproar in the States-General where Steyn utterly refused to use his influence, and Friesland, in its first ever open revolt against its stathouder, voted against it. With the matter now in the public domain, France had to take the umbrage expected of her, at which precise moment the English transport ships appeared off the coast, and there was an outcry against Anne as an unpatriotic Anglophile exceeding her authority.

Anne dashed off letters in every direction – confidentially to members of the States-General to explain the French attitude, to Bentinck and Steyn appealing for help and finally to Newcastle in London:

I am heartily sorry, my good Duke, that our people have been so ill bred and ridiculous as to put off sending the six thousand men, but the fear and terror all over the country is so violent that all my zeal has been useless hitherto.[4]

Steyn's refusal to give any lead, or even express an opinion, despite her entreaties, tore their relationship to shreds again, and English fury was expressed by Ambassador Yorke in an explosive interview after the transport ships withdrew. According to Bentinck, Yorke had arrived at his post convinced that all his predecessors were fools and that he would be the one to shake some sense into the Dutch. His overbearing manner and his 'black humour' made enemies everywhere, and though he was quite reasonably riled at having been kept in the dark over the secret agreement, and as a former aide-de-camp to Cumberland shared the latter's exasperation with his sister, his conduct towards Anne was disgraceful. She told Brunswick afterwards that he was so insolent that she was glad the door was shut and no one else could hear him; with increasing self-discipline, however, she seems to have managed to keep her own temper. She asked him about the fine print of the Convention of Westminster (the recently signed pact between England and Prussia) which had obvious implications for the Dutch, and he refused to answer. When she told him she feared for the peace of Europe, he replied tersely that that peace was already lost. 'Oh no', replied Anne, 'I don't think so, and I would be very upset if that were true.'[5] Yorke's response was that once it might have bothered him, but now he couldn't care less and would be delighted if peace were destroyed... it is somewhat surprising to find his memorial tablet at Wimpole Hall near Cambridge commending especially the urbane diplomatic skills of Joseph Yorke.

Newcastle, who greatly disliked Yorke, would certainly have disagreed with his sentiments as much as their form of expression. The French declared war in the late spring of 1756, but to his relief seemed content to keep the conflict away from mainland Europe, increasing their activity in North America, where English access to the Great Lakes and the St Lawrence seaway was lost, while the strategically important island of Minorca in the Mediterranean fell after a seventy-day siege. But at least, Newcastle consoled himself, the alliance with Prussia would keep Frederick under control and prevent trouble nearer home. However, at the end of August this happy delusion was shattered as 'in the prototype of all Blitzkriege'[6] Prussia invaded neutral Saxony, ransacking the Dresden archives to discover the Austrian-Saxon plot for Prussian partition which had forced him 'reluctantly' to war. The Elector of Saxony himself had little interest in anything but his vast collection of Meissen porcelain: an English ambassador had written in 1747 of his 'large house built in bad taste [where] about fifty people sit down at table and starve in state for the meal is always cold and the wines abominable'; but since his daughter was Dauphine of France, his status as King of Poland was guaranteed by Russia, and the Empress was bound to defend one of her Electors, Europe must erupt into war.

So England found herself dragged into the maelstrom on Frederick's coat-tails. For the Republic, however, the option of neutrality was a real one; more secure and self-confident than it had been for many years, it now sought under Anne to exploit this war to develop its own colonial trade. The pressures it had long endured from both France and England were lifting – the latter under-standing that her own resources could ill afford a relationship which had yielded so little over the years, and the former perceiving the advantage to burgeoning trade if she could use neutral Dutch carriers on the 'free ships, free goods' principle. But there was a stumbling block because such a new situation required the disturbance of what Bentinck referred to as 'the sleeping cat treaties'[7] of the previous century with England about trade protection.

London was willing to renegotiate, but a powerful lobby of merchants in the States-General, whose jealousy of their English rivals had been fuelled by the decline in their share of the markets, seized the opportunity to propose punitive sanctions. Steyn once again proved useless, and with Anne at Soestdijk nursing her young son through a severe attack of measles and refusing point-blank to return to the capital, Brunswick was left to deal with Yorke: '[He] came to see me as usual without having anything to say but vent his bile on Steyn… he was beside himself.'[8] Brunswick made soothing noises to the effect that 'this is the constitution and we must live with it', but Yorke's panicky reaction was mainly due to his own feelings of insecurity after a tart rebuke from Newcastle:

> Your recommendation of the advisability of an amicable agreement must occur to everybody. But we are not advanced by that. I was in hopes that you would have proposed some methods of doing it… Allow me to observe that you either do not quite understand the situation or are unwilling to enter into it because you decided beforehand that it was impossible to find an expedient for it.[9]

The matter was so important that George wrote personally to Anne, 'I wish, my dear daughter you would work on [this], and believe me full of friendship my dear daughter.'[10] In private he expressed himself rather differently: 'Needless would it be,' wrote Yorke, 'to enumerate the overflowings of the royal breast.'[11] The matter was to drag on for years.

Notes

[1] Nijhoff, op. cit., p.57
[2] Ibid. p.57
[3] Baker-Smith, op. cit. p.164; AMON, IV, III, CDLXVI
[4] AMON, IV III D
[5] Ibid., DXXII
[6] MacDonough, op. cit., p.248
[7] AMON, IV III CDLXVIII
[8] Ibid., DXLIX
[9] Ibid., DLXI
[10] KHA, Anna, 430
[11] AMON, IV II CCCLXX

Chapter Twenty-three

George was by now well into his seventies, enjoying the respect and deference which old age always brings a monarch. He was still irascible – prone to curse and kick the furniture – and he still expressed his opinions in public and with great passion, Pitt having replaced the late Prince of Wales as the main object of detestation; but he was riding out domestic political difficulties with resignation and relative calm. Newcastle's administration 'was suffering that public odium which not infrequently afflicts English governments at the start of a war for which they have neglected to make proper preparation'[1] and the manoeuvres to strengthen his hold of the House of Commons by the inclusion of Pitt, 'the man to whom the nation instinctively looked to stop the rot,'[2] were complicated by royal prejudice and political infighting. The waters were further muddied by the old Hanoverian tradition of suspicion between ruler and heir.

The future George III attained his legal majority on his eighteenth birthday in 1756, but the previous concern about the problems of a regency now shifted into direct tension between the King and Leicester House – once again 'the pouting place of princes'. Augusta had played the role of dutiful daughter-in-law since Frederick's death, but she had not concealed her contempt for George and her opinion of 'the weakness, meanness, cowardice and baseness of the Duke of Newcastle' from her closest friends; she tightly controlled all contacts between her son and the outside world: 'the young people of quality were so ill educated and so very vicious, that they frightened her'; and Cumberland's genuine efforts to relate to his nephew were spurned.

Augusta knew that her son was immature and easily influenced, so that it was up to her to find him a mentor whom she could trust to guide him both morally and politically, and she turned to the Earl of Bute, whose commitment to Leicester House had been demonstrated when he refused to seek advancement elsewhere after Frederick's death. The latter's somewhat dismissive remark that 'Bute was a fine Showy Man, who would make an excellent Embassador in a court where there was no Business'[3] did not seem to worry her; it merely meant that he was not tied down by the restricting practicalities of government but could rise above them to mould the Prince into a patriotic and moral king. There was also the rumour that 'the Princess Dowager has discovered other attributes [in Lord Bute] that the Prince her husband may not perhaps have been competent to judge'. George's efforts to detach his

grandson from Augusta by offering him a separate establishment were in vain:
Lord Waldegrave was begged

> to assure His Majesty of his being deeply penetrated with … the sense he has of
> His Majesty's tenderness towards him … but the Prince flatters himself that
> His Majesty will permit him to continue with the Princess his mother[4]

Augusta's attitude to her sisters-in-law was equally hostile: Caroline's
declining health and increasing bulk meant that she rarely made any effort to
relate to anyone, while Amelia, though she was to prove an indulgent great-
aunt to George III's children, was not considered an appropriate role model for
her nieces. Grafton was still her constant companion and at church services
she would sweep up the aisle accompanied by four or five dogs, glaring down
any hapless cleric who dared to protest. Her Rangership of Richmond Park,
and her efforts to bar public access there made her deeply unpopular; but her
ever-strident voice, raised to a new pitch by increasing deafness, could be
influential with her father, and she was still cultivated by ministers as they
jostled for office. Pitt finally engineered the resignation of Newcastle and
consented to serve – for the moment – under the Duke of Devonshire – 'a
Whig grandee of blameless character, spotless repute and minimal
understanding';[5] and his shortcomings were reflected in a Speech from the
Throne, which the King privately termed 'stuff and nonsense… and greatly
beyond his comprehension'.[6]

Devonshire's first problem was to determine the fate of Admiral Byng. The
Admiral had been sent to defend the island of Minorca, but his ten ships of the
line failed to engage the French warships besieging the garrison, and when he
turned round and headed back to Gibraltar without ever making contact with
the valiant eighty-year-old commanding officer, General Blakeney, the latter,
starved of supplies, had, after seventy days, to sign an honourable capitulation.
Minorca had been a vital strategic toehold in the Mediterranean, and public
opinion in England was incensed as the newspapers raised temperatures in the
coffee houses against 'Mr B—, chef d'escadre of the middle seas'.[7] In vain
Byng protested that he had led an undermanned scratch fleet and that the
decision to return to Gibraltar (the safety of which had also been in his remit)
had been a unanimous one by all his officers: his defence was held to be 'an
empty laboured piece of obscurity and subterfuge', he was burnt in effigy in
every town in England and his court martial, though it found him guilty of
negligence not cowardice, had then no alternative but to sentence him to death
by firing squad.

Government ministers and the King himself sought to save him, but the
verdict could only be overturned by an Act of Parliament which would never
pass the House of Commons. Amelia's opinion chimed with Voltaire's

memorable phrase that Byng's fate was '*pour encourager les autres*': as she announced to Horace Walpole, 'Indeed I was for it, the officers would never have fought again if he had not been executed.'[8] The Admiral submitted to his fate with remarkable calm: the night before a friend visited him and in an elaborately casual manner asked, 'Which of us is the taller?' Byng laughed. 'Why such ceremony? Let the man come in to measure me for my coffin'.[9]

Next morning on his own quarterdeck at Portsmouth, he sat on a chair and was persuaded to be blindfolded lest his eyes should upset the men's aim, saying, 'Very well, if it will frighten them let it be done; they would not frighten me.'[10]

Newcastle was to bounce back. He so revelled in the bustle and importance of high office that after thirty years he could not forego power for long, although it meant working with Pitt, and he even began a crash course in colonial geography: 'Ah, yes, to be sure, Annapolis must be defended, indeed it is vital that we keep Annapolis – but pray tell me, where is Annapolis?'[11] He wrote in the summer of 1757 that 'Mr Pitt and I are equally pleased with each other… We go on well beyond expectation', and even George was impressed when Pitt at last seemed to be taking the dangers to Hanover seriously, Parliament having agreed a sum of £200,000 'for the just and necessary defence and preservation of His Majesty's electoral dominions and towards the discharge of his obligation towards Prussia'. The Duke of Cumberland was appointed to command an Army of Observation, i.e. a purely defensive force, and he left for Germany after holding a great levee in his rooms at St James's, where his sister-in-law and nineteen-year-old niece, the Lady Augusta, bid him farewell.

He arrived in Hanover to find chaos. The horses he had been promised were non-existent and he had to buy them for himself and his staff. There was neither bread nor forage, his brother-in-law of Hesse refused to accept his authority, and, worst of all, the Hanoverian ministry was so terrified of what Frederick of Prussia might do next that they were considering a negotiation of neutrality rather than fighting. As the Duke wrote to a friend when he heard that a French army of 100,000 men was on the move towards him, 'How all this will end God knows,' and he actually wished he was back in private life at Windsor. Such uncharacteristic lassitude and depression must have been partly rooted in his physical health: to his constant pain from the Dettingen leg wound was now added a tendency to the severest bouts of asthma. Since he was too heavy to sleep on a camp bed, he would use a leather-covered chaise longue, and two valets must wait by his side all night to help him turn over or to prop him up to ease his breathing. Joseph Yorke in The Hague kept in touch with his old chief, and took it upon himself to approach the French ambassador there to request a supply of Eau de Luce, to prevent the Duke 'smothering himself'.[12] A large supply of the remedy was authorised for delivery by Louis XV himself and sent across enemy lines to Hanover before Cumberland left for the front in Westphalia.

While Cumberland tried to concentrate on the problems he faced, his cousin Frederick was defeating (though at terrible cost) the army of France's ally, Austria, at the battle of Prague. The English were exultant – the diplomatic revolution was bringing them at least reflected glory and 'the admiration we already had of His Prussian Majesty's heroism' was raised to fever pitch.[13] He became London's darling, and the newspapers reported the story of an 'Unknown Lady' who wrote to Frederick complaining of fraudulent behaviour by the director of a Prussian china company who had confiscated her shares: 'By return of the post she received an apology, return of her shares and promise of punishment for the offender.'[14]

Anne, too, was corresponding with Frederick. They had remained personally close and continued to share their passion for music, but the content of their letters at this time was much more serious. The Hague's reputation as 'the whispering gallery of Europe' and her own interest in foreign affairs enabled Anne to tap into many foreign secrets. One cannot tell at this distance whether it was family feeling or hope of future gain which prompted Anne to risk the hard-won acceptance of Dutch neutrality by warning Frederick of an imminent and totally unexpected Russian campaign against him. She impressed the utmost secrecy on her cousin. 'I am writing without the knowledge of any minister of the Republic,' she explained, and she begged especially that Gronsfeld, Dutch ambassador to Berlin, should be kept in the dark. Within three days Frederick replied:

> Nature has given me a sensitive soul and a grateful heart. As a man who regards ingratitude as the greatest of vices the memory of so noble and generous a gesture as yours will never be forgotten until the moment of my death.
> Your faithful brother and cousin, Frederic.[15]

Later in the month Anne sent news of the temporary postponement of the Russian attack and of the negotiations between Russia, Austria and France over money and troop numbers. Frederick's own 'secret service' was highly developed, but it is likely that Anne's detailed statistics gave him information he was unable to glean for himself. He wrote to her again during the siege of Prague, telling her of his worries. If the city fell within three weeks all would be well, but if it held out longer his position would become desperate. For a man so personally secretive and jealous of his military reputation to write in such a frank manner of his fears shows the trust he placed in Anne (he once said that if his skin knew his thoughts he would tear it off), and, in turn, he never betrayed her, although he recalled their private correspondence with great emotion ten years later when his niece Wilhelmina married Anne's son, William.

The Austrian army had retreated into Prague and Frederick was hoping to emulate his great hero Maurice de Saxe who had taken the city in 1747 (he said that the great marshal's book on warfare, *Mês Reveries*, was always by his bed: so it was, but at his death its pages were found to be uncut).[16] But his position did indeed become desperate, for the Austrians continued to hold out, and as Russians, French and Swedes advanced on him from all sides through the summer of 1757, he was forced to keep dividing his army into ever smaller units which were often defeated.

He appealed to Cumberland for help, but the Duke was himself in desperate trouble. His forces were being driven back inexorably by the French, who had invaded Hesse, forcing his sister Mary and her father-in-law to flee, and were now threatening Hanover itself. Just outside the village of Hastenbeck he prepared for the last battle of his career. The terrain was a hostile mixture of small wooded hills and marsh, and as he spent three days in the saddle studying the lie of the land the wound in his thigh opened up and gaped apart to the size of a man's hand. As he reached some thick woodland on his right flank, he was prevailed upon to rest, and for once accepted the assurance of a Hanoverian quartermaster that it was impenetrable, without checking it himself. Through this the French advanced, and although Cumberland stood his ground for some hours under a hail of cannon fire which was judged the heaviest he had ever experienced, he was eventually forced to withdraw northwards, leaving Hanover wide open. Even now his discipline held: 'There was no confusion or break in squadrons or battalions... Troops never marched from a parade in better order.'[17]

The thought of an invading army in his beloved electorate was too much for George, and he ordered his son to assume electoral powers and make peace:

> I trust my affairs entirely to your conduct... As in the case of war I depend upon your courage and skill, so I now depend on your affection, zeal and capacity to extricate yourself, me, my brave army and my dearly beloved subjects.[18]

For the first time in his life, Cumberland had to negotiate rather than fight, and after such a heavy defeat he had few cards to play; the Convention of Kloster-Zeven, which he signed in September 1757, theoretically saved Hanover's territory and 'the brave army', but brought no glory and meant that George had to apologise to his hated nephew of Prussia for making a separate peace and receive reproachful letters from him to the effect, 'You are the cause of all the misfortunes which are about to fall on me'.[19] The King would have felt much better if he had known that Frederick was simultaneously involved in bribing Louis XV's mistress and making peace himself.

As he had been after Culloden, George was swayed against his son by public opinion. The people's foreign hero had been left in the lurch. The British Minister to Berlin wrote, 'I know not how to look the King of Prussia in the face' and government ministers deplored such a breach of faith. Cumberland received a furious letter from George referring to 'a convention shameful and pernicious… Come back at once by a warship and explain';[20] but he was quite unprepared for the reception he received as, resplendent in his best uniform, he walked into the cupola room at Kensington Palace where his father was sitting with Amelia. The King threw down his cards and refused even to look at him, announcing to the room at large, 'Here is my son who has ruined me and disgraced himself.' Then, as Cumberland tried to explain, he pushed him aside and stormed out, whereupon the Captain-General of the British land forces, keeping his temper and his dignity, told Amelia to tell their father that he resigned all his military appointments, summoned his carriage and returned to Windsor.

George's rage was, as so often, compounded by his own feeling of guilt. He had acted in panic, unconstitutionally and without his usual good judgement, in giving his full authority to a completely inexperienced negotiator. Pitt himself, despite his dislike of Cumberland, was brave enough to point out to the King that the Duke had been given very full powers to act in the way he saw fit.[21] Two months later, the Convention was repudiated on the ground that the French had committed some minor infringements of its terms, and though George tried to coax him back, Cumberland let it be known that he would only return to active service in the event of invasion; at the age of thirty-six he had effectively retired.

Notes

[1] Trench, op. cit., p.271
[2] Rayner, op. cit., p.250
[3] Waldegrave, *Memoirs*, pp.163–64
[4] Quoted by Trench, op. cit., p.268
[5] Ibid., p.274
[6] Davies, op. cit., p.310
[7] *Gentleman's Magazine*, July 1756
[8] Trench, op. cit., p.278
[9] Horace Walpole, *Letters*, pp.38–9
[10] Ibid.
[11] F McLynn, *1759*, 2004, p.97. For those of us who share the Duke's confusion, Annapolis is in Nova Scotia and thus crucial to the efforts to secure the St Lawrence seaway.
[12] Whitworth, op. cit., p.189
[13] Rayner, op. cit., p.258
[14] *Gentleman's Magazine*, June 1757

[15] AMON, IV III DCLXXXIII
[16] Baker-Smith, op. cit., p.171
[17] Chatsworth MSS 397/36
[18] RA 52970
[19] Whitworth, op. cit., p.198
[20] Trench, op. cit., p.284
[21] On the letter of recall to Cumberland from Holderness, expressing 'the King's surprise that you [signed] without ratification', Pitt minuted in his own hand: 'He had a full power.' Whitworth, op. cit., p.200

Chapter Twenty-four

Back in The Hague, such troubles served to validate the Dutch neutrality, and Anne continued to concentrate on what was to prove her lasting legacy to the House of Orange – the establishment of its great wealth second only to that of the House of Windsor. She targeted two main areas for her attention, both of them long mismanaged: the personal household accounts and the family's assets in terms of land, titles, indemnities and possessions.

No item in the first of these was too mundane for her attention. The state provided a monthly sum for the maintenance of the Household to be divided between such headings as kitchen, wine, storeroom, etc., and gradually Anne ensured savings on this of up to 3,000 guilders a month. Wine consumption, in particular, dropped sharply after William's death: a sample monthly bill in 1752 came to f. 1,463, comprising ten bottles of old Rhine wine at f. 12.10 each, nine bottles of champagne at f. 16.10, 245 bottles of burgundy for a total of f. 367 and 1,313⅓ bottles of red wine for f. 590. This compares with an average bill of f. 2,200 a month during the Prince's lifetime, and the saving need not be attributed to excess on his part nor by any diminution of hospitality – the French Ambassador commented that 'the Princess of Orange keeps a princely court'[1] – but simply to better management; before, perhaps, many two-thirds mysteriously disappeared into the kitchens…

The accounts give a picture of the range of food eaten in a single year: poultry, pork and game were the main meats, the previously popular beef having completely disappeared since seventy per cent of the cattle in Holland and Friesland had been wiped out by rinderpest and stocks had to be rebuilt. German-type rye and wholemeal breads were for everyday consumption, with the finer white French loaves reserved for special occasions. Dairy produce, especially cheese and cream, had an important place, and the chickens were fed on buttermilk. Milk was seldom used except for cooking and Professor Simon Schama records a physician's advice that if milk must be drunk, the mouth should be rinsed with wine afterwards.[2] F. 2,570 was spent on fruit, f. 2,777 on vegetables and f. 15,578 on sea fish, with f. 198 for crabs. Coffee, usually drunk heavily spiced with cinnamon or ginger, came to f. 500 while tea disappears from the accounts after 1752. The figures are so meticulous that there is even an allowance for 'maintenance of the cats', which remains at f. 6 every year from 1751 to 1759.[3]

In June 1752, hospitality was lavish as a deputation arrived from England to invest the young Prince with the Garter, and Anne set out to impress her compatriots. The ceremony took place in the Oranje-zaal of Huis ten Bosch, and was performed by Garter King-at-Arms. The four-year-old William probably wore the little blue and silver embroidered silk suit now preserved in the Rijksmuseum, and the fabric approximates so closely with the description of his mother's wedding dress that it is tempting to speculate that it may be the same. He revelled in the occasion since he already had a high opinion of his own importance; only a few months later he refused to have his mother present when a new ambassador came to pay his respects, asserting, 'This is my place not yours, I am the Stathouder, not you.'[4] Lady Sundon, long ago, had blamed Caroline for ignoring her daughter's arrogance in pursuit of metaphysical speculation, but Anne did not consider pride a fault at all; she fondly spread the story around the court, but William IV who, at his coming of age at eighteen, had insisted on including his mother in every celebration and whose sense of his position was always tempered by humility, would have been appalled. Petted and indulged as the longed-for son of elderly parents, the Prince had always been strong-willed; one of Anne's letters to her husband records a tussle, barely won, over eating up his carrots. The Utrecht deputy, Hardenbroek, had much to say about the young heir, all of it uncomplimentary, although his horror that William 'did not even respect his sister' and called her a beast displays a rather idealised view of sibling relationships.[5] Carolina was an affectionate, charming and biddable child, never showing the slightest resentment of her brother's status, and the two remained close throughout their lives.

The Hague's royal archives contain a massive inventory, which Anne ordered, of all the possessions of the House of Orange: these ranged from the magnificent Holbeins and Van Dycks at Het Loo (many of the latter family portraits) to the beautiful Correggio 'School of Love' now at the National Gallery. A Breughel drawing had especial significance, for her since William had bought it from an Antwerp dealer just two weeks before his death. It is a Last Judgement, executed in 1558 for reproduction as a print, and is now in the Albertina in Vienna. Christ presides over a seething mass of naked humanity: to the right angels welcome the saved, to the left fearsome beings with tails and dogs' heads force the damned into what looks like a cave but is actually the mouth of a great fish. This symbol, appearing in much of Breughel's work, is repeated in the foreground, where a fish lies gasping in the act of swallowing a man – his legs protrude from its mouth while a desperate arm wielding a knife emerges through the creature's gill. To modern eyes it is a grotesque piece, and even in the eighteenth century it must have been a strange purchase for a dying man.

William's personal possessions appear in the inventory also: his own Garter regalia and 'a toilette of cloth of gold trimmed with silver' (almost certainly his wedding outfit), in the same chest were stored a wolfskin muff, two mosquito nets and nineteen miniatures 'most of them immodest'.[6] A small box of lead toys and some scraps of wallpaper reveal a sentimental man, while his valuable collection of coins and considerable classical library were later enthusiastically expanded by his son.

All the family palaces were richly furnished. Anne's bedroom at Soestdijk was hung with a flower tapestry woven at Delft for William II, and her son slept in 'an English bed of white and yellow silk, hung with green silk curtains'.[7] Embossed screens of gold leather set off lacquered chests from the Indies, and priceless porcelain and silver plate were displayed on tables of walnut and strange Eastern woods. But palaces and their contents could not be all, as either good advice or Anne's own intuition prompted the study of long forgotten treaties, and this combing of personal and constitutional documents proved fruitful. It was discovered that the separation in 1702 of the personal and national obligations due to the Stathouder-King William III had meant that many of them were never fulfilled. Rent due for lands round the Meuse had been paid by the last Hapsburg King of Spain, the pathetic degenerate Charles II, from 1688 until his death in 1700. As family lands, the obligation now became due not from the Bourbon kings of Spain but from the Austrian Hapsburgs. Mismanagement by Friso and his mother Amalia meant that Marie Louise had never been aware of the debt, and it was left to Friso's determined daughter-in-law to present the bill to the head of the Hapsburgs – the Empress Maria Theresa herself.[8]

It was further discovered that by an agreement of 1697 France owed an indemnification of £700,000 to William III, of which only two-thirds had been paid. The States-General had, in fact, requested payment in 1714, but the French had managed to avoid it by arguing that it was only due to a ruling stathouder. The distinction between money due to the state and to the family was important, but in the task of providing for her son's future Anne realised that it was irrelevant; the calling in of old family debts augmented the already considerable Orange wealth, but money she could claim for the Republic might be even more valuable in terms of both short-term political goodwill and long-term national survival.

The severe financial problems of the Republic were common knowledge in Europe: 'The merchants and dealers have not the trade they used to have and the little money that is left them is risked in lotteries.'[9] These lotteries were now used as a matter of course by every province to augment the already enormous tax levy; the States of Gelderland agreed one of f. 760,000 to be used for dyke repair. Crippling taxation produced predictable results: evasion on a massive scale (a tax on playing cards had to be abandoned when it was discovered that it was costing f. 100,000 to collect f. 30,000), uneconomic wage increases and a 'brain drain'.

The rise in wages pushed manufacturing costs to an uncompetitive level and still gave very little spending power to stimulate a home market: ordinances that 'only silks and stuffs of the manufacture of the country' should be worn proved futile.[10] Familiar protests to the modern ear were heard that the much admired charitable relief, for which the Dutch were renowned, now demanded an unsustainable tax level, and 'many private persons are leaving because taxes, customs and excise are so heavy, interests and rent so low'.[11] In 1751 the States-General had forbidden the emigration of textile operators, sawmill workers and rope makers; but it was too late, for the Dutch monopoly on textile finishing and paper making was already lost as the skills were taught abroad by emigrants. Forty years after Peter the Great had come to Amsterdam to learn shipbuilding, Englishmen were being enlisted in the yards to teach new techniques. National disasters posed further problems: the rinderpest epidemic undermined the only thriving area of the economy, and floods through the 1730s had forced remittance of taxation and necessitated vast sums for the rebuilding of the sea defences.

Since dredging techniques were inadequate, the new foreign ships with deeper draughts and greater carrying capacity could no longer be accommodated, and the country's exclusive role as a world carrier was lost. The new generation of those merchant families whose hard work and capital investment in industry had been the key to Dutch success were now using their wealth for money lending or foreign investment; capital was no longer seen as for the public good but for private gain. Dutch bankers in London lived sumptuously in great houses in Putney or Fulham and held 22.7 per cent of England's public debt. Back home the oligarchs lived behind discreet facades on the canals, concealing their priceless possessions from the public gaze, the only outward sign of a family's increasing wealth being a move to one of the newer houses with five windows instead of three, but still built high: paying more than the barest minimum in land tax was anathema.

The English custom of making one's money in the city and then moving to a great estate in the country was quite alien to the Dutch: power and influence depended on keeping your finger on the pulse of town life, not on land. When in England, however, they did as the English; Joshua Vanneck received a knighthood for his services to finance and retired to an estate in deepest Suffolk, where his son later built an enormous Palladian mansion, giving 'Capability' Brown his last commission. The aristocracy were everywhere tearing down their Elizabethan houses to build in the new style, and for most of them political interests took second place to architecture and landscape gardening. Cumberland certainly returned with relief to his works at Windsor;

Virginia Water was now well stocked with fish, and his landscaping was coming on well. He commissioned Thomas Sandby to build him a Chinese style temple on one of the islands he had created connected to the shore by a delicate one-span wooden bridge; inside a great room in scarlet and green with touches of gold formed a background for porcelain from the Chelsea factory he was still supporting. He also bought an old Thames barge which he transformed into a Chinese junk with japanning and lacquer work and 'no expense spared' – a visitor declared his achievements 'magnificent beyond description' and greatly to be preferred to Blenheim.[12]

The Duke lived here in almost total retirement, welcoming old friends such as Joseph Yorke and taking no part in politics. However, in the autumn of 1757 he occasionally visited his sister Caroline before she died in December. She was only forty-four, but her hypochondria had for a long time been absorbed in serious illness which was probably emphysema; like her mother she lingered on, and when the doctors finally told her there was nothing more they could do, she accepted it with relief: 'I feared I would not have died of this.'[13] She was buried at a private ceremony in the Henry VII chapel at Westminster Abbey on a bitterly cold January day – the most obscure member of a forgotten family.

Mary was now living in exile in Hamburg with two of her sons and her father-in-law. Since she had fled before the French in such haste, most of her possessions were left behind and she was practically destitute. Pitt urgently convened a session of Parliament to grant her an initial payment of £20,000 and thereafter an annuity. Her continuing popularity in England served the family well, since her two sons drew on the latter for seventy years. Pitt's skilful management of Parliament was not matched by his personal relationships with the royal family: he and Cumberland existed in mutual distrust, his flowery rhetoric still incensed the King, even though its content was now more to his taste, and he had antagonised the young Prince George who, still under Bute's control, was criticising the new involvement with Germany in terms which would have outraged his grandfather: 'that horrid Electorate which has always lived upon the very vitals of this poor country'.[14]

George was now almost blind and very deaf but he retained all his old vigour and force of expression when military affairs were discussed, or when Pitt roused him to more than usual anger. Newcastle still dreaded being summoned, as he so often was, to act as mediator: 'The Closet is all window, and His Majesty keeps all sashes up... so there is no avoiding the draught.' The death of his oldest friend, the Duke of Grafton, in 1757 hit the King hard, and Amelia, also mourning Grafton, and the faithful Lady Yarmouth, gave him 'the only comfortable two hours I have in the whole day'.[15] Cumberland rarely came up to London, observing events from his Windsor retreat with the eloquent attitude of a military man, 'God knows how these motley politicians will ever get themselves or the great vessel they steer out of the black storm they have led us into.'[16]

Notes

[1] Baker-Smith, op. cit., p.149
[2] S Schama, *Embarrassment of Riches*, 1987, p.172
[3] KHA 470
[4] Nijhoff, op. cit., p.25
[5] Kramer op. cit., p.143
[6] S Drossaers [ed.], *Inventarissen van de Inboedels in de Verblijven van de Oranjes 1567–1795*, 1974
[7] Nijhoff, op. cit., p.25
[8] Baker-Smith, op. cit., p.151
[9] *Gentleman's Magazine*, May 1753
[10] Baker-Smith, op. cit., p.152
[11] *Gentleman's Magazine*, August 1754
[12] Whitworth, op. cit., p.158
[13] Charteris, op. cit., p.52
[14] R Sedgwick [ed.], *Letters of George III to Lord Bute*, 1939
[15] Trench, op. cit., p.296
[16] Sandwich Papers, Mapperton MSS

Chapter Twenty-five

The years of Anne's regency saw the resolution of a problem which had haunted the United Provinces for nearly fifty years: 'that ancient patrimonies of the House of Orange were in foreign hands.'[1] By a tortuous genealogical thread through Anna van Egmond, the first wife of William the Silent, the French Princes of Isenghien held various properties within the Republic; while William's 1732 agreement with Prussia, although it had neutralised claims to the succession, had given away palaces and estates in the province of Holland. For a country desperate to maintain its territorial integrity by defensive means, foreign enclaves belonging to possibly aggressive princes were an uncomfortable risk.

Moves to buy off the French princes had been initiated before William's death. The latest one was an old man with only nephews to succeed him, and on a visit to him William wrote to Anne that he had high hopes of buying the properties back, observing, 'He is like all French princes, that is to say he spends more than his annual income.'[2] In the event he proved more stubborn and greedy than they expected, and Anne was only able to make the settlement ten years later.

But of course the real worry was Prussia. Her refusal to accept William III's will had cast a baleful influence over the country, and the lawyers had long advised that the grievance was genuine, not just because her kings were descended from an elder daughter and Friso from a younger one, but because Frederick Henry had, in 1654, left a specific written instruction that if his son died without a male heir everything must revert to that elder daughter. Although in the event it was his grandson William III who died childless, the point was arguable – whatever one thought of Prussian methods. Frederick the Great's actions showed his long memory for Prussian rights and his disregard for international agreements when it suited him, despite a radiation of honest innocence; so Anne, feeling confident of his personal regard, decided to use this to serve national as well as family interests and remove a possible danger.

After much hard work by the lawyers, a Resolution of the States of Holland was ratified by both Frederick and Anne: in it the King gave up for himself, his heirs and successors, all his possessions within the province 'with all furniture according to the inventory'.[3] The price was 700,000 guilders for the property and 5,000 for the furniture, but the deal met with such general approval that the States-General, 'glad to be rid of so formidable an inmate',[4] voted a large sum towards it out of public funds.

The two palaces which Anne thus acquired were Honselaersdyck and the present Noordeinde. The former had been built by Frederick Henry between 1620 and 1640 among sand dunes three miles north of The Hague; it was a severe grey stone building set four-square round a central courtyard, but inside it was magnificent since proceeds from the Dutch capture of a Spanish silver fleet in 1628 had paid for a wealth of paintings. One artist, Gonzalo Coques, was commissioned to produce ten works portraying Amor and Psyche: uncertain of the story or simply lacking in imagination, he secretly commissioned another artist in Antwerp to do the initial sketches for him, and having collected them, travelled to the palace and happily transferred them to canvas. They were nearly complete when Frederick Henry arrived to inspect progress, accompanied by his secretary Constantine Huygens – the latter was a polymath and was able, helpfully, to point out to the Stathouder that the designs were straight copies of a series by Raphael.

By 1754, however, the glories of Honselaersdyck were long past; it had been occupied sporadically by members of the Prussian royal family, but little had been spent on maintenance, while furniture, paintings and even the gilding and stucco work had been stripped out and taken to the Sanssouci palace in Potsdam.

The Noordeinde Palace in the centre of The Hague had been built in 1540 and was the childhood home of Frederick Henry and his mother Louise de Coligny, fourth wife of William the Silent. He had used it as a grace and favour house after her return to France, and Henrietta Maria spent a year there in 1642 while the Civil War raged in England; it had been newly restored for her, but she apparently left it in such a state that another restoration was needed. Through the early part of the eighteenth century it was used by the Prussian King on his infrequent visits to the capital (his 1711 agreement with Friso was due to be signed there), and between 1740 and 1743 Voltaire, at the time Frederick the Great's close friend, lived there, complaining of leaking roofs, split panelling and rotting floors.

Both palaces, therefore, offered what a modern estate agent would doubtless term 'an investment opportunity' and Anne relished the challenge while meeting it frugally. The old formal gardens at Honselaersdyck, by now a wilderness, were sold off to neighbouring farmers on condition they were used sensitively, and this money paid for restoration of the building. Two sides were demolished, the remainder repaired to receive new murals and plasterwork, and it became Carolina's summer residence after her marriage. Noordeinde, in the centre of The Hague, was more of a problem because the Binnenhof apartments were still all the family needed within the capital. Anne utterly refused to countenance its demolition, although she was continually pressed to do so, and a basic repair of the structure was carried out before the building was 'put to sleep': its great days came when the Dutch monarchy was established in 1815 and needed to distance itself from the seat of government, and the 450-year-old palace has recently been lavishly restored again.

Anne was determined to emphasise the symbolism of what she had done, and she planned a great theatrical gesture. Three days after the Prussian treaty was ratified, an elaborate ceremony was staged at Honselaersdyck where guests enjoyed a great feast, after which Orange flags were unfurled from the towers, drums rolled and trumpets blared while cannons, laboriously towed out from The Hague, fired a salute to mark the return of Orange property to Orange hands. She continued her property transactions throughout the 1750s, selling off some scattered estates which were difficult to administer and using the money to increase the family lands round existing palaces; there is no doubt that her shrewd management and rationalisation secured the Orange inheritance at a most crucial time and laid the foundation for the family's enormous wealth today.

Despite the pressures on her, Anne always tried to keep the summer months sacrosanct to spend in the country with her children, year after year refusing the most urgent pleas to return to the Binnenhof. Her relationship with her daughter was always good, but William was a real problem. He was spoilt and indulged until his behaviour became so bad that even his fond mother realised that he needed a firm hand, and a French refugee named Joncourt was appointed his preceptor: 'a learned, wise, virtuous and religious man',[5] he embarked on a similarly rigorous and disciplined educational regime to that which Anne herself had experienced. Anne imparted her own love of music and art to both children – Carolina's harpsichord playing was much praised and the young Mozart was invited to her court, while William's management and expansion of the Orange picture collections was one of his few unqualified achievements.

As children do, William picked up on many of the adult tensions around him. Brunswick heard that one morning at breakfast he suddenly asked his mother if she wanted him to love her. After receiving the expected reply, he told her that she couldn't love her own father because she hadn't seen him when he recently passed through the country and announced triumphantly, 'So I warn you, while you don't love your father, I shall not love you.'[6] Anne must have often felt near despair as she struggled on: that unfailing good humour and cheerfulness which had always so struck observers disappeared at her husband's death, and through the course of the 1750s her energy and powers of concentration seemed to dwindle. She took far longer to master documents and briefs than before; she slept badly and it was noticed that her head would frequently droop and her feet dragged as she walked. The general slowing down of a woman still in her forties, previously remarkable for her mental and physical energy, prompts one to look beyond the bereavement and 'liquid in the head' which her physicians diagnosed. Her post-mortem indicates thyroid deficiency, which leads to lethargy and anaemia and its characteristic neck swelling could lead to a drooping head. Later, as the disease progresses, the legs become swollen and the heart begins to fail, death usually coming from a heart attack.

For the first years after her husband's death, Anne obstinately refused to make any decision about the question of a regency. But her failing health while William was still under ten and their return to Leeuwarden for a long visit with an emotional reunion with Marie Louise changed her mind, and by 1755 the two functions which Anne had combined were directed to be separate at her death. The political role of the Stathouder would be left 'on hold' while Brunswick continued in the military role as acting Captain-General. The personal guardianship of the children was to be divided between him, Marie Louise, and – rather surprisingly – George. She may have calculated that this would ensure a friendlier English attitude, but the King was already seventy-two and would outlive her by a bare eighteen months.

Anne now turned her attention to another obligation which these regency arrangements would not necessarily affect – the marriage of her daughter. Perhaps she looked back to her own youth and the prospect which had so alarmed her, of being a dependent at her brother's court. Her financial organisation had already ensured her daughter's wealth, for she would inherit lands and goods quite separate from William's, and her own dowry, which was still largely intact, would go to Carolina rather than to him, but she was looking for some kind of independent position. She did, in fact, float the extraordinary idea of dividing the stathouderate again, giving Friesland and Groningen to her daughter with the title of *Gouvernante*: George termed it 'the wildest project he ever heard' and nothing came of it, but it shows the extent of Anne's concern that she should even contemplate such a split after so many years of struggle to unite the provinces. An even wilder project had concerned the colony of Surinam.

This South American possession had been exchanged by treaty with the English in the seventeenth century for New York, and had become the black spot of the Dutch tropical empire, renowned, as C R Boxer put it, for 'the sadistic cruelty, pig-headed selfishness and short-sighted cupidity of successive generations of its planters and their overseers'.[7] By 1749, 1,500 Europeans (mostly Dutch but including Germans, French and some Sephardic Jews) dominated 30,000 Negro and Indian plantation workers under a Dutch governor. William's success in May 1747 had been welcomed there, even the slaves wearing orange cockades when the news reached them three months later. After the Prince's death, a certain Salomon du Plessis appeared before the

States-General to file charges against the Governor, and while these were being investigated, he was received by Anne many times in private audience. Apart from the constitutional impropriety of her action, it seems another example of her misjudgement of character. The du Plessis family had a reputation in Surinam for feathering their own nest, and Salomon's daughter, Susanna, is notorious to this day for her cruelty: while travelling by river boat, she was once irritated by the wailing of a baby and gave orders that it should be wrenched from the mother's arms and thrown into the water. Anne's discussions with Salomon seem to have centred on constitutional change whereby the colony would be transferred to Orange control, presumably as a personal possession for Carolina.

In the event all charges were dismissed and the young Princess was spared such a doubtful inheritance. In truth, as Anne came to realise, her daughter's only chance of true security lay in the right marriage, and this was a responsibility which only she could shoulder. Since Carolina was five years older than William, she was likely to be well past marriageable age by the time he himself could take the initiative, and as far as the guardians were concerned Brunswick would have more than enough on his mind with his military and political responsibilities, Marie Louise was cut off in Friesland, and George could hardly be expected to worry about a faraway granddaughter whom he had never even seen.

The possibility was discussed of Carolina marrying her cousin William Henry, Frederick's son, born in the same year of 1743; but although Anne's old hostility to her brother and all his works had faded, she specifically rejected an English connection. She had been careful to make the child thoroughly Dutch: all her correspondence with her father and grandmother are in that language, and her German and French were much better than her English. Carolina's dynastic importance until William had a family of his own dictated a match with no political implications. She was no beauty, having inherited her mother's figure and her father's face, but the liveliness and sweetness of temperament which contemporaries remarked upon are apparent in her portraits. As early as 1755, Anne had fixed on Prince Charles Christian of Nassau-Weilbourg, then aged twenty, as the perfect match for her twelve-year-old daughter.

In the thirteenth century, two brothers had divided the Nassau inheritance between them: William's German lands had come to him as the sole survivor of one branch, and Charles was the senior member of the other, so that if Carolina should become stathouder the family lines would be united and strengthened, since Charles's possessions, east of Koblenz, were extensive and adjacent to William's Siegen and Dillenburg. Since Charles was already serving in the army of the Palatinate, Anne reckoned that he could switch to the army of the States, which would give Carolina a reason for maintaining a base in the Republic. His ancestor had had the worst of the land deal and he was far from rich, but this was also seen as being in his favour: Anne could offer a generous dowry, and she argued that his lack of fortune would make Charles more 'pliable',[8] and thus a support for William rather than the threat which might be posed by a powerful brother-in-law.

The Prince was invited to The Hague and acquitted himself well, kind to Carolina, deferential to Anne and amiable to everyone else. Anne was delighted with her choice and threw herself, as usual, into precipitate action. The permission of the States-General was needed for the marriage, and Anne had ample experience of the trouble caused by lack of consultation; but, carried away by her enthusiasm, she began to press ahead on her own. She sent the hapless youth on a tour of her family, including George in London, with a handwritten letter pressing his case:

> I must establish my daughter, she is very young but the position of our house in the Republic makes me anxious for her to stay there to support the well-intentioned and discourage faction.

A lengthy recital of Charles's virtues ended with a rather sheepish, 'I hope you will find that I have not said too much in his favour.'[9]

Rumours abounded in The Hague, where her marked attentions to him and his to her had been noted. Steyn was told nothing, but she wanted Brunswick's approval to get Charles an army appointment: he was summoned to an audience and found an excited Carolina in attendance, so he knew what was coming. Anne was so nervous that she could not bring herself to broach the matter and, to his mounting amusement, Brunswick was kept in inconsequential conversation for nearly an hour. At last he rose to leave and was nearly at the door when, in response to her daughter's whispered plea, Anne blurted out her idea that the Prince should enter the Republic's service; he told her it was not for him to say, and she laughed and made him a mock curtsey.

It was correct that she needed no permission to make what military appointments she chose, but the actual marriage was a very different matter, and she needed all the help she could get. Instead, she seemed deliberately to alienate rather than persuade: the influential *burgemeester*, Hop from Amsterdam, who ventured to raise the subject was told, 'These are my children, what business is it of yours?'[10] Quite apart from the rash stupidity of the remark itself, the account of the whole interview shows Anne at her worst. People often found her speech difficult to follow since she had a habit of speaking through her teeth and barely moving her lips; Hop was extremely deaf and she spoke much faster than usual, making no secret of her impatience with him. Her husband's personal courtesy and informality had been appreciated; he would often meet visitors at the door and escort them to their carriages afterwards, while enquiries after their families and health would precede any discussion of business. Anne could never forget she was royal, and her stiffness and concern for status ensured that audiences were usually conducted with formality and brevity.

Her secretary, Larrey, was the only person she took into her confidence about the marriage, and although he was powerless to stop the bandwagon, he did his best to slow its headlong flight. He pointed out frankly at an early stage that the alliance would bring little lustre to the stathoudership, and from a financial angle 'thrusts Princess Carolina into mediocrity'.[11] He also raised the religious issue, which Anne seems barely to have thought of in her reckless haste: Carolina must marry within the Reformed Church because her children would inherit if William died childless, and not only was Charles a Lutheran, but the Reformed Church was barely tolerated in the lands he controlled. Larrey's memoir to Anne delicately hints that both the confirmation of succession in the female line and the religious restrictions had been passed only during the first flush of enthusiasm for the House of Orange in 1748, and if the latter were not adhered to now 'there is a risk to the prospects of Princess Carolina from those who might seek to invalidate the resolutions in question.'[12]

Far too late, Anne informed Steyn of her plans, and the Pensionary found it 'not only surprising but beyond belief that she should have done so much on her own.'[13] She had made a hostage to fortune, and the States-General now had a hold over her which it would not hesitate to use. Charles totally refused to change his faith, and by the time he was prevailed upon at least to allow his children to be brought up in the Reformed Church, relations between Anne and the States were so bad, because of her inability to renegotiate the trade treaties, that any discussion of the marriage was blocked. Three years dragged by, and by the summer of 1758 she was failing fast, and Bentinck warned London that, 'She believes she is dying and is preparing herself.'[14]

Notes

[1] *Gentleman's Magazine*, August 1753
[2] KHA, Willem IV, 171
[3] Extract Resolutie of the States of Holland and West Vriesland, 9 August 1753
[4] *Gentleman's Magazine*, August 1753
[5] Ibid.
[6] Nijhoff, op. cit., p.26
[7] C R Boxer, *The Dutch Seaborne Empire*, 1973, p.169
[8] Baker-Smith, Anne of Hanover, p.176
[9] AMON, IV, III DC
[10] AMON, IV, III, DXCIX
[11] Baker-Smith, op. cit. p.178

[12] AMON, IV, III, DXCVII
[13] Ibid.
[14] AMON, IV, III, DCXC

Chapter Twenty-six

The long-standing failure to reach agreement with England over commercial affairs came to a head in 1756 when the war between England and France broke out. The French had relaxed their navigation laws and issued licences for neutral shipping to carry their goods, and since the Dutch had virtually creamed off the whole of this advantage, they had been able to take over most of the French trade in the West Indies and North America, bypassing English blockades. The English argued that since the Dutch had refused to supply troops for the continental campaign, they had lost the reciprocal right to protection for their shipping. The Dutch held that this was a unilateral decision, and until the treaties had been renegotiated the 'free ships, free goods' principle stood. The English possibly had the better case, but they largely obscured it by their actions: Dutch ships on the high seas were repeatedly boarded, searched and harassed by both government cutters and illegal privateers, and 240 vessels were seized within six months and their cargoes confiscated. Not surprisingly, Dutch merchants were so incensed that any rational discussion of the issue was out of the question while such tactics continued.

Deputations of merchants came to Anne from Amsterdam and Rotterdam, demanding increased protection for merchant shipping, and accusing the English of 'piracies which would dishonour Algiers'.[1] They complained afterwards that she had shown contempt for their problems, because after the briefest of audiences she delegated the meeting to Larrey; in reality this was for health reasons, since she was now barely able to stand for more than a few minutes. The States-General was due to meet in the first week of December 1758, and she sought some English concession, even if only about compensation, 'to put an end to the clamours and complaints of those seamen who suffer unjustly'.[2] She argued that this would enable the political problem to be addressed, but London viewed the issue the other way round: a political agreement must come first: 'The Princess Royal must bring the Republic to absolutely renounce all trade and traffic with the French colonies in the West Indies.'[3] As soon as that was done, sweetness and light would follow. As far as compensation was concerned they would promise nothing, offering the familiar disclaimer about the independence of the judiciary. The instructions to Yorke about the illegal privateers were ridiculously ingenuous:

And the Dutch merchants could do no greater pleasure to the King than by enabling His Majesty to trace such offenders and bring them to justice by giving viva voce evidence against them, without which as you know it is the happyness of this country that no man can be punished.[4]

Anne knew herself trapped, and the emotional letter she hurled at Yorke showed she was near breaking point:

Nothing ever hurt me more than these English government orders. Not only my authority, but the protestant cause and the union of the sea powers will be quite forgot. You know what unreasonable people we have to do with and next week [at the States-General meeting] all our enemys will be in array expecting to take fire. England is offering nothing, I am helpless… my heart is so full, I could not help writing you my mind which I hope you will forgive.[5]

Even Yorke was touched and sent a warning letter to London, while Bentinck, who was still in close touch with Newcastle, went further: 'Not only her credit and authority must be lost for ever, but what she is now forced to undergo will kill her.' He was right.[6]

She suffered almost continual fevers and her body swelled; while terrible nightmares dominated what little sleep she could snatch. As her weakness increased, personal rather than political obligations dominated her mind and she made a desperate appeal to Brunswick about Carolina's marriage. Pressing his authority to its limit, Brunswick got States-General approval for the princess to marry a Lutheran; but still permission for the marriage to Charles himself was withheld until, on Brunswick's advice Anne made only her second appearance before the assembly to make the appeal in person. As he had calculated, the sight of her 'with staggering step and death in her eyes'[7] had a profound effect, and as she was helped out of the Chamber, the deputies gave unanimous agreement.

She managed to take part in the Christmas and New Year celebrations at Court, but a detailed account of 'Her Royal Highness's last illness' records that on 5 January she awoke with a great pain in her side, a cushion of herbs was pressed to it, but she fell heavily when she tried to stand.[8] The next day William was assuring Marie Louise that 'Mama continues to do well'.[9] The doctors had swathed her swollen legs in bandages and placed her in an arm-chair from which she managed to sign the marriage papers with Larrey guiding her hand. She remained upright in the chair for three days, which so stiffened the legs that she could no longer bend them; on the evening of 9 January a servant heard her scream with pain, and as he knelt beside her with a footstool she told him, 'I have no fear of death, I have been ready for it for too long and I know where I am going.'[10]

She drifted in and out of consciousness for many hours but then rallied and summoned her chaplain to pray with her, saying, 'I am ready to go when God calls me.' The ladies and gentlemen of the Household filed into the room and she thanked them for their service, with a special word for the faithful Larrey; then the children were called and she held them both by the hand. 'May God make you as good and happy as I would wish,' she said, adding that she left them above all in His protection although they should look on Brunswick as their earthly father.[11] Finally Brunswick himself arrived, in great haste, having delayed to ensure the ratification of the marriage agreement, and she breathed the deepest of sighs and fell into a peaceful sleep. The doctors left, Brunswick drew William away, and Carolina and Charles supported her for three hours until the breathing suddenly ceased.

The usual post-mortem was published which gave 'dropsy' as the cause of death. The spleen and liver were sound but she had three gallstones, the lungs were bluish both inside and out and the heart was much enlarged. She lay in state at the Binnenhof, as her husband had done, but the crowds, it was noted, were far greater for her than for him. The floor of the *lyk-zaal* was covered in black baize, and black velvet curtains braided with silver framed the bed where the body lay in a white satin gown with frilled sleeves and a lace cap. A balustrade of fretted silverwork, showing crowned skulls, surrounded the bed, and it was flanked with church candelabra giving pyramids of light. Crowns everywhere symbolised her royal birth – silver ones on sconces, painted ones at the head of the bed, and one of jewels and orange velvet on a cushion at its foot, from which was draped the violet and ermine robe she had worn for her wedding almost twenty-five years before. Members of the Household, the women heavily veiled, sat in the shadows.

Anne's funeral took place at the end of February, and once again the States-General voted its entire cost – 70,000 guilders – from public funds. By dawn on a day that was mild and very still, officials and soldiers milled into position around the Binnenhof, and the long procession set off around nine o'clock led by a squadron of dragoons and one hundred Swiss Guards. Servants, cellarers, pastry cooks and dancing masters carried the badges of their trade, and heralds bore the arms of Orange and of England, as well as Anne's personal quarterings of Brandenburg and Celle, Brunswick and Hanover. The ermine-draped coffin – a sign of her royalty – was borne on a funeral coach with eight horses and forty pall-bearers. The eleven-year-old William, wearing his Garter star, walked between Brunswick and his future brother-in-law as far as the city walls, where they transferred to a coach for the remaining short journey to Delft. The whole route was lined with trainbands, who turned in to follow the procession as it passed. In Delft the cobbled streets and bridges had been boarded over to provide a smooth surface, and twenty-one-gun salutes from each of the city gates marked the arrival of the cortege at the door of the church, with its soaring Gothic tower. The vault lay ready, flanked by soldiers, and there was a chair 'in case His Highness the Stathouder should need it',[12] while his mother, Princess Royal of England, Princess of Orange and Gouvernante of the United Provinces, was laid to rest beside her husband.

Frederick the Great wrote an official letter of condolence to the States-General, but also sent a personal letter to the Republic's ambassador to Prussia, saying, 'I have lost a friend whose generosity and wisdom was unsurpassed and whose strength of spirit deserved my respect.' As the preacher of Anne's eulogy at the English Church of Rotterdam said, 'The praise of so illustrious a prince is praise indeed.'[13] The sermon took as its text, 'The memory of the just is blessed', and amid the commonplaces – 'the Glory of the State, the Charm of Society and the Ornament of her Century' – there were many spontaneous touches: she was 'utterly averse to indolence and dissipation, filling up every portion of her time'; 'a generous as well as a zealous protestant who was a great friend to religious liberty'; and 'she had the true interest and prosperity of this republic much at heart, she laboured incessantly to promote it and it was the burden of her life that she had not a success equal to her wishes and her pains'.[14]

An English minister might be expected to deplore 'the tainted breath of self-interest and the equally malignant one of faction'[15] which had shackled Anne's efforts in her adopted country, but even the *Hollandsche Historische Courant*, a newspaper never noted for its balanced attitude to the House of Orange, paid generous tribute:

> A princess who in her tenderest years already showed an upright and sincere piety, a princess who in all the blows of life showed a steadfast resignation, a princess skilled in different languages, a princess who although born and bred in another country was in no way an enemy to ours.[16]

Anne had worked hard for that last recognition in particular, and it was probably the epitaph she would most have wished in her unique role as the only English princess ever to rule in her own right in a foreign country.

Notes

[1] *Gentleman's Magazine*, June 1758
[2] AMON, IV III DCXC
[3] Ibid., DCLXXXIV
[4] Ibid., DCLXXXVI
[5] Ibid., DCLXXXVIII
[6] Ibid., DCXC
[7] J Naber and L de Neve, *De Vorstinnen van het Huis van Oranje-Nassau*, 1898, p.180

[8] KHA, Anna, 404
[9] Ibid., 430
[10] Ibid., 404
[11] Ibid.
[12] KHA, Anna, 407
[13] Benjamin Sowden, *Funeral Sermon of HRH Anna, Princess of Orange*, 4 March 1759
[14] Ibid.
[15] Ibid.
[16] KHA, Anna, 407

Chapter Twenty-seven

The year of Anne's death, 1759, became known in England as 'the Year of Victories'. As Horace Walpole remarked, 'one was afraid of closing one's eyes for fear of missing one.' From India to Canada, from the West Indies to Germany, the French were defeated on land and humiliated at sea. The two greatest victories came towards the end of the year. In November, in 'one of the great naval victories in world history',[1] Admiral Hawke destroyed nine French warships which had taken refuge in the supposedly inviolable Quiberon Bay in Brittany. In an extraordinary display of courage and seamanship, he manoeuvred his fleet through a ferocious westerly gale along a shoreline studded with reefs and shoals. Like the German Grand Fleet after Jutland, the French could not put to sea again for the rest of the Seven Years' War.

Two months before, James Wolfe had led his redcoats up the Heights of Abraham and taken Quebec, dying in the hour of victory. It had been a desperate and rash attempt, but success (and death) pardons all, and when strategists in London queried his judgement the King let it be known that if Wolfe was indeed mad, then it was a pity he had not bitten his fellow generals.

George's own life was drawing to a close. Augusta's steady insistence that her son should spend as little time as possible at court, the deaths of four of his children within eight years and his own failing health made him a sad and isolated figure in the year of victories, though he would occasionally appear on the Kensington Palace balcony to acknowledge the crowds. In August 1760 he was deeply shaken when Cumberland suffered a stroke and could no longer visit him in London, and on 25 October 'Young Hanover Brave' died of a heart attack at the age of seventy-seven.

The English custom of a private funeral was observed, and late one November night, Cumberland, as chief mourner, stood for two hours in the icy Henry VII chapel of Westminster Abbey. A massive figure muffled in a black cloak with a five-yard train, he drew all eyes as the yeomen of the guard carrying the leaden coffin swayed and stumbled and cried out for help under the weight. As Horace Walpole put it, 'His face bloated and distorted with his late paralytic stroke... he stood over the mouth of the vault into which, in all probability, he must himself so soon descend.'[2] But Walpole was premature: after fifteen years, Culloden was at last forgiven, and Cumberland returned to the heart of public life as a revered elder statesman.

The new King, George III, showed his uncle great respect and government ministers relied heavily on his advice and experience. Even his sister-in-law's antagonism seemed to have faded: when George married Princess Charlotte of Mecklenburg-Strelitz, Augusta pressed Cumberland to accompany her to the bedding ceremony. 'Madam,' was the reply, 'of what use could I possibly be? If she were to cry out, I could not be of any assistance.'[3] Ten days later, the coronation of King and Queen was a disastrous affair. The Earl Marshal, Thomas Howard, Earl of Effingham, admitted his many mistakes but was able to reassure the King that he had learned a great deal, and the next coronation would run much more smoothly.

Queen Charlotte was scandalised by the raffishness of London society, and as she abolished gaming at Court and economised by providing no food for guests, Cumberland and Amelia escaped to be fêted at private house parties in the country. Stowe, with its temples and follies, was a great favourite, though not with Horace Walpole:

> Twice a day we made a pilgrimage to every heathen temple in that province they call a garden, and there is no sallying out of the house without descending a flight of steps as high as St Paul's.[4]

In the autumn of 1765, Cumberland was heavily involved in government discussions over the Stamp Act, which had been passed at the beginning of the year. This extended the existing stamp duty on newspapers and legal documents to the North American colonies and had met with no opposition in Parliament and little attention anywhere else. But it was the fuse which ignited the American War of Independence, and the colonial resolution demanding no taxation without representation, caused a crisis in London. The Cabinet were due to meet at the Duke's London home on 31 October, but as they arrived, Cumberland collapsed. The Dukes of Newcastle and Northumberland had to help his servants carry the enormous body to a couch, but he was dead at forty-four.

His old adversary outlived him by twenty years. The 'Bonnie Prince' roamed Europe, abusing the mistress for whom he had abandoned his wife and, more often drunk than sober, continued to boast of 'my friends in London', but there were none to listen. The House of Hanover had finally triumphed, extinguishing the romantic aura of the Stuarts and the glamour of their dying Jacobite fall.

Mary, as the last survivor of those 'Daughters of Great Britain' who had married abroad to strengthen their family's prestige, died peacefully at her castle of Rumpenheim in 1772. Her elder son succeeded his Catholic father as Landgrave of Hesse in 1786, but her two younger sons inherited the pensions which Pitt had procured for Mary from Parliament. Since Charles lived until

1836 and Frederick survived into his ninetieth year of 1837, Britain paid dearly for a marriage which had been originally intended to provide mercenaries at reasonable cost in time of war. From Scotland against Charles Edward in 1746 to the south coast of England in 1756 against an expected French invasion, the Hessians had received their subsidies and barely raised a sword.[5]

Augusta died a month after Mary of cancer of the throat. She had already lost four of her children and there were rumours that their deaths were due to scrofula – 'the King's Evil' – which she had brought into the royal family. She had become deeply unpopular and this possibility was openly discussed, as was her relationship with Lord Bute, and her coffin was booed as it passed to the Abbey for burial.

Three of her surviving sons were already upsetting their brother, the King, either by secretly marrying commoners (whom they had previously flaunted as mistresses) or by being cited in aristocratic divorce cases. The jury thoroughly enjoyed themselves when Lord Grosvenor claimed damages from Henry, Duke of Cumberland, for seducing his wife. Assignations had taken place above a milliner's shop in Pall Mall, and the listening owner recounted to the court how she had heard the bed crack among even more disturbing noises.

Such exploits paled, however, beside the scandal caused by Augusta's youngest daughter, Caroline Matilda, born four months after Frederick's death. She had been despatched in floods of tears to marry her first cousin, Christian of Denmark. Louisa's only surviving son was an outstandingly good-looking but diminutive man, who had long shown disturbing signs of insanity. When he became King, he appointed as Prime Minister his physician, Count Struensee, and in an eerie rerun of the story of George I and Sophia Dorothea, the young Queen had embarked on a blatant affair with the Count. Her lover was condemned to death and Caroline imprisoned in the fortress of Kronborg. When the doughty English ambassador threatened to train gunboats on Copenhagen in her defence, she was released and sent to Hanover, where she settled in the city of Zelle (birthplace of Sophia Dorothea).

Her two sisters-in-law married their cousins of Hesse, with whom they had played as children, and settled into the claustrophobic world of the tiny German states, managing to maintain their independence through Napoleonic turmoil. Anne's daughter, Carolina, was also lucky. Her mother's dying choice of Charles of Nassau proved to be a good one and their tiny court east of Koblenz became a cultural centre of some importance as she patronised both Haydn and Mozart.[6]

For Anne's son, a far more turbulent future was in store. William was a clone of his father without the charm, 'a vacuum at the head of state.'[7] He was stubborn, lazy and indecisive, asserting his rights and prerogatives while doing very little to earn them. He had hoped to marry Caroline Matilda, but while he agonised over the idea she left for Denmark and he eventually married Frederick the Great's niece, Wilhelmina. This brought him a wife who would repeat his mother's mistakes. Strong-willed and intelligent, Wilhelmina gradually asserted authority over her flaccid husband. Joseph Yorke, still ambassador at The Hague, was shocked during one audience when William prevaricated over a decision and his wife cut in, 'It is not necessary to delay. I accept it.'[8]

The anti-stathouder opposition strengthened into virtual civil war. The rumours of William's illegitimacy resurfaced with increasing force and as Wilhelmina – like her late mother-in-law, a foreigner with little understanding of Dutch institutions – took control, William relapsed into apathy: 'Let them just drive me out of the Republic. I ask nothing more.'[9] His wish was granted. In 1794 the 350-year-old institution of the stathouderate was abolished, the House of Orange dispossessed, and William fled with his family to England and exile at Hampton Court.

The masculine and eccentric Amelia was the last survivor of the old generation. Horses were still her passion into old age and she would always get in and out of her carriage in the stable yard, so she could inspect them properly. An admirer wrote: 'She has her ears shut to flattery and her heart open to honesty… yet she never forgets she is the King of England's daughter.' An absent-minded companion once helped himself from her snuffbox, whereupon she threw it into the fire.

Amelia was always close to George III's many children, and Lady Mary Coke recounts a visit in 1773 by the three youngest, Augusta, Elizabeth and Ernest, then aged four, three and two, to her house at Gunnersbury. Their great-aunt's insistence on formal dress was evident and the children were carefully dressed for the occasion, with 'the two Princesses in a great many diamonds', but she laid on a skittles alley for them.

> The whole apartment above stairs was open for them to play in, and a long table in the great room covered with all sorts of fruit, biscuits, etc., of which they ate very heartily. They stayed for two hours without tiring Her Royal Highness or themselves and said they were sorry to go.[10]

Shortly before she died, Horace Walpole reported, 'I was sent for again to dine at Gunnersbury and was forced to send to town for dresscoat and sword.' The meal lasted a long time, 'since the Princess eats and talks a great deal.' Another guest was the 26-year-old Prince of Wales, already deeply in debt, 'always in a dazzle' and pursuing a Catholic widow, Mrs Fitzherbert. His great-aunt's home obviously provided a congenial refuge from parental disapproval.

Warned by her doctor at the end of October 1786 to expect 'dissolution' within three days, Amelia remained perverse to the last, and survived for over a week, dying on Cumberland's anniversary, with her hands folded over the miniature of her only suitor, Frederick the Great, who had died two months before. 'If she is not buried beside people she approves of,' wrote one of her nieces, 'she will make a great noise at the raising of the dead.'

This death marked the passing of a lost generation. Amelia's great-nephews and nieces would continue to provide notoriety and scandal enough in the years to come to ensure their place in history, but she and her sisters have been long forgotten and her brothers too often maligned. This particular Hanoverian family has been in the shadows of the eighteenth century, but richly deserves a place in the sun.

Notes

[1] F McLynn, *1759*, 2004, p.379

[2] Letter to Horace Mann, November 1765

[3] Quoted by Whitworth, op. cit., p.212. This remark has been attributed to his nephew, Henry, who succeeded to the title on the Duke's death (and was only fifteen at the time). It is just one example of the confusion caused by the genealogical elision resulting from the death of Frederick, which has led so many writers to merge three generations – more easily done, admittedly, since the same names reappear.

[4] Lewis, op. cit. 39. 127

[5] Frederick made some contribution to English history since he was grandfather to Queen Alexandra.

[6] For genealogical enthusiasts, their youngest daughter was the great-grandmother of Queen Mary.

[7] Rowen, op. cit., p.196

[8] Hardenbroek, op. cit., i 371

[9] Ibid., iv, 604

[10] Quoted by Flora Fraser, *Princesses*, 2004, p.34

Bibliography

Archival Sources

Althorp, Spencer Papers

British Library, Longleat House, Portland MSS 111, fol.29

British Museum, 1418.d.40
  MSS 103.k.27

Cambridge University Library, 'Gratulatio academicae Cantabrigiensis auspicatissimus Gulielmi principis Auriaci et Annae Georgii II nuptias celebratis', 1733

Chatsworth MSS, 397/36

Dorset County Records Office, D86/X4

East Suffolk County Records Office, Albemarle Papers

Koninklijk Huis Archief, The Hague:
  470
  A, 17, 412
  Anna van Hannover, 404, 407, 430
  Johan Willem Friso, 2017 I
  Willem IV, 22, 170 I–III, 171 I, 172, 306
  Archives de Maison Oranje Nassau

Manchester City Council Education Dept., 'Jacobites in Manchester'

National Archives, MSS of Earl of Egmont, HMC, 1920, 304, 1717, fol.78, 1712, 1713
  HMC, XV, 6, 26
  Add MSS 32694
  Add MSS 32 700
  Historical MSS Commission II, 1925
  HMC Lothian MSS

Oxford Dictionary of National Biography, 2005

Public Record Office, London, Lord Steward's Department, MSS 13/15, fol.97

Royal Archive, Cumberland Papers 3/36, 4/209, 4/30, 9/99, 57/200

Royal Archive, Windsor, Add 28/149

Royal Archives, 54026, 52970

Royal Artillery Institute, Woolwich, *Diary of Royal Artillery Officer Wood*

Sandwich Papers, Mapperton MSS

Stuart Papers, 35/77

Secondary Sources

Arkell, R L, *Caroline of Ansbach*, Oxford, 1939

Baker-Smith, V, *A Life of Anne of Hanover, Princess Royal*, Leiden, 1995

Barnouw, A J, *The Pageant of Netherlands History*, New York etc., 1952

Baron Bielfield, *Letters*, 1770

Bocage, Madame du, *Letters Concerning England and Holland*, 1770

Boxer, C R, *The Dutch Seaborne Empire*, London, 1973

Burton, E, *The Georgians at Home*, London, 1967

Campbell Orr, C, [ed.] *Queenship in Britain*, Manchester, 2002

Campbell, R, *The London Tradesman*, London, 1748

Carlyle, T, *Frederick the Great*, 1858

Chance, J F, [ed.] *British Diplomatic Instructions 1689–1789*, Royal Historical Society, 1926

Charteris, E, *William Augustus, Duke of Cumberland*, London, 1913

Chesterfield, P S Earl of, *Miscellaneous Works*, London, 1778

— *Common Sense: Or, the Englishman's Journal*, London, 1737

Chevenix Trench, C, *George II*, London, 1975

Clark, J C D, [ed.] *Memoirs and Speeches of James, 2nd Earl Waldegrave*, Cambridge, 1988

Coxe, W, [ed.] *Memoirs of Horatio Lord Walpole*, London, 1808

Croker, J W, [ed.] *Letters of Alexander Pope*, London, 1886

—, *Letters to and from Henrietta Howard Countess of Suffolk*, 2 vols, London, 1824

Cumberland and Westmoreland Antiquarian and Archaeological Society, *Transactions*, X, 'Clifton Moor'

Daiches, David, *Bonnie Prince Charlie*, London 1973

Defoe, D, *A Plan of English Commerce*, London, 1728

De-la-Noy, M, *The King Who Never Was: The Story of Frederick, Prince of Wales*, London, 1996

Deutsch, O E, *Handel: A Documentary Biography*, London, 1955

Drossaers, S, [ed.] *Inventarissen van de Inboedels in de Verblijven van de Oranjes en Daarmede Gelijk te Stellen Stukken, 1567-1795*, The Hague, 1974

Drummond, J C, and A Wilbraham, *The Englishman's Food: Five Centuries of English Diet*, London, 1957

Fraser, F, *Princesses: The Six Daughters of George III*, London, 2004

Geyl, P, *The Netherlands in the Seventeenth Century*, London, 1964

—, and C Gerritson, [eds.] *Briefwisseling en Aanteekeningen van Willem Bentinck*, Utrecht, 1934

— *Willem IV en Engeland tot 1748*, The Hague, 1924

Goslinga, A, *Slingelandt's Efforts towards European Peace*, The Hague, 1915

Griffith Davies, J D, *A King in Toils*, London, 1938

Harris, G, *Life of Lord Chancellor Hardwicke*, London, 1847

Hatton, R, *George I*, London, 1978

Henderson, A, *History of the Rebellion*, London, 1753

Lord Holland, [ed.] *Memoirs of James Lord Waldegrave*, London, 1821

Horn D B, *Great Britain and Europe in the Eighteenth Century*, Oxford, 1967

—, *The British Diplomatic Service 1689–1789*, Oxford, 1961

Huffel, W C van, *Willem Bentinck von Rhoon*, The Hague, 1923

Huizinga, J, *Dutch Civilisation in the Seventeenth Century and Other Essays*, [ed.] P Geyl and F W N Hugenholtz, London, 1968

Israel, J, *Dutch Primacy in World Trade*, Oxford, 1989

Johnson, S, *London*, London, 1738

Krämer, F J L, [ed.] *Gedenkschriften van Gijsbert van Hardenbroek*, Amsterdam, 1901

Kroll, Maria, *Sophie, Electress of Hanover*, London, 1973

— *Letters from Liselotte*, London, 1975

Laprade, W T, *Public Opinion and Politics in Eighteenth Century England*, New York, 1936

Leeb, I L, *Ideological Origins of the Batavian Revolution*, The Hague, 1973

Lenman, B, *The Jacobite Risings in Britain*, London, 1980

Lewis, W S, [ed.] *Selected Letters of Horace Walpole*, London, 1926

—, *Letters of Horace Walpole*, London, 1937

Lodge, Sir R, [ed.] *Private Correspondence of Chesterfield and Newcastle 1744–46*, London, 1930

MacDonough, G, *Frederick the Great*, London, 1999

Maclean, F, *Bonnie Prince Charlie*, London, 1998

Marples, M, *Poor Fred and the Butcher*, London, 1970

Marshall, D, *Eighteenth Century England*, London, 1962

Marshall, R, *Bonnie Prince Charlie*, Edinburgh, 1988

McLynn, F, *1759: The Year Britain Became Master of the World*, London, 2004

Michael, W, *Beginnings of the Hanoverian Dynasty*, London, 1936

—, *Englische Geschichte im 18 Jahrhundert*, 5 vols, Berlin/Basel, 1896–1955

Naber, J W A and L de Neve, *De Vorstinnen van het Huis van Oranje-Nassau*, Haarlem, 1898

Newin, T, *The Butler's Recept Book*, 1719

Nijhoff, D C, *De Hertog van Brunswijk*, The Hague, 1889

Osborn, E, [ed.] *Political and Social Letters of a Lady of the Eighteenth Century*, London, 1891

Patten, R, *History of the Late Rebellion*, London, 1717

Pennant, T, *Account of London*, London, 1813

Pevsner, N, *The Englishness of English Art*, London, 1964

Picard, L, *Dr Johnson's London*, London, 2000

Quennell, P, *Caroline of England*, London, 1939

Ralph, J, *A Critical Review of the Public Buildings in and about London and Westminster*, London, 1734

Rayner, R M, *European History 1648–1789*, London, 1954

Reid, S, *1745: A Military History of the Last Jacobite Rising*, London, 1996

Rowen, H H, *The Princes of Orange*, Cambridge, 1988

Saussure, C de, *A Foreign View of England in the Reigns of George I and George II*, [ed.] Van Meyden, London, 1902

Schama, S, *The Embarrassment of Riches*, London, 1987

Schutte, G J, 'Gouvernante Anna' in *Vrouwen in het Landsbestuur*, [ed.] C A Tamse, The Hague, 1982

Sedgwick, Romney, [ed.] *Some Materials towards Memoirs of the Reign of George II by John Lord Hervey*, 3 vols, London, 1931

—, *Letters of George III to Lord Bute*, London, 1939

—, *The History of Parliament: The House of Commons 1715-1754*, 3 vols, London, 1970

Sinclair-Stevenson, C, *Inglorious Rebellion*, London, 1972

Speck, W A, *The Butcher*, Oxford, 1981

Spencer Cowper, C S, [ed.] *Diary of Mary, Countess Cowper 1714–20*, London, 1864

Stevenson, G S, *The Letters of Madame*, New York, 1924

Szechi, D, [ed.] *Letters of George Lockhart of Carnwath*, Edinburgh, 1989

Tamse, C A, [ed.] *Nassau en Oranje in de Nederlandse Geschiedenis*, Alphen aan den Rijn, 1979

Temple, Sir W, *Observations on the United Provinces*, 1703

Thackeray, W M, *The Four Georges*, London, 1861

Thomson, K, [ed.] *Memoirs of Viscountess Sundon*, London, 1847

Walpole, H, *Reminiscences*, [ed.] Paget Toynbee, London, 1924

Walters, J, *The Royal Griffin*, London, 1972

—, *Splendour and Scandal*, London, 1968

Ward, A W, *The Electress Sophia and the Hanoverian Succession*, London, 1903

Wentworth, P, *Letters to Lord Strafford, 1711–37*, [ed.] J J Cartwright, London, 1883

Wesley, J, *Journal*, London, 1827

Lord Wharncliffe, [ed.] *The Letters and Works of Lady Mary Montagu*, London, 1837

Whitworth, R, *William Augustus, Duke of Cumberland*, London, 1992

Wilkes, J H, *A Whig in Power*, New York, 1964

Wilkins, W H, *Caroline the Illustrious*, London, 1901

Williams, E N, *Ancien Regime in Europe*, London, 1970

—, *Life in Georgian England*, London, 1962

Willson, B, [ed.] *Life and Letters of James Wolfe*, London, 1909

Young, Sir G, *Poor Fred: The People's Prince*, Oxford, 1937

Brice's Weekly Journal, 8 April 1725

Derby Telegraph, 23 April 1869

Gentleman's Magazine, June 1736, December 1736,
    August 1737, September 1737, November 1737,
    January 1738, March 1738, November 1738,
    April 1739,
    February 1740,
    July 1741,
    November 1742,
    July 1743,

December 1745,
May 1746, August 1746, October 1746,
April 1747, June 1747,
July 1748,
April 1749, July 1749,
May 1753, August 1753, September 1753,
August 1754,
July 1756,
June 1757,
June 1758

Daily Advertiser, 3 March 1731

Daily Courant, 19 October 1714

Saturday Evening Post, 23 September 1714

Universal Spectator, January 1731

Index

870565

Printed in Great Britain by
Amazon.co.uk, Ltd.,
Marston Gate.